CREATIVITY UNLOCKED

An Inside-Out Approach to a Life of Joy and Purpose

CHRIS LUMRY

Creativity Unlocked, An Inside-Out Approach to a Life of Joy and Purpose
Copyright © Chris Lumry, 2022

All rights reserved. No part of this publication may be reproduced, stored in or introduced into a retrieval system, or transmitted, in any form, or by any means, (electronic, mechanical, photocopying, recording, or otherwise), without the prior written permission of both the copyright owner and the above publisher of this book.

The scanning, uploading, and distribution of this book via the Internet or via any other means without the permission of the publisher is illegal and punishable by law. Please purchase only authorized electronic editions, and do not participate in or encourage electronic piracy of copyrighted materials. Your support of the author's rights is appreciated.

Published and Produced by OneStepGrowth LLC.

OneStepGrowth LLC
1095 Hilltop Dr. #328
Redding, CA
www.onestepguides.com

Cover Design by Chloe Wengerd, Chris Lumry, and Hayley Janzen with Hope Charged Creative
Interior Layout by BookBloks.com

Paperback ISBN: 979-8-9863328-0-2
eBook ISBN: 979-8-9863328-1-9

Printed in the United States of America

TABLE OF CONTENTS

DEDICATION	**V**
FOREWORD	**VII**
1 | CREATIVITY UNLOCKED Embrace your multifaceted creative nature	1
2 | MINDSETS UNLOCKED Upgrade mindsets and create from worth, not for it	17
3 | EXPRESSION UNLOCKED Quiet external pressures to find what brings intrinsic joy	37
4 | PROCESS UNLOCKED Develop a step-by-step approach that serves your goals	55
5 | HEALING UNLOCKED Address blockages and pain that hinder your journey	73
6 | COMMUNITY UNLOCKED Understand roles for life-giving interactions	87
7 | CONNECTION UNLOCKED Discover the secret sauce of thriving creativity	99
8 | SPIRITUALITY UNLOCKED Connect your creativity to something deeper	115
9 | CHILDLIKENESS UNLOCKED Experience the benefits of a lighthearted approach	135
10 | NARRATIVE UNLOCKED Adopt new viewpoints that reframe the story of your life	147
11 | REDEMPTION UNLOCKED Uncover treasures amidst daily pains and difficulties	165
12 | REFINEMENT UNLOCKED Upgrade your expressions from a place of love and rest	181
13 | AUDIENCE UNLOCKED Share your creations and enjoy the process	195
14 | LONGEVITY UNLOCKED Choose pacing and priorities that allow you to flourish	211
15 | LEGACY UNLOCKED Recognize creativity's long-reaching impact and meaning	225
ACKNOWLEDGEMENTS	**243**
ENDNOTES	**245**

For Josh, Kinsey, Chris, Carly, Trevor, Chrispus, Guido, and many others whose time on this planet ended far too soon. Your stories continue to inspire. Thank you for the love you shared with the world.

FOREWORD

The beauty and power of our creative nature lie in its ability to bring about something new. New experiences. New joys. New solutions. New art. New relationships. New ideas. New purpose. To create, in a broad sense, is to bring something into existence.

If you are reading these words, it's because consciously or subconsciously you are hungry for something new. It may be a new way to activate delight or purpose, a new hobby, new inspiration for a current project, a new solution for a challenge, new fulfillment in your career, new hope for a world spinning into chaos, or a new approach to what you love that allows for greater joy and longevity. You may not know exactly what you want or need—only that it's different from your current experience.

To embrace and benefit from the new, there must be space for change. That which is present or old must be open for examination. You do not need to drop all of your existing perceptions or processes to unlock creativity. But as you hold them with an open hand, they can turn, spin, expand, transform, even float into something more beautiful, more potent, and more fruitful than before.

There are pieces within your creative nature that you have not seen before—keys that you hold to unlock goodness, beauty, and practical change for your life and those around you. If you invest in this process, what you discover will surprise you.

That's why I've written this book: to help you explore your own story and consider how your creative nature can be more deeply unlocked and enjoyed. To highlight the universality of creativity and share a scientific and narrative-driven rationale for celebrating and intentionally engaging this aspect of your humanity. And to invite you into adventures, big and small, that bring euphoric experiences where you feel fully alive. Though our stories differ, we have more in common than you might think—starting with the versatile, ubiquitous gift of creativity wrapped in our beings.

> You and I both need the joy and purpose that our creativity is designed to bring.
>
> You and I both need the permission to explore, experiment, and grow.
>
> You and I both need the hope that what we have experienced thus far is not the limit of what can be created.
>
> You and I both need the opportunity to continue writing, and rewriting, the stories of our lives.

> Let's get started.

CREATIVITY UNLOCKED

Embrace your multifaceted creative nature. It is one of the most ever-present and powerful aspects of your humanity, no matter your context. Unlocking your expressions can transform your daily life.

The Case for Creativity

Taking time to consider your creativity may not seem like a top priority in today's fast-moving world. Technology is developing more rapidly than ever, giving us much to do, explore, and keep up with. But your creative nature holds great importance for daily joy and a purposeful, fulfilling life.

Creativity is transformative. It turns materials, places, situations, and even challenges into something new. It's our creative nature that both solves problems around the house and offers hope for broader societal challenges. You are reading this via a technological contraption, whether a book or screen, that was the outflow of multiple people's creative journeys. Think about that for a second: you're drinking coffee, checking social media, filing reports at work, bombing down a ski slope, or savoring guacamole because someone chose to create. From steamships to smartphones, soliloquies to space exploration, creativity continues to profoundly impact the experience of life on this planet.

Human creative potential is the greatest untapped resource in the world. But this immense possibility for innovation is not the focus of this book, at least initially. What we're prioritizing are the internal benefits of unlocking this aspect of our humanity. Properly activated, our creative nature can spark joy and add meaning in the midst of life's daily uncertainties. When we build, make, design, speak, share, praise, elevate, or refine something in a way that simply makes us smile, it satisfies a part of us that is hard to quantify. Our expressions can spark experiences where we feel fully alive and bring fresh motivation for our goals. Creativity reminds us of the treasure within ourselves and others, no matter our current context. It is evidence of the innate value of every person.

In an era when many feel increasingly isolated or divided, creativity is an important channel for meaningful connection with ourselves, others, and that which is greater than us. This inherent human quality can strengthen emotional health in a modern culture that is inundated by jarring news and facing significant challenges. Yes, the world needs the problem-solving power of your creativity, but *you* need it first: for the joy and purpose it can activate. Approaching life through a creative lens can help you navigate change in accordance with your values and priorities, especially in a world where technological, economic, and political contexts are continually shifting.

In addition to these benefits, creativity holds keys for personal growth. When facing a short-term obstacle or long-term problem, we need to be able to diagnose what is wrong and identify tools or practices that can bring a solution. But we also require something beyond analysis: the motivation, the energy, and the perseverance to implement the needed changes. We can know the answers but still struggle to implement them, especially when the journey gets scary or hard. Where do we find the missing motivation to move forward? What is lacking? The answer is hope, which is more than a transient feeling or a resonant slogan. It's the expectation of future good that motivates us to take our next step forward.

Life-giving experiences of creativity are a powerful tool for activating hope and strengthening resilience. When we find delight and goodness via our expressions in the present, it subconsciously strengthens the belief that similar and greater experiences are available in the future. Someone who is at a low point in their journey is going to have a lot more motivation to keep going if they can engage with an activity that sparks joy or meaning.

All of us go through hard times, and none of us have arrived as fully developed human beings. If you have, you can stop reading now and go eat some ice cream. For the rest of us, the music we make, the education we're gaining, the family we love, or the hobbies we're enjoying can help us keep showing up in difficult seasons. In the midst of challenges, we can all too easily deprioritize our expressions. Or we feel unworthy of the creative goodness that sparks hope and motivates persistence. But developing fun, fulfilling routines for our expressions helps us persevere through hard times. We can build *joy capital:* stockpiles of experiences of delight and meaningful connection activated through our creativity. Then, when adversity arises, our perception and ability to respond are vastly different. Problems look more like blips on a map full of meaningful creativity versus the latest addition to a landscape overwhelmed by difficulty.

Life-giving experiences of your expressions hold answers for the places where you feel stuck or that are in need of change. Playing a sport, painting a picture, or doing something new at work that makes you smile may not seem important, but the joy you experience can strengthen motivation for growth. Researchers at Drexel University have shown that moments of creative insight initiate a sense of pleasure by spurring brain activity in the orbitofrontal cortex, which is also responsible for the good feelings that come from delicious food or substances.[1] Activating your expressions can offer a natural reward that fuels your journey. Think of creativity as an irrigation system that, when properly connected, pumps refreshing water (joy capital) that supports fruitfulness in dry seasons and prevents sparks from turning into fire. Of course, there may be some work needed to dig up and upgrade the apparatus.

When we are regularly creating in ways that make us feel fully alive, we have more to share with others. Joy helps fuel gracious interactions and reduces the likelihood of choices we might later regret. Whether you're a busy professional who is outwardly achieving but inwardly looking for more fulfillment, a parent hustling to keep it all together, or an artist stuck at some point on your dream project, unlocking the joy and purpose that are possible through creativity holds tremendous benefits for your life.

Everyone Is Creative

There are numerous reasons why people aren't experiencing creativity as the transformational superpower described above. The first one is simple: many people don't recognize that they are creative beings already expressing themselves. Whether via routine activities or longer-term projects, we are experiencing this aspect of our nature in physical, internal, online, and even virtual spaces every day. It's hard to appreciate or upgrade something that we don't think exists.

When reflecting on creativity, does your mind jump to a definition of the word that excludes your hobbies or passions? Maybe you don't think this book is for you because you're "not creative"? You're not alone. A 2016 survey by the tech company Adobe found that only 41 percent of respondents worldwide described themselves as creative.[2] It is a common misconception due to many factors, including definitions prevalent in current culture that constrain creativity to artistic expression. This innate human quality encompasses much more. Let's look at the definitions of "create" in the Merriam-Webster Dictionary:

To *create (transitive verb)*:
1. To bring into existence
2. To invest with a new form, office, or rank
3. To produce or bring about by course of action or behavior
4. To cause or occasion
5. To produce through imaginative skill
6. To design

Though some schools of thought on creativity focus on specific components like problem-solving or artistry, we'll continue to use the first and broadest definition above: to bring something into existence. The fact that you're not a photographer, vocalist, or sculptor does not mean that you aren't creative! And if you are an artist, your creativity extends far beyond your craft! Recognizing the possibilities for joyful, meaningful creativity through non-artistic activities is important for all of us. It's time to dump limited perspectives that disqualify your gifts and rob your process. No matter your past awareness, there are current expressions to celebrate and explore in your life.

Experts in psychology and the human brain embrace similar definitions of creativity. Cognitive scientist Art Markman shares a broader viewpoint in the book *Tools for Innovation*:[3]

> Every day, we use language to speak sentences that have never been spoken before. We express thoughts that have never been expressed. All of this is so deeply ingrained that we don't notice how creative it is.

Professor Robert E. Franken, author of *Human Motivation*, defines creativity as "the tendency to generate or recognize ideas, alternatives, or possibilities that may be useful in solving problems, communicating with others, and entertaining ourselves and others."[4] Researchers Michele and Robert Root-Bernstein, authors of *Sparks of Genius*,[5] also affirm this wider view, writing:

> It's too bad that when considering what endeavors may be creative, people immediately think of the arts. It's the problem-solving processes they exhibit rather than the content or craft that make them so. Just about anything we do can be addressed in a creative manner, from housecleaning to personal hobbies to work.

Sure, your childhood crayon drawings were creative, but so is making lunch for a friend, going back to school for a new career, solving a crossword puzzle, mentoring youth in your community, walking in a city park, experiencing a movie, even reading these words. Take note: actions do not require intention to be "creative." People who don't think they are creative are actually creating every day, in multiple formats; they just don't realize it.

The question is not *if* one is creating, but *what* and *how* they are creating, and whether they are benefitting from the process. Every day, people are raising families, accomplishing tasks at work, navigating relationships, making art, engaging in hobbies or new experiences, solving problems, and more. Many just don't take a moment to explore whether they're expressing and producing in alignment with their goals and needs. Or they don't have a process that effectively unlocks the joy and purpose their creativity can hold. Here are a few eclectic examples of creativity in daily settings that can help increase awareness of your creative nature:

- An interior designer lays out a professional space to facilitate teamwork and flow.
- A grader operator skillfully creates a precise measurement for a new road.
- A soccer player executes a trap and pass that enables a goal.
- An elementary school teacher works with a family to develop a learning plan specific to the needs of a student.
- A customer-service representative takes time to understand a customer's situation and address a frustrating experience.
- A consultant refines a PowerPoint deck to more clearly and impactfully communicate data.
- A shopper figures out the most time-efficient path at the grocery store.
- A painter mixes oils into new colors.
- A hiker plans out and completes a multi-day adventure.
- A parent devises strategies to help their kids better navigate bedtime.
- An architect reviews progress in a new building construction.
- A delivery technician ends their day with surfing.
- A barista uses playful visuals to share daily specials in their coffee shop.
- An analyst upgrades the design and structure of a spreadsheet.
- A volunteer prepares meals for disadvantaged children at a local shelter.
- An engineer restores an old piece of furniture.

After reading this list, where can you identify aspects of creativity in your life? Take a few moments to reflect on creative activities in different parts of your weekly schedule. Recognizing existing expressions strengthens our ability to upgrade our experiences.

Collecting Keys to Unlocking Creativity

If I could wave a stick over your head to transform your process or had a machine that could laser off the limitations robbing your creativity, I would use it. But the creative growth journey doesn't work that way. Instead, it mirrors human development. In order to expand our creativity, we must consume nutrients and engage with new ideas. Growth requires moving out of old stages or understandings and putting concepts into practice. We must go on adventures, big and small, and be part of a community—a family—that encourages and sees us through difficult moments.

In this book, we will look at science, we will explore intangible and spiritual aspects, we will activate and practice our expressions, and we will talk a lot about meaningful connection. This is the quality that fuels creativity and that many sources indicate is associated with fulfilling, fruitful lives. You'll learn from the findings of scientists who study the creative ability of thought to spark new experiences via the brain's neuroplasticity. These pages hold practical keys and activating tools that draw from the field of behavioral psychology. You will also engage with research findings from experts on the topics of creativity and connection, including some from the incredible individuals who indirectly helped inspire this book. Throughout these chapters, I will pull from my own story and invite you to return to yours, for that is the central line that links all of our creative outflows. New experiences of specific expressions can spark exploration of your broader narrative and transform how and what you create every day.

Even though there is work ahead, I have good news for you: this journey can be full of surprising amounts of joy and fun. As a fellow traveler, I am here to encourage and guide you into experiences that can bring greater delight and meaning while hopefully sparing you unnecessary pain. You can go at your own pace, based on your interests, capacity, and goals. Approach these concepts like an experiment: test them and see what they bring about. Some may need time and practice before they produce, depending on your current context. Our Creativity Unlocked workshop participants have found that the more they invest in this process, the more they receive from it.

You can also think of this book as a collection of keys. There are sleek and light ones, and others that are larger and weightier, because they work on different locks. Some will open the proverbial doors around you presently, providing clarity for next steps. Others you are adding to your keyring for future challenges or innovative projects for which you are unknowingly training. All will help unlock insights into what makes you tick and what fuels your fire as a creative being.

Together, we will investigate where mindsets, past experiences, and processes have limited your creativity and its benefits. We will identify and activate expressions that spark intrinsic motivation. We will consider how to healthily engage with community, feedback, and audiences in ways that support your progress and your wellness. And we will see how our creative journey can hold new narratives and redemptive aspects that help strengthen longevity and legacy.

There is a purpose in the sequence of chapters. However, if you get stuck, feel free to skip around and return to sections as needed (that's how I read). Unlocking creativity can be both sequential and ordered or abstract and sporadic. And it is a journey that you have permission to explore from a relaxed, restful posture.

Creativity Fuels Thriving Lives

This book is closely tied to the work I've done over the past few years that helps people rediscover their creativity. Via workshops and our Creativity Unlocked app, I have had the delight of empowering business owners, artists, academics, tech workers, healthcare professionals, and others to unlock passion and momentum in their expressions via these concepts. It has truly been an honor to see inspiration sparked, ideas conceptualized, milestones reached, and projects launched. Most of all, my heart soars as I see people experiencing greater joy and meaning in the process. You will hear the stories of several workshop participants sprinkled throughout these pages, as well as those of others I have stumbled upon whose processes already embody these principles.

CHAPTER 1 | CREATIVITY UNLOCKED

In addition to this work around creativity, I have served as primary interviewer and story editor for the last four years for a nonprofit, OneStepHope. We capture inspiring written and filmed stories about addiction recovery and mental health that reframe these topics and reduce stigma. Our storytellers represent a range of socioeconomic, geographic, and racial backgrounds. Each has rediscovered hope and passion for life through their journey. All have experienced pain or trauma that contributed to substance or mental health challenges, though you would not guess that from meeting them. Early in our work, it became clear that our participants were each saying yes to something positive in their lives, not just no to a substance or behavior. At some point, I realized that all of our OneStepHope storytellers were creating something—whether through a career, art, nature adventures, relationships, service, or a better future for their families.

For example, Ryan is a father and husband who finds joy in hunting and running a successful electrician company. He built his business from just himself to a dozen others after recovering from a seven-year opioid addiction that led to him living in his truck for a season. Ebony is an author, mother, and advocate whose journey to sobriety empowered expressions beyond what was previously possible. She is now seeing change in cycles that affected her family across generations and has written a book. Doug grew up in a small town where he felt like a black sheep. Coping with substances led to DUIs and addiction, until he found a twelve-step community that provided tools and led to a faith awakening. With this supportive community, Doug completed a degree in design, which eventually led to a career at a top firm in his industry. Rhodalynn found great healing from panic and anxiety-related challenges through dance, which helped spur the founding of an organization that helps women connect authentically.

In the midst of these storytellers' respective challenges, activating their innate creative nature played an important role in sustaining a healthier experience of life. Each described both internal shifts and external support as being crucial for their personal growth, and many highlighted creative expressions that have added motivation and purpose to their journeys. The delight and satisfaction experienced are often personal, or *intrinsic*, meaning that it naturally occurs in the activity or experience regardless of reward or recognition received. We'll talk more about this important concept later, because internal motivation is at the core of flourishing creativity.

In case you're wondering, you don't need to have experienced significant trauma or struggle to benefit from unlocking creativity. You also do not need to be a natural virtuoso or formally trained in a particular competency. The benefits of creativity are not just for those in the shiny penthouse or those who have been wowing audiences with karaoke routines since the womb. They are available for anyone willing to engage. We are all creating via a range of expressions that are informed by our unique backgrounds and passions.

Introducing Your Creativity Guide

Not too long ago, I was an operations manager at a large tech company who would have laughed at the idea that I was creative. I had no idea how much delight and fulfillment could be found by embracing a new approach to my expressions. A series of life-changing experiences sparked this shift from a self-proclaimed "non-creative" to someone who prioritizes creating opportunities for joy and meaningful connection every day. Beyond filmmaking and writing, I love to strategize, play sports, hike, make music, tell dad jokes, and engage in authentic conversations with people. The heart-alive moments and delight found even in small steps and wobbles have spurred the discovery of creative identities and projects beyond what I knew possible.

To be clear, my credentials don't include Pulitzer Prizes, a PhD, Oscar nods, tens of thousands of followers, profiles in business magazines, or even a book deal. People wouldn't recognize the name of my music alias and I haven't been talking with world leaders or taking selfies with Steph Curry. This book is built on something eminently more accessible: practical step-by-step tools and concepts that give you the means to consistently claim delight and bring creative purpose into your weekly routine, without the approval of the Academy. Externally measurable achievement, recognition, and financial success are what culture prioritizes, but they are *not* required for satisfying and delightful experiences of your expressions. Here's a wild truth: you can find an

CHAPTER 1 | CREATIVITY UNLOCKED

approach to creativity where you are fulfilled and delighted regardless of the reach or the audience. Intrinsic joy and satisfaction can be both fuel and fruit of life-giving expression.

Looking back, I can now see how an over-focus on achievement in my younger years choked out creative awareness and restricted activities I could enjoyably experience. Expressing myself in certain ways then felt fraught with risk, so deprioritizing interests was not only safest but also sensible. I didn't then know that a new approach and practical tools could help me *love* projects and the creative process regardless of the outcome. Like many of you, I was impacted by marketing messages that highlighted glitzy experiences and personal accomplishment as necessary for happiness, only to find them disappointingly unable to meet my deepest needs.

Consider this book a preventive tool to keep you from arriving at a future stage of life wrestling with a sense of dissatisfaction and emptiness, despite a plate of achievements others value. One such painful season brought me to the deepest lows of my life. My multiple Ivy League degrees, tech job in Silicon Valley, social impact work with large foundations and charities, and opportunities to visit dozens of countries checked the boxes I thought defined success. But a sense of emptiness grew, leaving me increasingly unsettled and hopeless. Coping mechanisms became addictions that progressed to the point where I did not know if I could come back from them. These lowest moments unexpectedly triggered the steps toward life-changing discoveries that would spark joy-filled creativity. A Monday night blackout and drunken phone call from a bus stop led to getting help and so much more. Through a recovery journey, the gift of an awakening brought a new understanding of myself, healing to unrecognized pain, and an unlocking of creativity. Now I get to activate a whole range of passions that bring delight and satisfaction on a daily basis. The adventure continues more than six years later.

The joy and purpose I find in the creative process, whether in work or hobbies, continue to fuel ongoing growth. It has been a virtuous loop: the healing I experienced sparked delight-filled creative expressions, which continue to motivate personal development through the messy and imperfect parts of life. At times, I encounter obstacles, stumble over pain, or face reminders of the past that are heavy. But embracing my creativity has helped me navigate these challenges and even glean from them. Beautiful new things are springing forth from places that once felt most broken.

I used to live counting down the days until the *next* thing: the next trip, the next escape, the next achievement, the next reward. Now I can see and seize the opportunity to create meaningful experiences throughout my days. A new approach rooted in connection has helped me become more present and actually enjoy the process. There are chances to create each day, whether that's through volunteering in my city, designing online product experiences, hiking in the woods, or dancing in my kitchen with my Baby Yoda travel mug full of Earl Grey tea.

Start Fresh Today

Our backgrounds and interests may be different, our passions unique, our stories a world apart, but what we do have in common is our innate creative nature. Whether you express yourself through sock drawers, sonnets, snow machines, soup recipes, or spreadsheets, you are a creative being. There are opportunities closer than you think, small and big, to incrementally add delight and purpose to your daily activities. This book will not fix every external challenge you're facing. But it will facilitate internal experiences and offer tools that can help you navigate current situations with hope and fresh vision. The keys in these pages will help you discover new aspects of yourself, your creativity, and your community. Something as simple as setting aside thirty minutes a week for a creative outlet that brings you genuine delight can profoundly benefit your life.

So, why wait? Discover the space decorator, rhyme spitter, overseas adventurer, romantic poet, or social impact activist within you waiting to be joyfully activated. Learn how to enjoy and explore your current expressions. Celebrate the passions and interests that specifically bring you purpose and meaning. Get ready to uncover more of the treasure that lies inside of you and the unique ways that you can release beauty and love into the world.

Your expressions represent a unique sound that is meant to be heard, whether by one person or a multitude. It's not too late, even if you

CHAPTER 1 | CREATIVITY UNLOCKED

feel like you are at square one. Join me in this adventure of unlocking creativity, and see how it benefits your story, one step at a time.

Each chapter holds a short activation that will help you put key concepts into practice. It concludes with a story of someone activating life-giving creativity in their daily life. For more exercises, tools, and community, check out the Creativity Unlocked App.

> 🗝 **ONE-STEP ACTIVATION**
> Make a list of at least ten non-artistic ways that you are creating each week, and choose one to activate with intention, energy, and focus.

CREATIVITY STORIES

ZACH | AEROSPACE ENGINEER

Aerospace engineer and concrete sequential thinker Zach faced a hurdle to enjoying his creativity that affects many: "For most of my life, I didn't think I was creative because I had defined that quality to consist only of the arts. I had a limited understanding." For Zach, rediscovering his creativity challenged lies that he believed about his own potential and provided avenues to pursue passions that continue to bring deeper meaning.

Engaging with the content from *Creativity Unlocked* and participating in a workshop brought a new perspective for his engineering work. "I began to recognize that my favorite parts of my job were the most creative parts, like solving problems, taking ownership of projects, collaborating with teammates, and iterating on solutions. There was also a personal satisfaction in helping build something bigger than me." Recognizing the fulfillment that came through individual contributions caused Zach to see creativity as a crucial element for satisfaction in work regardless of the role, including as a manager.

In addition to career settings, Zach took significant steps around another creative passion. Recognizing that he didn't need to have all of the answers in himself empowered progress on a dream project. "*Creativity Unlocked* helped me understand how to blend my own skills and passions with those of others." This key enabled Zach to conceptualize and publish a children's book, which had been on his heart for years but felt implausible. "The themes of creating a healthy community and recognizing legacy sparked an idea." Zach remembered as a kid how much he enjoyed the art that his father had made but never published. "I decided to use his goofy, engaging drawings, now forty years old, to make

Zoochini, a picture book about a zoo full of rare vegetanimals [vegetable animals] and fruitimals [fruit animals]."

For Zach, the writing experience has been a wonderful source of connection with his dad. He loves getting to read to his son and daughter a book that he wrote that incorporates the work that brought him so much joy as a kid. "You never know how the creative seeds you plant, the small expressions that you make, may bless others." Practical steps to activate joy through his recently rediscovered creativity continues to open new possibilities for meaningful experiences at work, in family, and via other expressions.

MINDSETS UNLOCKED

Upgrade mindsets and create from worth, not for it. Creativity starts with your internal reality, so it's time to ditch the limiting thoughts that are bogging your expressions down. In this chapter you will learn how to unlock new mindsets and add ease, delight, and meaning to your expressions.

Check Your Lenses

Lenses shape the way we see, whether within our human eyes or attached to a camera or telescope. What is perceived can be magnified or shrunk, dimmed or brightened, clarified or obscured. Not all lenses benefit our vision. Sometimes they need to be cleaned or replaced entirely. Just as there are tools through which visual clarity can be restored, so too we can learn how to recognize and shift how we perceive our creativity. Your mindsets about yourself and your creativity are lenses that profoundly affect your expressions and your process.

Picture your favorite garden or another relaxing nature scene. Imagine the golden light of early morning or the rich tones of sunset illuminating plants and trees, bringing reality into gorgeous contrast. Remember the smells of flowers, vines, or even the soil itself. Is there water nearby? Can you hear the trickle of a stream, the breeze blowing through the leaves, or the pleasant buzz of the creatures that inhabit this space? Now, look for your favorite flower. Savor its sweet scent. In your imagination, feel the warmth and peace of this place.

Now, return to the present. What if this blissful image could be a picture for what your creative process feels like? The goal of this chapter is to help you begin to experience more of your expressions in a way that looks and feels full of joy, wonder, curiosity, and ease. Think back to your last genuine moment of delight, where life felt beautiful and wondrous. It may have been minutes, days, months, or even years since you have been able to return to a similar emotional state. Unlocking your creativity can increase the frequency of these sensations. Before thinking about the outcomes or end products, this picture represents the refreshing, delightful experience that simply creating can become.

Does this sound too far-fetched for you? Don't close the book just yet. For many of us, our creativity has been more stressful than enjoyable, more exhausting than recharging. There might be a range of questions and contradictory thoughts flying through your mind right now. The sting of rejection, the sense of failure over uncompleted projects, uncertainty and insecurity around giftings have marked the creative journeys of many. If past events have made your expressions the opposite of a tranquil garden, you're not alone. Previous experiences of discomfort and pain may be shaping the lenses through which you see yourself and your creativity.

The garden image above reflects a mindset I am choosing to embrace. It's also a picture of how I experienced creativity as a kid. Many of us have had similar experiences of carefree, childlike, joy-filled expression, whether with a paintbrush or on the basketball court, even if we don't remember them well. The emotions of these moments are a reminder of what is possible. It doesn't mean that golden sunlight or easy flow are always the picture of my process. There are days and weeks when I have to more intentionally apply the practices in this book to return to creativity rooted in joy and ease. But the work is paying off. The garden is more representative of my process every day. And new mindsets and other keys have helped bring this shift and fuel life-giving exploration, far more than old perspectives that emphasized difficulty.

New perspectives come from new thought patterns and can help you discover a new approach. Many of us have set our expectancy around creativity to the level of our past experiences or those of others from whom we have learned. But the past emotions and difficulties of our creative journeys do not have to be the leading attributes of your present and future expression.

The Power of Thoughts, Words, and Mindsets

Have you ever witnessed someone respond to an event or piece of news completely different from you? They likely have a different mindset or belief informing their reaction, which they have either subconsciously learned or proactively chosen. Our perspectives and thought processes color our understanding of every situation we encounter. Each of us has a unique internal operating system that is impacted by our core beliefs, current needs, values, and past experiences. It's one of the reasons why two different people can go through similar circumstances and have vastly different feelings or results.

Your creativity actually starts with your internal reality. Thoughts and words are expressions you release into the world, and they bring something new into existence for yourself or others. Think about how your emotions can abruptly swing based on a comment from someone or a seemingly random thought. One minute your countenance lights up because of a wonderful memory, and the next moment you feel the swirl of negativity after ruminating over someone's social media post. Yet, activate a positive memory, a kind action, or an expression of gratitude, and your perspective and emotions can shift again. Embracing the power of thoughts and mindsets is a key for unlocking more life-giving experiences of creativity.

I have good news for you: the lenses through which we see can change. New mindsets can jumpstart our creativity. Science continues to reveal the power in our brains to replace negative thought patterns with ones that positively affect our experiences. Your brain is neuroplastic, meaning that it is continually changing. "Habits of thinking need not be forever. One of the most significant findings of psychology in the past twenty years is that individuals choose the way they think," states Dr. Martin Seligman, pioneer of positive psychology and author of *Learned Optimism: How to Change Your Mind and Life.*[6] Dr. David Eagleman, neuroscientist and author of *Livewired,* notes that our brains have 86 billion neurons and trillions to quadrillions of synaptic connections: "[They are] living, dynamic, electric fabric. Every experience changes us."[7] Neuroscientist Dr. Caroline Leaf explains in her book, *Switch on Your Brain,*[8] that "[t]houghts are real, physical things that occupy mental real estate. Moment by moment, every day, you are changing the structure of your brain through your thinking. When we hope, it is an activity of the mind that changes the structure of our brain in a positive and normal direction." No matter your current lenses, the creative power of your thoughts holds great potential for upgraded emotional experiences of your expressions.

Recognizing Our Lenses

Hopefully, the visualization exercise above provoked to the surface some of your perspectives about creativity. Did the idea of the delightful garden resonate or rankle? Do you see your creativity as a joyful experience or as a slog? A duty? A gift? A painful corridor to a future dream? Something you still struggle to see within you? A burden too large for you to bear? Sadly, negative thoughts and words have shaped mindsets about creativity for many. Past rejection or disappointment can affect our actions in profound ways, whether explicitly or subconsciously. It's one of the reasons why a focus on weaknesses and limitations in creativity may feel more natural than awareness of strengths and opportunities. If you are struggling to activate an artistic expression you enjoy or can't find motivation for a personal or professional goal, there is likely a limiting mindset that needs an upgrade.

Shifting mindsets happens not through denial of reality but through reexamination of it. Change happens step by small step. Simply telling myself that I'm an NBA-caliber basketball player is not going to help me immediately hit every bucket or get me a spot on a team. But proactively building mindsets that value my long-term health and give me permission to enjoy or explore a sport can change my experience of the gym and fuel delight and growth beyond what seems possible. Personally, I have seen intentional practices around building new thought patterns tremendously impact how I experience songwriting, organizational leadership, taking risks, and other creative expressions.

Tangible experiences work in concert with new mindsets to unlock creativity. As we build new thought patterns about ourselves, activating expressions can reinforce these shifts. If I begin to explore a new lens for myself as a songwriter, a positive experience of making music can strengthen this perspective and inspire more creativity in this area. It's a virtuous loop that opens up whole new possibilities.

An important, foundational mindset for unlocking our expressions is that we can create from an awareness of our innate worth. Many have struggled with the creative process because they are consciously or subconsciously trying to prove their value or that they are enough. Yes, our creative choices are powerful and can have a great impact on our lives and those of others. But our outflows are not an ideal foundation on which to base our value. There will always be more that can be done to improve, perform, refine, produce. A final, satisfying point of "arrival" or "making it" does not exist. Finding our value in what we create may seem appealing and can even be motivating for the short term. But it all too easily becomes an endless hamster wheel of proving ourselves and believing that the next "level" of creativity is what will bring the security and significance we seek. Instead, what people actually need is a new starting posture.

We can transform our process by celebrating that our creative nature reflects the innate significance we carry. You don't have to work exhaustingly to prove your worth. Your creative outflows do not define, determine, or justify your value or significance; they simply reveal that it's already there! Intentional practices can help build or strengthen this essential mindset, and we will return to it throughout this book. It will unleash new freedom and joy for your creativity.

Shame: The Creativity Killer

Rooting our creative exploration in a foundation of innate value counters one of the most toxic ingredients for internal realities and creative processes: shame. Many fears and limiting perspectives come from experiences or beliefs rooted in shame—e.g., the feeling of not being enough, of being unwanted or alone. Noted researcher and speaker Dr. Brené Brown has done incredible work on the topic of shame and its antidote, connection. We'll borrow her definition and her helpful distinction around guilt. According to Dr. Brown, guilt can be "adaptive and helpful—it's holding something we've done or failed to do up to our values and feeling psychological discomfort... Shame is much more likely to be the source of destructive, hurtful behavior.... [It is] the intensely painful feeling or experience of believing that we are flawed and therefore unworthy of love or connection."[9] Elsewhere, she writes that "shame corrodes the very part of us that believes we are capable of change."[10]

Seeing ourselves as lacking value and incapable of change keeps us stuck, even at times when it's clear that our behavior is creating costly, unpleasant consequences. Shame contributes to insecurity, diminishes our value and potential, and leads to isolation and negative thoughts. Shame defines you by your weaknesses and the worst moments of your past, instead of seeing those events as opportunities for healing, restoration, and growth. It can paralyze us with fear or pressure hyperactive performance that brings stress and burnout. Coping mechanisms, addiction, escapism, passivity, and depression can all be fueled by these deep experiences of not feeling "enough." Shame's oppressive ideas can subconsciously motivate lots of "doing" or "achieving" in order to make up for your past or to somehow be enough. It is exhausting, and it poisons aspects of life meant for our good, like the processes of receiving feedback and working toward self-improvement.

Reflect on the questions below, and jot down what comes to mind.

- ❖ Where have you struggled with the idea of being creative because you feel like you don't have anything to offer? Have you ever *not* done something you wanted to do because you saw someone doing it better than you thought you could?
- ❖ Has it been hard to invest time or resources around things that bring you joy because it feels "selfish" or less important than other priorities? Where has the fear of what others might think limited your expressions?

- Do regrets or negative thoughts about yourself or your past ever leave you feeling stuck or unable to move forward? Have you ever thought that your poor choices or something that has happened to you disqualifies you from good experiences or your dreams?
- Where does the pressure to have things "perfect" or "better" slow down your actions or reduce your beliefs that good things can happen today?
- Are you subconsciously avoiding good things or life-giving experiences because hardship feels more deserved? Are you punishing yourself by not moving forward?
- Do you have an unrelenting urge to work, grow, or heal faster than you are currently?
- Has your desire to prove yourself or achieve led to choices that consistently hurt key relationships or your own wellness?

Shame is the common root underneath these experiences. There is probably shame influencing your life in some form. Just because it's not immediately visible doesn't mean it's absent. For many of us, shame is like carbon monoxide—a silent, invisible killer that we can lack the awareness to see. Or we may allow shame-influenced limitations around parts of our lives because of the sense of the perceived value or safety they provide. One example is partnering with shame to diminish or judge ourselves first in an effort to avoid risking the pain of others doing so. Another example is overworking and undermining our own wellness or relationships because we constantly feel behind. Accomplishing tasks becomes a means for comfort to cover where we believe we are inadequate. Finally, shame contributes to resistance to change in our lives, including our creative processes, because it feels scary to admit when we are wrong or where our misinformed choices have played a role in our pain. That which is incredibly good and fruitful can subconsciously seem unappealing because it might require acknowledging and grieving what was missed.

I have good news for you: experiences of the joy and redemptive aspects of creativity can far outweigh even this real experience of pain. The journey to freedom from shame is far better than suffering in Stockholm Syndrome-like experiences where we allow and even defend the very forces that limit and ultimately oppress our creative expressions. Your answers to the questions above might indicate areas of unworthiness, insecurity, and pain waiting to be healed. Don't be afraid; you're not alone in this—we *all* have them, and we are *all* on this journey. There is hope: a life without shame and with thought patterns that support and spur creativity is possible.

Practices to Kick Shame in the Face and Upgrade Mindsets

To address and upgrade mindsets influenced by shame, we must first recognize the creative power of our thoughts and words. Our current mindsets about ourselves and our creativity are reflected in what flows through our minds and out of our lips. These ideas are the blended, shaken-and-stirred mixture of past and present experiences and information. Many of us are unaware of how we are already creating, whether intentionally or passively, in this area. The result can taste pleasing and sweet or coalesce into something sour or even downright nasty. I don't think I'm the only one who has gotten stuck in a cycle of thoughts or participated in self-talk or conversations that felt as enjoyable as drinking a mixture of old socks and squid. We can find new recipes for our mindsets that in turn shape what flows out of us so that what we bring to the world is something that people, including ourselves, can enjoy.

Let's look at some practices that can help us address shame and build healthier mindsets that support flourishing creativity. The activities in this toolkit are listed in an intentional sequence, but you might find yourself bouncing around based on your current need or the thought pattern you are shifting. For instance, connecting with a trusted friend or a counselor may help you specify how shame is contributing to a particular limiting mindset. Or positive, reinforcing experiences of your creativity may be helpful for fueling greater compassion for yourself and others. If you find yourself stuck, try mixing it up with a different practice or combination. As you progress on your journey with creativity, you may find yourself returning to tools for deeper engagement.

Recognize the influence of shame. It's difficult to address a problem that we pretend doesn't exist. The first step of building new mindsets and beliefs about your creativity is to recognize the old ones. Vocalizing a specific limiting mindset or belief system helps us to both understand that we have a need and identify a targeted solution. Take account of what comes out of your mouth regarding your expression. Consider where you can let go of negative words and shift your focus from difficult experiences or missed opportunities to the creative possibilities that lie before you. For instance, in situations where something went wrong and the idea "I'm a failure" is barking loudly, explore a new perspective. Here are a few examples: failure isn't final; it's a data-rich opportunity for learning. Failure means we are trying and that we have found limitations to current capacity, skill sets, or opportunities. Failure experiences do not have to define us; they present chances for growth and innovation.

It's important to apply this practice to specific thoughts instead of contradicting negative emotions. Dr. Mark Noble shares why in the book *Feeling Great*: "This rewiring of the circuits in your brain can only occur by focusing on the negative thoughts and not by focusing on emotions… because statements about your feelings are inherently true, so if you try to challenge your feelings, then your efforts probably won't be effective…. But the distorted thoughts that trigger these feelings can be fairly easily challenged. The negative thoughts are the neuronal networks we [need to] target for modification."[11]

Examination of thoughts hindering your expression chips away at what keeps you stuck. Is there a stress-causing expectation you have put on yourself or that you feel from others? Do certain situations or problems fuel procrastination or flood your mind with disappointment or pain? Where do you find yourself worrying about messing something up? Your answers might indicate a perspective that can shift and areas of unworthiness, insecurity, or pain that need not be permanent. Growth and healing are possible. Writing out bits of your internal monologue brings clarity by highlighting what supports your creative goals and what could be upgraded. It's not uncommon to recognize an initial shame-linked mindset and then discover that there are multiple layers of limiting mindsets or beliefs, often tied to pain. Input from a trusted friend, trained professional, or supportive loved ones can help.

Choose a new thought that supports a healthier mindset. In places where limiting mindsets or hindering beliefs have been identified, we can replace these ideas by intentionally partnering with new thoughts. Choosing a new, positive affirmation about yourself or your situation activates your creative power to shift your internal reality. Craft affirming statements that are not so distant or unrealistic that they feel impossible but that are still aspirational in the direction you want to grow. In *Atomic Habits,* James Clear highlights this concept of cognitive congruence by encouraging intentional thoughts that support a new understanding of oneself but can still be fully believed: "When you start to speak positive words that are rooted in honest thinking, you literally destroy the toxic memory and grow a beautiful new memory to replace the painful and oppressive one.... Congruent thinking, not positive words, creates the necessary changes in the brain."[12] Here are some examples of affirming statements that can support cognitive congruence in your creative exploration. Feel free to use these or write some of your own. The more personal and relevant they are, the better.

- I am designed to enjoy, experience, and create things that represent beauty and goodness in the world.
- I am worth investing in, even if I don't always feel that way.
- I make powerful choices to have new thoughts about myself and my creativity.
- I do not have to measure up to anyone's standards of excellence or beauty.
- I am willing to go on a journey of learning to experience and walk in compassion and kindness.
- I have permission to freely explore and experiment with my creative expressions, regardless of whether they lead to something bigger.
- I am willing to embrace new, life-giving ideas and beliefs about myself and my creativity.
- The very challenges that have limited my creativity can become places where I release hope, goodness, and joy into the world.

Consistent repetition of affirmations can change what we think and ultimately what we believe about ourselves and our creativity. Set a consistent time each day to speak out loud affirmations that you need to hear, and repeat as necessary.

Connect with community. Dr. Brené Brown writes that "the very best thing to do in the midst of a shame attack is totally counterintuitive: practice courage and reach out!"[13] She shares powerfully about the importance of meaningful connection through vulnerability and acceptance in her book *The Gifts of Imperfection*. Community helps us remember that no matter what we are facing, we are not alone in the process. The experience of human connection implicitly attacks the lies that we are not enough or that we are isolated. This step could look like reaching out to a loved one, joining a support group, meeting with a counselor, or simply doing something fun with friends. It doesn't have to be serious to be powerful. Conversations with others can spark clarity. Trusted friends can provide space to process, help you verbalize what you're experiencing, or identify a beneficial mindset shift. The more you practice reaching out to others for help, the easier it becomes.

Practice self-compassion, acceptance, and grace. The permission to be exactly where we are, and know that we are loved, helps quiet flight-or-fight responses and makes space to thoughtfully address what we're experiencing. If the other tools on this list aren't helping, this is a good place to start. Connection can be experienced and felt in the midst of uncertainty, imperfection, or mistakes. Each of us can benefit from having an established process for handling situations when things go wrong. Experiences of acceptance and love freely given in the midst of our mess or failure are also called grace. In chapter 5, we'll talk more about this concept, the scientifically indicated benefits of forgiveness, and its power for unlocking creativity. Experiences that help us love ourselves in healthy ways, regardless of our limitations or imperfections, naturally strengthen our ability to love our expressions.

Take action to address shame triggers. Experiencing compassion, acceptance, and grace does not mean ignoring what is wrong. All of us have been impacted by hurtful, imperfect choices made by others *and* ourselves. We can't just paper over pain or trauma, or pretend an ongoing negative situation is going to magically change. As we do the work to replace toxic thoughts with healthy mindsets, we can make practical choices about our activities and environments that result in fewer shame triggers within our own brains and bodies. This might look like implementing boundaries in relationships or shifting how and where we spend our time. Reducing exposure to people, environments, and behaviors that spark shame or reinforce negative mindsets helps accelerate growth and healing. Consider where tangible changes could better support the new thought patterns you are building. If you're not sure where to start, ask someone you trust for ideas, and experiment with small changes.

Seek positive, reinforcing experiences. We can repeat "I am enough" until we're blue in the face but not actually eliminate shame's lingering influence unless our words are accompanied by experiences that support these words and remind us of our inherent value. The internal work flows into the external. Taking tangible action aligned with new mindsets about ourselves and our expressions strengthens neural pathways that increase the joy, hope, and freedom we experience. By all means make time to practice and delight in activities you love. These life-giving experiences build positive affect—aka the expectancy of good things to come—which is associated with flourishing mentally and emotionally.[14] So make, build, paint, write, sing, problem-solve, learn, or say something that makes *you* smile.

As you explore these ideas, keep in mind that additional support for your personal journey may be necessary. You might need help navigating your thoughts and feelings, or be in a stage of your journey where control of your choices and responses is more difficult. Additional services and care can help you heal and grow, especially if you have a mental health or substance abuse challenge. There is no shame in being in that place. Support groups, mentors or coaches, and counselors or therapists can help you navigate shame-filled areas of perception and the pain that has shaped them. New, life-giving experiences of compassion, acceptance, and grace are possible and can lead to deeper sources of connection and security. Taking the important steps to seek help demonstrates the power of your choice. Getting support not only strengthens your ability to explore your creativity but also benefits other parts of your life.

CHAPTER 2 | MINDSETS UNLOCKED

Five Key Mindsets to Upgrade for Unlocking Creativity

Before we explore specific creative themes and activities that bring joy and satisfaction, we're going to further develop and practice affirmations that strengthen mindsets supportive of our expressions. Having a personal list will help you align with the values and perspectives you aspire to have, instead of falsehoods or limiting perspectives. The very thoughts or ideas that have hindered your creativity can be helpful ingredients for building your own list. Simply write out an opposite statement. These affirmations don't have to be long, fancy, or complicated. The tips below, from the book *The Success Principle* by Jack Canfield[15], can help you get started:

- ❖ Use "I am…" statements.
- ❖ Use positive framing—the word "no" or "not" does not appear in the statement.
- ❖ State goal or desire as if it's already achieved or reality.
- ❖ State specific positive affirmations about yourself and your creativity in the present tense.
- ❖ Use brief and memorable wording.
- ❖ Focus language on yourself, and not other people.
- ❖ Use specific action words.

Not every personalized affirmation has to follow all these rules, but they're a good starting point. Now, let's upgrade five key mindsets in areas where people commonly have false beliefs affecting their creativity. These are also some of the lies I believed about my creative process, where intentional work has unlocked permission and ability to explore and deeply enjoy expressions.

Common False Belief #1: "It's too late for me to embrace my creativity or try something new."

Truth #1: "I choose to recognize my existing creativity today and celebrate the opportunity to find expressions that bring greater joy and purpose."

Our brains are more resilient and creative than we realize. If we're breathing, there's still time to activate creativity in new ways. Instead of seeing this exploration as something new, remember that you *already* are creating each day. It's just a question of awareness and impact. Jumpstart your creativity by focusing on one channel for positive expression today.

> *False Belief #2: "The delight and meaning of creativity are only available for certain activities and limited parts of life."*
>
> *Truth #2: "I am a multifaceted creative being. I celebrate that I am creating via daily routines, relationships, experiences, hobbies, and even responsibilities that feel boring."*

From simple tasks like commutes or running errands to conversations with coworkers or loved ones, opportunities for creativity abound. Recognizing them is the first step toward increasing the life-giving benefits that our expressions can bring. If you have used a narrow definition for creativity, start by broadening your language. Whether you're an auto mechanic, a camp counselor, an investment banker, a factory worker, or a stay-at-home parent, you're expressing aspects of your creative nature every day, just maybe not in ways that are as enjoyable as they could be (yet).

> *False Belief #3: "My past situations, contexts, and choices have set a course for my creativity that is unchangeable. I've missed the boat."*
>
> *Truth #3: "Experiences of joy-filled, meaningful creativity beyond what seems possible now are waiting for me. The unique details of my story contribute to the depth and flavor of my expressions"*

No matter our environment, background, or level of resource, we are part of creating the world around us. The challenges we have faced around our expressions or our contexts do not determine or reduce our value. Fresh experiences of acceptance, grace, and compassion empower a positive growth mindset about this reality instead of discouragement.

I doubt I'm the only one who has made poor choices or foolishly poured gasoline on situations that turned sparks into dumpster fires. These moments are not ideal, but they do reaffirm our creative power. As you continue through the unlocking process this book supports, the parts of life that have felt most difficult and tender can become ingredients for heart-alive, meaningful creativity in surprising ways.

> *Common False Belief #4: "I cannot claim to be creative, or have a specific creative identity, until I have reached a certain level of productivity or recognition."*
>
> *Truth #4: "Embracing creative identities fuels my exploration and enjoyment. I am creative. I am a leader, a songwriter, a good friend, a _____, a _____, a _____ [replace or fill these blanks with words that resonate with your journey]."*

Many have been taught that one must complete a book before they become a writer, or achieve a level of financial sustainability before they call themselves a businessperson. This viewpoint is understandable and needed in some settings—we do want our doctors to be well-trained, for instance. But this approach may not be ideal for supporting every creative process. If our creativity is inherent within us, could certain expression-related identities also be? Public speaker Wendy Backlund uses a powerful picture to illustrate this truth: we still call an apple tree an apple tree when it doesn't exhibit visible fruit. The presence or lack of output doesn't change its identity. The same is true for your creativity. Rediscovering interests, passions, and goals via the ongoing unlocking process can inspire new creative identities for you, whether or not their fruit is visible yet.

> *False Belief #5: "My creative process is always going to feel like this: difficult, uncertain, stuck."*
>
> *Truth #5: "I am excited to discover greater joy, ease, and freedom via my expressions, and I choose to be open to change and growth. My creative future is better than I think."*

Mindset shifts can transform not just what we create but also how we experience the process. Even if you are advanced in your craft, there are opportunities for greater delight and ease in the actual experience of creating. I am convinced that discovering more joy in the creative process, and not just the outcome, will change individuals and the world. Take a deep breath. Let the reality of your innate value and beauty, the wonder of creativity, and the excitement of possibility stir fresh hope in you today. You don't have to have all the answers. Simply taking the brave step to admit where you feel stuck and want to explore something new is an incredible success. You are loved, and you were designed for the gifts you have been given.

These examples are a starting point. You will benefit from continuing to refine and upgrade affirmations as your expressions and context evolve. Use language specific enough to resonate. For instance, I've added "I'm a writer who cheerfully creates worlds with words," "I proactively create positive atmospheres in my workplace and home," and "I choose to look for joy, purpose, and beauty in every creative process" to my list. When I say them, there is now a deep sense of resonance that did not exist around these ideas a few years ago.

Rewiring Your Mindsets and Strengthening Your Foundations

Your beliefs and mindsets likely will not fully shift in a day, a week, or even a month. It takes time and intention to build a new approach. Continued experiences of connection, love, and acceptance are part of the healing process from old thought patterns that have shaped our brains' neural pathways. Don't give up on the process; more joy and hope are possible. Integrative medicine pioneer Dr. Andrew Weil explains this concept in his book *Spontaneous Healing*: "Neuroplasticity means that emotions such as happiness and compassion can be cultivated in much the same way that a person can learn through repetition to play golf and basketball or master a musical instrument, and that such practice changes the activity and physical aspects of specific brain areas."[16]

The very places where you now feel most uncertain around your creative identity or expressions can become your areas of greatest strength.

Keep exploring, keep experimenting, and you'll start to taste more of the life-giving fruit of creativity. Intentionally practicing new mindsets and affirmations will translate into courage to discover experiences that make your heart come alive.

As you continue on your creative journey, you may hear again the accusatory whispers of shame and hopelessness that question your value or your creative nature. Though it may feel hard at times, stay connected to words and affirmations rooted in grace and hope, step by step. You *are* creative and worth fighting for. Your expressions matter, and you have permission to learn, to grow, to not get it right or perfect. Continued exploration and expression offer opportunities to learn how to deal with negative thoughts and beliefs in healthier ways, instead of medicating or stuffing them down. Whether these whispers tell you that you are behind, not enough, doomed to fail, bound to screw up, insignificant, or whatever *blah blah blah* they yap, just remember: there is another perspective and thought you can embrace. As the classic sports adage goes, sometimes the best defense is a good offense. When under fire, lean into proactively enunciating affirmations for current and future situations, or find someone you can encourage. The next chapter will provide clarity around themes to prioritize: the unique collection of expressions that bring intrinsic joy and satisfaction and that help you feel fully alive.

✒ ONE-STEP ACTIVATION

Choose one of the limiting mindsets that resonates with you personally and build an affirmation that replaces this lie with truth. Practice speaking it out loud every morning this week. Get the Creativity Unlocked app to access more mindsets and affirmation tools.

CREATIVITY STORIES

NATHAN | DELIVERY WORKER & ARTIST

Nathan is a spoken-word artist and musician whose expressions add joy to his current roles as an apprentice and a delivery driver. Intention around his mindsets has shifted his understanding of creativity and impacted his approach: "Recognizing that creativity is a part of me, regardless of whether or not I make something, has helped lift pressure off of my processes. Creativity is inborn in me. It is something that I have carried from birth to now, in my twenties."

Nathan describes how this internal change from a focus on productivity to one rooted in identity has helped him find joy-filled, meaningful expressions in different situations. "My creative nature shapes how I see: people, problems, ideas. There are seasons when I am bursting with artistic expressions like poetry and song, and others when it is not flowing in that same way. I can have 'good' or 'bad' days in terms of what I make or write, but it doesn't change who I am as a creative person." Nathan sees creativity activating whether he is crafting a lyric or having a meaningful conversation with a friend.

One of his creative gifts is bringing a fresh viewpoint to difficult situations, though at times it hasn't felt like a blessing. "Growing up, I didn't always understand how different my perspective was. Some people couldn't understand my thought process, though it did lead to me being put in higher level classes." His different viewpoints even led to misunderstandings with people he was close to. But they have also been a blessing. "Recently a friend of mine was going through a rough time, and I got to creatively share words of comfort and encouragement that helped her reframe a problem and shift her viewpoint into hope. This is a regular occurrence in my friendships."

Though Nathan's job is not focused on his longer-term artistic goals, everyday experiences of creativity fuel joy in his current season. "I'm in a mentorship program where I have to do a lot of administrative tasks. Leaving inspirational quotes and messages in the midst of this mundane work helps to energize these activities." A similar approach helps brighten his work as an Instacart shopper. "It was not the most enjoyable role, but then I started integrating music and dance into my grocery shopping and delivery trips. On a recent drive, lyrics for a spoken word about racial injustice and healing began to flow out of me. I was so personally moved that I got emotional, even as I was driving around and dropping off milk and frozen pizza."

Still, Nathan's favorite days are those when he gets to make music. "They hold these wondrous moments that are hard to describe with words. It's like a door opens up in my mind. Memories, ideas, inspiration, clarity flow through, as if I'm exploring a new world. It's beautiful." He likes to compare the emotions of these days to the giddy state of a kid about to go to a Six Flags theme park. "These opportunities are refreshing, especially when there are difficult things happening in the world." One of his favorite creative moments came while forced to isolate during the pandemic. "Moments with my guitar led to unexpected creative flow and opportunities to record a song in the midst of the challenges of that season," Nathan shares.

Though his creative passions have not paid him a dime yet, Nathan is undeterred. "I know that I know that I know I am creative. Call a spade a spade. Music, art, spoken word are a significant part of my calling, but they are not its entirety." He loves to encourage others in their creative pursuits. "Whether your favorite expressions are professional or a side hobby, keep finding and exploring your creative flavor. Champion your creative identity and power. Who are you to hold back the gifts you have been given?"

EXPRESSIONS UNLOCKED

Quiet external pressures to find what brings intrinsic joy. An overemphasis on reward or recognition can crowd out the delight and satisfaction of creativity. In this chapter, you will unlock expressions that provide intrinsic motivation and spark resonant heart-alive moments.

Exploring Intrinsic Motivation

Do you have a secret passion for *Star Trek*, fifteenth-century Italian art, single-source coffee beans, capoeira, hibachi grills, or Arianna Grande's music? Embracing expressions that spark intrinsic joy and satisfaction, regardless of whether anyone affirms or rewards you, is essential for lifegiving creativity. The more we love and enjoy what we do—the process, and not just the outcome—the more creativity will help us flourish in everyday life. Finding this internal resonance helps us take action, avoid distraction, navigate external pressures, and much more.

In our Creativity Unlocked workshops, the permission to prioritize intrinsic joy and personal satisfaction is one of the concepts highlighted by participants as most transformational. It's a simple but powerful key. Many of us have missed out on delight and momentum in our expressions because of an over-focus on what we think others value or approve of, at the cost of what most moves our hearts. Or we have not made time to find and celebrate the activities, topics, and contexts that bring us joy.

It's like falling in love. Tasks and longer-term commitment are easier when motivated by passion and joy. Prioritizing intrinsic motivation will help you reclaim fun and ease in creativity. For years, my need for external validation made exploring new or underdeveloped expressions like creative writing difficult. Putting words on the page often felt uncertain, even painful. Today, I've fallen in love with the writing process, largely through a fiction project on which I've been working for five years. Writing in this genre brings me the same warmth and enjoyment I experienced reading in my youth, and that is success, regardless of its completion or reward by readers. It has not been published or read by many, but the story's ideas, contexts, and characters all stir a sense of personal delight and are thus intrinsically motivating. The old me would have thought it *crazy* that I could enjoy a project with this trajectory—heck, I didn't think I could stick with something for that long. This process changed my perception of how creativity can feel.

Intrinsic motivation is crucial for unlocking creativity. Don't rush through this chapter. Together, we will create space to recognize and quiet external pressures. We will identify clues that point to what makes your heart come alive, and spark fresh hope for your creative exploration. The very factors or qualities that may have made you feel different, or even like an outsider at times, are an integral part of your authentic creativity that can hold great fulfillment. Celebrating your uniqueness will help enhance your process and give permission for others to recognize theirs too. Plus, the external results and rewards you experience will be more achievable and enjoyable when your expressions are rooted in authenticity and personal satisfaction.

Breaking the Mold

Picture your creativity like a tree. The branches heading in different directions are your expressions. The trunk and root system consist of your creative identity and mindsets. Support from others is the sunlight that helps growth, and the inner joy and satisfaction of creativity are the water that will nourish you day in and day out. Some branches will naturally extend and develop. Other expressions may not grow as strong or bear fruit. But they're all still a beautiful part of the tree's shape. Not all have to be productive to be important.

What is the stencil that you have felt pressure to fill via your expressions, whether in work, family, hobbies, or other settings? Many of us have tried to force ourselves and our creativity into someone else's design, and we've become frustrated, or worse. We end up lopping off interests and passions that bring us joy but seem unimportant to others. Or we glue on branches that we feel like we're supposed to have, instead of allowing natural growth or a healthy grafting process. Granted, there can be great value and fruitfulness in following and learning from the creativity of others. Not all structures of tree growth are as beneficial or fruitful; there can be good reasons to intentionally shape or prune your creative tree. But, if you find yourself lacking passion or joy in your expressions, check to see if it's because you're trying to fill a shape that doesn't fit you. Heck, you might be a whole different species. A pear tree is going to have a difficult time becoming a sequoia.

Overemphasizing the metrics of success provided by external sources can cause us to miss out on deeper levels of fulfillment and joy. I recently had lunch with a new friend who has written and released multi-platinum hit songs and experienced this reality firsthand. "I couldn't believe how unfulfilling and empty [the multi-platinum hit] felt," he shared. "I just felt the pressure to do it all again." In the same conversation, this artist talked about how meaningful less flashy activities had become: spending time with his wife and kids, being intentional about friendships, and savoring vulnerable, heartfelt sessions with songwriters. Yes, the rewards and recognition that our expressions attract matter. They can greatly impact how, where, and what we create and experience. But they are not what ultimately brings fulfillment. There are more than enough cautionary tales to remind us that notoriety, financial success, or even impact on the world does not guarantee creativity that is satisfying, joyful, or supportive of our wellness.

"People move from grade school to college to the workplace and are trained to focus on external motivators," shares Meredith Neumann, a licensed therapist and entrepreneur. After ten years in private practice, she started Scaling Within, a company that helps other entrepreneurs and business leaders strengthen their internal capacity and sustain external growth in their professional lives. "People often underestimate their own creative potential because of this overemphasis on an external locus of control that feels out of their hands. Rediscovering intrinsic motivation can open up whole new avenues and possibilities in the workplace, in hobbies, and in one's personal life."

Even if you already have a creative outlet or two that you're passionate about, there are likely additional themes or outflows to discover. We can become so focused on the few we know that we stop exploring new expressions that can add even more delight and satisfaction to our lives. Embrace the ongoing, unfolding journey and discover more joy and purpose via your creativity.

Finding Creative Themes

Before identifying more personally satisfying expressions, let's clarify the difference between external and intrinsic motivators. The former are received from others: reward, compensation, attention, validation, energy, feedback, recognition. The latter are naturally experienced within, regardless of an outcome: joy, satisfaction, excellence, meaning, wonder, curiosity, learning. External motivators are not bad in themselves, but they can easily be overemphasized. Our society likes to measure pretty much everything: return on investment, followers, sales, health metrics, statistical performance, engagement, profit, impact—the list goes on. This framing adds pressure to settle for stifled experiences of creativity that prioritize a quantifiable metric or that check a box, instead of leaving more space for intrinsic motivators like delight and authenticity. Re-prioritizing this inner motivation can unlock new experiences of ease and freedom that supercharge our expressions.

Pull out a piece of paper and pencil and journal through the questions below. They are designed to help you identify and activate greater intrinsic motivation in your creativity. The questions may stir ideas and memories that feel outside of your comfort zone or that are inaccessible at your current stage. That's okay. The goal is to pull back the curtain on conscious and subconscious creative passions that inform new, refreshing expressions in multiple parts of life.

These open-ended prompts are a starting point for brainstorming. Follow the flow, and give yourself permission to answer with the understanding you have today. Don't overanalyze your answers or shut down your thinking because it seems unrealistic. You will have a chance to interpret and apply the results after.

- *What experiences, places, creative influences or memories make your heart come alive?* Make a list. Where have you had those skin-tingling, I-can't-believe-I-get-to-do-this, deeply fulfilling moments? What activities make you lose track of time? These can be experiences that happened through your own creative expression or through somebody else's.

- *What expressions or activities would you enjoy even if no one ever saw or knew the outcome?* Write down two or three that come to mind. Look for hobbies, memories, or places that bring you enough delight or satisfaction that you feel no need for recognition or validation from others. What do you not need compensation or affirmation to enjoy doing?

- *What do you enjoy learning about for fun?* Which topics get you stuck in Wikipedia rabbit trails or YouTube wormholes? Take note of subjects and skills that spark natural curiosity. It could be a person, event, or era. Or you might be drawn to activities, problems, or other areas of study.

- *How would you spend your time if you had all the money in the world?* Think about how you would structure your life and what dreams you would pursue. Helping others? Being the parent at every one of your kids' sports games? Learning to cook Indian cuisine? Working on a novel? Showing others beautiful parts of your neighborhood or distant places? Taking people on rejuvenating nature adventures? Building a company that makes a world-changing product? Allow yourself to dream about what could be without any pressure for a tangible, practical, or financial outcome.

- *What brought you joy as a child?* Before you learned what attracted external validation or reward from others, what did you like to do? What were you drawn to? These early-in-life moments often indicate areas of passion undiluted by the pressure to please others, live up to a perceived image, be "practical," or prove yourself. If joy-filled memories from childhood aren't readily available due to your story, think about the most delight-filled moments you have found as an adult, free from others' expectations.
- *What experiences do you believe you're supposed to enjoy but you actually don't?* Are there hobbies, activities, or aspects of culture in which you participate because it seems to be what a certain type of person is supposed to do? Look for where your life feels more like performance or checking a box than true enjoyment. Do you create or hold back from certain tones, channels, or styles because of what others might think?

Interpreting Your Responses

Feel free to spend as much time with the questions as needed. They may lead to more questions or reflective ideas. Remember that there are no wrong answers. Allow your mind the freedom to explore. Once you have a bunch of ideas written out, reflect on what you have collected. Look for patterns. These can indicate creative themes that stir intrinsic joy, satisfaction, or curiosity. A theme could be an activity, a type of experience, a skill set, a topic of interest, a people group, or a place. Find what is life-giving for you, that doesn't come at the expense of others' or your own wellness. Are there other previous experiences that align with or confirm these passions?

Your answers may not indicate a single literal application or expression right away. They likely will point to multiple possibilities. For instance, if a heart-alive memory that you captured involved playing with building blocks as a kid, you might find intrinsic joy through activities that involve design, organization, or making something with your hands. If you get really excited when reminiscing about your favorite outdoor concert, creative themes for you could include music, art combined with nature, or creating special moments of connection with others through events. This is where pattern-recognition and reflecting across your life can be helpful. The points of light that are highlighted begin to indicate clearer shapes and ideas, just like constellations.

Look for and follow clues that surprise you. They are great to note for exploration. These discoveries may benefit from additional attention, since they weren't already on your radar. It's not uncommon for people to discover new, resonant themes simply by making space for reflection.

Here are a few examples that demonstrate how varied and abstract themes or expressions can be, divided into a few categories for clarity:

Abstract Qualities and Skills

- Bringing order to chaos
- Making new friends
- Pushing yourself to the limits of your capacity
- Making processes more efficient
- Pursuing harmony among different viewpoints
- Breaking new ground
- Doing in-depth study and examination of a topic
- Helping people achieve their goals
- Brainstorming new ideas
- Competing for a prize
- Solving problems
- Reaching a feat that seemed impossible
- Structuring information for ease and fluency

Topics & Interests

- Ancient archaeology
- Comic books
- Anything to do with birds
- Pacific Northwest forests

- Racial justice
- Computers
- Jazz music
- Eighteenth-century philosophers
- Neuroscience
- Global economics
- Latin dance
- Seashells

Activities

- Practicing meditation and spiritual practices
- Creating colorful art
- Fixing a vehicle or machinery
- Recycling used clothes
- Developing training curriculum for a school
- Writing fiction novels
- Collaborating with a close friend on a house project
- Teaching kids your favorite game
- Making a sale or purchase at work
- Hosting memorable parties with other people
- Rock climbing or other adventure sports

As you brainstorm themes, take note of places where there is a spark of interest or excitement but also resistance, questions, concerns, or fear. The barriers may indicate that something valuable lies on the other side. What is most vulnerable for us is often most precious. You may find indicators of life-giving expressions that have been hindered or forgotten due to unresolved pain. Are there themes that spark intrinsic joy that you haven't felt permission to explore? Unaddressed experiences of confusion, disappointment, and rejection frequently prevent pursuit of life-giving expressions and dreams.

The more you allow yourself to explore and not feel pressure to justify or explain what you find, the easier discovery becomes. If the process feels uncomfortable at first, don't give up. Instead, be encouraged. You are on the pathway to experiencing more of what truly makes you come alive. You don't need to try to predict where it will take you.

Exploring the Tension Between Internal and External Motivations

The answers to the first five questions give clues about creative themes rooted in intrinsic motivation. The final question spotlights where your priorities may have been shaped more by external factors than what brings personal delight and meaning. Your motivations are a blend of many factors, so it's unlikely that any activity purely falls into one category or the other. As you can see, these questions and answers are not intended to make things black or white. You may experience joy for a mixture of reasons around any given activity. It's okay if the source is not entirely clear.

While this chapter is focused on internal motivators, that doesn't mean external ones are unimportant. There can be significant and necessary activities that may not spark great passion or joy directly but that bring meaning and satisfaction due to the people you care about. Or they enable you to fulfill a responsibility in family, work, or community. For instance, washing the dishes or running errands are not typically heart-alive experiences, but they support and strengthen healthy relationships and households, which bring longer-term joy and fulfillment. This recognition of purpose can provide unexpected motivation in seemingly mundane tasks. Recognizing aspects of one's creative identity in a profession or family role can deepen a sense of intrinsic motivation for parts of life that don't seem as exciting.

You can also find ways to increase creative joy and satisfaction while still honoring your responsibilities or doing things that bring reward or recognition. Look for places for incremental change: add a podcast or music you love to a commute, introduce your kids to a favorite sport or movie, give yourself a creative reward after finishing a work project. Small adjustments can enhance the delight you find in the checkout line, getting coffee with a friend or coworker, or on a Saturday you spend helping your kids with homework. These creative elements can be helpful fuel when things get hard or when the responsibilities you carry are less fun. There are more ways to discover joy in daily routines than may currently be seen.

Remember the phrase "audience of one" as you explore existing and new expressions. Recognize that you can discover opportunities to make more of what you personally love within your unique opportunities and capacity. Value your voice, and focus on what moves you. Sing until you get the same feeling you got listening to your favorite music; code in a manner that the targeted problem is solved in a way that feels satisfying; facilitate team-building in a way that aligns with what has benefited your career. Dance, make, fix, write until you find that sense of resonance. If you have previously been over-focused on the responses and desires of others, this may feel new and even awkward at first. The places where thoughts or pressures from external demands try to keep crowding out intrinsic motivation are opportunities for greater personal discovery. Focus on the internal benefits that your expressions can bring. As your value for your unique approach grows, you'll find that your freedom of expression increases too.

Connecting Dreams with Current Opportunities

Your answers to the questions above may have revealed goals or dreams that feel impossible to achieve in your current situation. Don't be discouraged or dismiss your answers! The ideas and thoughts still hold keys of truth for you, no matter how far off they seem from your present circumstances. This exercise is designed to spur both long-term goals *and* the discovery of life-giving outlets accessible in the short term. Sure, not every application of this expression may be possible right now. Nevertheless, some are! What *can* you begin doing now? How can you start expressing yourself creatively in a related manner?

Returning to the building blocks example, there are ways you can scratch that itch today, depending on the specific theme identified. It could be working with your hands, exploring a design, or finding satisfaction in the pieces coming together. Activating an expression could look like constructing a shed or a bird feeder, reading a book, taking a course on architecture, or putting extra effort into decorating your bedroom like your Pinterest dream.

Experimentation is a great way to identify which aspects of your creative outflows, outlets, and channels provide the most delight and satisfaction. Start trying things and see what you enjoy. Don't get stuck in analysis paralysis or worry about what others will think. Not everyone will share your passions; in fact, most may not. Instead of feeling hurt, let that reality remind you that you truly are unique and have something special to release into the world. Your greatest dream may not be feasible initially, whether due to a lack of available time, resources, or confidence that it's worth the investment. But success is just taking the next step in front of you and staying aware of what is truly bringing you life.

Your capacity for fulfilling experiences of creativity will increase as you become aware of where you have experienced limitations. You may find a level of satisfaction in present activities, but realize that there are other themes and expressions that bring greater joy and meaning. It's possible to be incredibly productive (and creative!) in your work or hobbies but not actually as intrinsically motivated or satisfied as you could be. Readjusting priorities can provide space for fresh heart-alive creativity. However, not all outflows of your themes will be beneficial or possible in your current context. For instance, family responsibilities may be need to be prioritized over a massive, immediate career shift to follow a newfound passion. There may also be resources or tools not yet discovered that transform your present experience or empower small steps forward. As you explore, make time to reflect on both your current opportunities and future goals for your expressions and your broader life.

The Kid Who Secretly Loved Dance Music

My hope is that you find creative passions that make you stop and stare, that you crave like I crave In-N-Out burgers, that bring a joy that keeps you up at night. Electronic dance music is one of those creative themes for me. I have loved this genre since I first heard it in my early teenage years. It brings me back to my first crush, junior high dances, memorable family trips, and key moments that shaped the course of my life. I can rock out in a solo dance party at my house at almost any time.

In my youth, songs by Alice DJ, Basement Jaxx, Daft Punk, and others brought floods of joy, excitement, and inspiration. I don't have words to fully describe it, beyond that my heart feels really alive.

For years, I listened to the voice of shame and felt I had to downplay my passion for electronic music because it wasn't the music the "cool" kids listened to. I didn't see any future purpose for this interest (it didn't check any external validation boxes). I developed a subconscious hesitation around it, even in the years after it became more popular in the U.S. Fear of others' judgments and my own internalized insecurities limited exploration and enjoyment of a passion that today brings great joy, via multiple types of expression. I had no clue that I would one day get to write and make songs in this genre and encourage and support other artists.

Intentional exploration started during my recovery journey in 2016. Listening to electronic music brought positive, joyful experiences, often with spiritual connection, meditation, and prayer. Throughout my life, EDM song lyrics had spoken messages of hope and love into key moments within difficult seasons. As I experienced my own healing process, I began to see how electronic music could connect to my newfound passion for mental, emotional, and spiritual health. A sense of calling grew as my heart stirred for the thousands of people I had partied alongside at clubs and festivals, some of whom I knew must be experiencing addiction and other challenges.

One night, while brainstorming a non-musical, recovery-related social impact idea, I felt a sudden flash of inspiration while listening to Swedish House Mafia. Though at the time I didn't believe I was personally musical anymore, I started jotting down lyrics. I had learned music theory by playing the trumpet and baritone in middle school and singing in high school, but I hadn't formally performed or trained in a decade. A few weeks later, I felt an unanticipated excitement in sitting down at a piano and plunking on the keys, though I'm not trained on the instrument. The joy I experienced in each small step encouraged me to keep going and prepared me for what was to come.

A serendipitous introduction soon after led to my first out-of-the-blue songwriting session with someone else. The intrinsic joy, in the form of a natural and spiritual high stronger than I knew I could feel via music, brought confirmation that this theme needed to be part of my life. This turned out to be a life-changing heart-alive experience, which I'll share more about in a later chapter. It inspired tangible actions that enabled further exploration of dance music as a life-giving hobby. As my confidence and self-acceptance continued to grow, I began to invest more time and resources.

The discovery of intrinsic joy and heart-alive experiences helped motivate practical changes needed to prioritize this expression. I removed activities that I was doing out of a perceived obligation to keep up appearances and old hobbies that weren't life-giving anymore. At times this has been easier than expected, and in other seasons more difficult. Decreasing time spent watching sports and television and picking my spots for nightlife or other social activities has provided additional capacity to make music. Removing hangovers from the equation also helped. The more intrinsic delight, meaning, and momentum I experienced around dance music, the easier it became to prioritize. I was not just saying no to less-fulfilling endeavors; I was saying yes to something superior.

Recognizing electronic dance music as a theme, and not just a specific activity, fueled life-giving expressions even when I wasn't writing it personally. I started by making playlists and incorporating the sound more into my daily activities. A chance meeting through friends who worked in tech led indirectly to other opportunities. Through these new friendships I got to help start an online community that supports the wellness of professionals working in the world of EDM, starting with their spiritual lives. I still pinch myself because I have so much fun facilitating calls for people who are creating in this genre. It's an honor to provide a space where they can feel seen and loved. The process practically demonstrated how several of my creative themes (e.g., dance music, spiritual wellness, connecting people) could intersect and bring incredible heart-alive moments. There are more ways to activate a passion than can be seen at first glance.

The creative freedom and delight discovered through this specific theme have inspired experimentation that would have similarly felt off-limits, implausible, or too distant. Growth in one area increased permission to explore and prioritize other expressions that sparked intrinsic motivation and passion.

Trial and Layer: Exploring the New

There are heart-alive experiences waiting for you. This process is about trial and layer, not trial and error. Seize the opportunities to discover more about what brings you heart-alive creativity every day. You're not in search of one end-all, be-all solution. Take out the "right" and "wrong" thinking from your vocabulary around creativity; there is much to be discovered in nuance. Having a negative experience with a particular format of an expression doesn't mean you have to disqualify a theme. Your dislike of sketching with charcoal doesn't mean you can't enjoy drawing; you just may need colored pencils or even a digital tool. You might greatly enjoy writing blog pieces but not have a passion for prose. Or you could love engineering work that contributes to new products far more than that which tests existing ones. Specific aspects of creative outflows can also complement or reinforce another. For instance, finding delight in sketching buildings may reinforce that both visual art and architecture are life-giving themes for you. It's all valuable information for your journey.

Taking note of these details in your heart-alive forms of creativity can make you aware of opportunities that you've not previously activated. Lean into these moments with gratitude for the opportunity to explore, not with a sense of having missed out. None of us gets it perfect right away. It is much more life-giving and beneficial to approach this learning from a perspective of thankfulness instead of getting stuck in "shoulda, woulda, coulda" thinking.

Deep experiences of intrinsic joy through creativity require the capacity to feel. Our wide-ranging emotions powerfully influence the flavors with which we create: sour, spicy, salty, sweet. This variety of experiences is part of the beauty of being human. While I will be sharing a lot about joy and satisfaction because of how they fuel creative processes, it's also important that we feel permission to express our full range of feelings. They complement each other in the development of a fulfilling meal. Authenticity in creativity can deepen its potential for beauty, hope, and healing. For instance, the inspiring recovery stories that we capture at OneStepHope include both painful losses and wondrous discoveries, horrendous situations and profound healing.

Personally, I connect most to art that carries tension. I enjoy making music that expresses deep longing, references authentic challenges, and explores unconditional love and new possibilities. As you upgrade your creative process, you will likely have opportunities to explore deeper and more authentic feeling. Just stay aware of whether you are emotionally connecting in a way that serves your journey. It can be more life-giving than it has been in the past.

Identifying creative themes that spark joy and satisfaction is an ongoing process. You likely won't be able to try every new expression right away, so it's important to record ideas as you explore and experiment. This is the purpose of the Resonance Map, a customizable tool that can support your ongoing journey. Access a copy or learn how to make your own at www.onestepguides.com/creativity-unlocked-book. If you get stuck in exploring themes or in identifying expressions, ask a friend for ideas or download the Creativity Unlocked app for content and community that can jump-start your journey. A creativity consultant or mindsets coach can also help you identify practical ways of applying your passion. Finding intrinsically motivated expressions is one of the most important parts of rediscovering creativity. But it's possible to identify the "right" themes and still be limited in the joy, ease, and satisfaction experienced based on your approach. Upgrading our creative process is what we will address in the next chapter.

⚷ ONE-STEP ACTIVATION

Indulge in a creative theme that brings you delight. If you can, pick one that has been under-prioritized or that may not be known or appreciated by others. Set aside at least fifteen minutes and allow yourself to enjoy the activation without any need for an outcome.

CREATIVITY STORIES

JESSE | AUTHOR

By the summer of 2020, author Jesse had fallen into a rut of work that lacked joy. As the creator of The Seabirds Trilogy, a young-adult historical fiction series, and a professional editor and ghostwriter, she had been aware of and active in her expressions for years. But something felt different. "Even though I appreciated my clients, my work felt heavy and dull, missing the spark that I had previously known. I had become so focused on work for others that I had put off more personal dreams, dreams that I believe I was born for. The Creativity Unlocked Workshop came at an ideal time."

Through her engagement with the curriculum and the community, Jessie rediscovered a childlike approach focused on intrinsic joy, which refreshed her process and sparked inspiration. "I had begun to think that certain creative channels would always lead to experiences of drudgery." This perspective contributed to Jesse pausing her efforts around screenwriting, a core passion, as other projects took over her schedule. "The permission to take a look at my process completely shifted my approach to work. I felt I was given a green light to rearrange my to-do list and give screenwriting its rightful place, front and center. As I began to re-engage creatively with my favorite writing form, I felt joy in my day-to-day work for the first time in several years."

Jesse found courage to step toward a dream project that had seemed unlikely by focusing on this simple idea of pursuing what brought her heart delight. "An excitement for this work returned, regardless of whether it ever saw the light of day. I felt set free from a sadness that had been holding me back, and the whole journey contributed to healthier approaches to relationships, collaboration, and other aspects of life." After shifting into this approach, an unexpected breakthrough occurred. "Funnily enough, and it certainly feels like divine timing, within a few months of this personal change, the door opened to acquire the life rights for the subject of the screenplay of my dreams." Jesse shared that upgrading her approach has enabled her to now enjoy the process of pursuing this project without carrying the weight of it, like she once would have.

Jesse's story is a wonderful example of the power of finding intrinsically motivating expressions. Her advice for people around their creativity is this: "Don't give up on the dreams that you're born for. Focus on what brings you intrinsic joy. Be intentional around trouble-shooting how you're creating, because it can benefit your process, and your life."

PROCESS UNLOCKED

Develop a step-by-step approach that serves your goals. Hurdles may present themselves that threaten to block or dull your exploration. In this chapter, unlock a process that honors your capacity and helps you navigate the imperfect parts of the journey.

Be Like a Baby Giraffe

Have you ever seen a newborn giraffe take its first steps? Find a video of one on YouTube, and get ready for fifteen seconds of pure joy. You're welcome.

Exploring and activating your creativity will feel similar at times: brave, wonderful, and wobbly. You may experience a whole range of emotions: uncertainty, exhilaration, fear, wonder, and much more. The wonderful natural highs of expressions that bring intrinsic joy are incredible. But there can also be low points, where you feel frustrated, confused, or disappointed. Moments of perceived "success" or "failure" serve as an invitation to upgrade your growth process, both around specific outflows and how you engage with creativity more broadly.

Don't be surprised if wacky thoughts cross your mind a few dozen or hundred times along the way—such as, *You're crazy to believe you can try this*, or *It's too late for you*. You don't have to let the voice of negativity win. There will be moments when you don't feel like you have the strength or the answers or when you need to lean into community. That's okay. You are still creative in the midst of these emotions, and there are still joy-filled experiences ahead for you, even if you can't see them in the moment.

The creative process doesn't have to be overwhelming. Recognizing the strengths and limitations of your current approach is an important aspect of experiencing greater joy, ease, and fulfillment in your expressions. The practical keys in this chapter, rooted in a "baby steps" approach, will help you build momentum, grow in healthy ways, find creative flow, and navigate the bumpy parts doing something new.

An Endless Blur of Possibility

Exploring creativity can feel a little like arriving at Disneyland with loved ones. There are an incredible number of options. You're aware of vivid sounds and experiences, many of which can trigger strong reactions. Thoughts race through your mind: *Is there enough time to really enjoy this? What will I do if someone gets lost? Where do I start in order to maximize the experience? How much will this all cost? How do I navigate what I like versus what others want? How can I fit in everything that I want to do or see? Will getting that slushy make me puke on Space Mountain?*

Okay, maybe not that last one. But, in your creative exploration, you may face questions about priorities, limited capacity and resources, incorporating others in your decisions, and defining success. Like Disneyland visits, the process can be highly emotional, and seemingly small factors can shift one's experience. Creativity connects deeply with one's sense of self and thus can stir all sorts of feelings. The positive ones are great for strengthening self-worth, sparking gratitude, and fueling momentum. Meanwhile, the heightened negative emotions can be challenging. Planning ahead and setting healthy expectations can help you avoid unnecessary pain and experience more fun throughout the journey.

CHAPTER 4 | PROCESS UNLOCKED

It is important to learn to stay in touch with your needs. The natural highs of creativity can sometimes paper over deficiencies in opportunities to process emotional pain or disappointment. At times, I have found myself so enthused by the purpose and delight of what I am building professionally or artistically that I end up underinvesting in my own wellness, leading to less-than-ideal decisions. If you are on an emotional health journey or have been prone to unwanted coping mechanisms or addictive cycles, it can be helpful to be aware of these possibilities. The practical keys below are designed to help you navigate the process in a way that supports your flourishing through the ups and downs. Remember, one of the most powerful ways we learn is through failure. There's so much hope and possibility, even when we hit a bump in the path. Remember the baby giraffe? Youngsters wobble at first, but not forever. Your creative steps won't always feel as uncertain as they may initially.

Eight Keys to Upgrade Your Creative Process

Applying the keys below will strengthen your process for any expression, whether you're initiating new experiences, building relationships, crafting art, serving an organization, or expressing in a different form.

1. Create achievable goals and practical plans.

Unrealistic expectations can be emotionally draining. They can also torpedo your best efforts to create. Remember, it's about *baby steps*. Our society is hungry for quick wins and overnight success, but discovery takes time, especially when intrinsic joy and meaningful connection are the aim. The practice of breaking bigger dreams or plans into *small wins* has been studied and shown effective by numerous researchers, including organizational theorist and psychologist Karl Weick.[17] Turning goals into achievable steps builds momentum for new habits and fuels motivation for further action.

For example, instead of launching into a new writing project by saying, "I'm going to finish a novel in the next six months," you can start with something more realistic and focused on a short-term output, like, "I'm going to write for thirty minutes twice this week." Consciously choose where you'll take the time from, and celebrate the trade you're making. Checking off each step provides a sense of satisfaction that fuels ongoing progress, whether creating in the arts or another space. If you're pursuing education or a new job, divide the long-term vision into smaller tasks that you can handle. This could include researching possible programs or workplaces, completing a resume or application, preparing for the interview, negotiating an offer, and starting classes or work. You can always refine and adjust the structure and goals you set. As you go, take note of settings, planning techniques, times of day, and environments that contribute to or hinder your process.

2. Give yourself permission to be imperfect.

Compassion is powerful and necessary fuel for your creative journey. If you're taking on an untried expression, or even trying a new approach to a format you know, it's likely going to go poorly at times. Please be kind to yourself! Don't spend your energy worrying about failing or being self-critical. Set your focus on learning how to move forward, even if that includes a stumble. Here's another helpful illustration from public speakers Steve and Wendy Backlund: one would not treat a child who is learning to ride a bicycle with the same negativity that many of us experience in our creative journeys. Can you imagine someone saying the following to a kid who has just tumbled over his handlebars: "I can't believe you fell. You should have known better. Maybe you just don't have the talent to be a bicycle rider?" That would be awful. Instead, we recognize the stage of development and comfort the child when they fall. Practice that tone of compassion with yourself. Recognize that growth comes through experimenting, whether or not you think the results were successful. Removing the pressure of perfection will make it easier to persist when you face challenges.

3. Embrace vulnerability and develop a plan for tough moments.

Newsflash: there will be steps in your creative exploration that feel vulnerable. You may not always know how to handle the situations or emotions you encounter, and that's okay. Having a plan in place will help you experience the tension without being shipwrecked by it. Over time, you can grow in comfort with uncertainty and with vulnerability. When things start feeling wobbly, draw from the steps below. If you have an overwhelming sense of stress or all-or-nothing thoughts, see it as an invitation to reset. You may have reached the extent of your emotional, mental, or physical capacity, or you may be feeling a bit overexposed. Pause what you are doing and follow these steps:

- Recognize and acknowledge your feelings.
- Remember that you're growing, trying new things, and stepping out of your comfort zone. You're moving forward.
- Take a practical step that helps you feel comfort and safety. Listen to a favorite song, engage with a life-giving spiritual practice, talk with a trusted friend, read something inspiring, or take a few minutes to engage with a hobby that is fun for you.
- Remind yourself of the experience, learning, joy, or growth that awaits on the other side of the vulnerability.
- Reaffirm a positive viewpoint about yourself and your creativity. Remember that it is part of your nature and reveals your value, no matter the outcome. Remind yourself that you don't have to get it perfect or somehow "arrive" to prove your worth. Revisit affirmations as needed.

As you progress in your journey, give yourself full permission to experiment and adjust your process. Some of the vulnerability "hangovers" we experience are hard to prevent, while others might be avoidable. The more you experiment and try new things, the more you will learn about your unique creative process and the more adept you'll become at handling the ups and downs.

4. Find the hidden benefits of limitations.

There are unexpected opportunities in situations where skills, resources, and even time are lacking. Necessity can truly be the mother of invention. Having fewer options provides the gift of focus and an opportunity to exercise your innovative, creative mind. Researchers like Daniel Kahneman and Barry Schwartz have shown that "choice paralysis" can occur when people have too many possibilities, which keeps them from making a decision and moving forward.[18] It may seem counterintuitive, but less can be more for your creativity, especially in early stages. Choose to embrace the three chords you can play on a piano or guitar, or the few colors or techniques you have for your visual art. Celebrate the limited time you have to prepare for an event or work project; you can still make something meaningful. Powerful poetry and lyrics can be written in the five or ten minute blocks of time you have. Too often, we put off our next creative steps with the excuse of waiting for a full toolbox or an abundance of time. Instead, start with what you have today.

Gratitude can shift your mindset from discouragement around what you're lacking to joyful experimentation with what is in your hands right now. You may not be able to execute your full vision, but you can still create using the same inspiration. For instance, if an elaborate dinner party or excursion isn't possible, start with a simpler gathering that brings you joy. Or, if you dream of building an organization focused on wellness for communities, start with an encouraging note for a single friend. If you're struggling with creative indecision, you may even want to intentionally set and enforce an artificial limitation. Give yourself a topic or theme you must create *and* within a time limit. Or choose one instrument, tool, or color. This can help keep you from overthinking and overanalyzing your creative outflows.

Focus on enjoying the sandbox in which you find yourself, even if you have a vision to reach the beach in the future. There is delight to be discovered around you today. You may even be unknowingly building the skill sets you need to thrive when you reach your dream context. The limited settings of sandbox seasons can provide opportunity to find greater clarity around which expressions actually provide intrinsic joy and satisfaction. Be intentional about your focus. Constantly looking at pictures of the metaphorical overwater bungalow or the Florida Keys won't help you benefit from the joy and meaning possible in the sandbox (hello, social media). Choose to embrace the moment you're in and grab those five, ten, or fifteen minute windows for expression that brings delight. What formerly seemed like scraps can turn into a bountiful feast that refreshes your soul.

5. Redefine success by celebrating every win.

Confident, joy-filled creativity is not just about refusing the voice of the inner critic; you *must* partner with new, positive ideas about yourself too. Recognizing qualities you can celebrate fuels courage and momentum. Day by day, you can strengthen beliefs around your creative expressions and grow in confidence around your dreams. Again, think of a child learning to ride a bike—or a baby giraffe learning to walk. How does a parent treat their wobbly progress? We celebrate like crazy!

In our society, many commonly struggle to see the gold in the midst of the process. Too often we are told that if something or someone is not perfect, it's completely devoid of good or redemptive possibilities. Though it may feel normal, this black-or-white thinking is simplistic and can make us dismissive, perfectionistic, judgmental, and cynical toward others and ourselves. It is terrible soil for growth! Placing judgment on quality in the early stages of exploration actually keeps us blocked up and locked away, because we could never be perfect enough to answer the cynical voice. So let's ditch it! A nuanced approach that recognizes positives and negatives within the messiness of growth will benefit your creativity. Focus on the wins you can celebrate when things don't go like you expect.

- ❖ I celebrate that I tried something new, regardless of the outcome.

- I am successful because I stepped out of my comfort zone and did my best.
- If I feel disappointed or let down now, that's okay. These feelings won't last, and they won't stop me from trying again when I'm ready.

The positive reframing of your own journey helps you navigate your feelings, which is the focus of the next key.

6. Distinguish emotions from facts.

Feelings are powerful. To thrive in creativity, you need to validate the emotions you experience as you explore. Just remember that your feelings and instincts aren't always objective or rooted in ultimate truth. How many times have you thought you failed something miserably, like a test or job interview, only to discover that you actually did well on it? Or vice versa? Am I the only one who has thought someone was upset with me only to realize that I was completely misreading the situation? Though feelings can helpfully indicate aspects of your current condition and capacity, they are not a fail-proof guide for creative growth. Sometimes they indicate the opposite of what is objectively true, especially when you're trying something new. There are times when you will need to lean into something more than your current emotions, whether it's a core value, inspirational quote, affirmation, proverb, or something else.

When attempting something new or vulnerable in creativity, don't judge your efforts by how you feel right away. Experiment with a twelve or twenty-four hour "no introspection" rule, when you intentionally give yourself space to celebrate your attempt instead of diving into constructive responses or negative emotions. If you're more used to critical thoughts, the "good" can be difficult to focus on. Take a break to do something fun, or ask a trusted friend for encouragement that helps you celebrate the steps you are taking. As you progress, you will learn what best helps you navigate the emotional aspects of creativity. Just be careful to not let short-term negative feelings blind you to the positive momentum of your journey.

7. Express gratitude that proactively counters comparison.

Self-doubt is not uncommon. Even those you now consider experts and professionals have moments of failure, insecurity, or starting again. Be aware that at some point you'll likely have negative thoughts flash through your head:

- *It's not as good as theirs.*
- *Why am I even attempting this?*
- *They've been doing this for so long. What's the point of me trying?*

When the voice of comparison starts to yap, take action with a different response.

- Verbalize the doubts you are feeling if need be, but don't stay there. Use positive affirmations that express thankfulness for your unique creative gifts.
- Proactively honor the beauty that others release into the world instead of allowing their gift to make you feel inferior. Celebrating others' outflows trains us to more easily celebrate our own, and vice versa.
- Exercise the power to ignore. Intentionally shift your focus or dive back into your own expression. Remember that you get to set the tone for your day.

Don't forget: *every single person had to start somewhere.* Remind yourself of what is fueling your expression: discovery, growth, joy, fulfillment, and other intrinsic motivations that are the natural products of your journey. This is for *you*, not your real or imaginary critics.

8. Follow the momentum.

As you explore creativity, give yourself permission to let go of expectations or thoughts driven by unhealthy pressure. Find freedom to explore in the reminder that you create from worth, not for it. You may find yourself led toward an expression that surprises you, or end up at a delightfully different outcome or destination. The process does not always unfold in a concrete sequential manner. Embrace the adventure, and follow the joy you find. This idea is true for both initial creative experiences and longer-term aspirations. Inspiration and momentum can come in ebbs and flows. If it lifts for a period of time, especially around a particular project, it doesn't mean that something is wrong. It might even be a signal that there are other aspects of your life or your creativity that need your focus.

As you explore expressions from a foundation of healthy mindsets, you might tap into flow states. These periods of ease, inspiration, and productive output are wonderfully fruitful, starting with the sense of satisfaction they provide. In the 1970s, scientists began to study the concept of flow, where one is fully immersed in their present activities. They found examples in sport, art, problem-solving, the workplace, and activities like rock climbing. Researchers say flow often includes heightened focus, clear direction, spontaneity, and awareness with a lack of self-consciousness. Challenges are recognized and solutions appear with ease. Flow state also can hold surprising directions, "rapid meaning-making," "effortless attention," and losing track of time.[19] Interestingly, subsequent research found that flow states involve both type I (automatic, intuitive) and type II (deliberate, analytical) thinking. The brain is able to focus on solutions while remaining open to originality and new ideas. According to researchers, flow states can arise out of periods of intentional preparation, effort, or unexpected moments, though the experience itself is often marked by an effortless feeling. The keys you are adding throughout these pages will help you find momentum in specific expressions and across multiple parts of life.

Embracing the Journey

Your creative journeys will likely contain advances and retreats. Mountaineers climbing the world's highest peaks almost never venture from base camp to the top in one go. They advance up the Himalayas step by step, setting up camps they return to as they acclimate to the environment. Your creative expressions may have seasons of rising, holding steady, or returning to a place of strength or comfort. There will be plenty of surprises. My goal is that you will develop a process that can sustain you over the long haul, including both adventurous moments and times of rest.

There are also moments for a mountaineer when success looks like calling it quits and waiting for another opportunity. When the conditions and the weather conspire to interrupt a summit attempt, a climber may decide that the best course of action is to halt an ascent or conclude an expedition. Though they may not have reached their intended goal, they know there will be an opportunity to climb another day, whether or not it's on the same peak. Sometimes momentum lifting indicates that it is best to move away from a creative project or partnership for a more prolonged period of time—whether artistic, relational, or experiential. This may be because we experience something that brings even greater joy or meaning, or because the current adventure doesn't support our growth or wellness. If you do shift your focus, don't quit on your creative potential! You are simply recalculating, and what you have learned will benefit you going forward. Who knows? New opportunities may arise to return and pick up an old project again, under more favorable conditions.

For the past several years, I've been working on a non-musical creative project with a friend that continues to take shape. The breaks between periods of creative flow have unexpectedly been some of the most important and refreshing times. The momentum would lift, the work would consistently feel like a slog instead of a joy, and we would sense the need to pause. Having someone with whom to process and identify these moments has been incredibly helpful. The in-between times provide opportunities to manage other parts of life, sow seeds for later creative adventures, rest, and have space from which to see with fresh perspective. These seasons also help me remember that my value and significance do not come from a piece of creativity, no matter how beautiful or potentially impactful it can be. My collaborator and I have been surprised at the clarity and joyful motivation that have arrived after each of these pauses. Fresh inspiration and ideas for constructive revisions have also flowed from our everyday experiences during these breaks. This pattern has been helpful for creative exploration and projects that are side hustles, as there have been seasons in which both of us need to focus more on income-generating opportunities.

My journey in making electronic dance music has also benefited from a similar approach. Baby steps helped shift this expression from delightful exploration to heartfelt passion and helped me navigate similar uncertain but fruitful starts and stops. Songs take longer to complete than I expected. Schedules don't align. Pauses and detours arise from other priorities. I'll go months without writing. Tracks I've helped create still haven't launched three years later. But because I experience intrinsic joy and delight (and now recognize songwriting as a creative theme), I can stay connected to deep gratitude for every experience that helps fuel the process. It is no longer a question of *if* I will make music, but simply how and when, because it is a clear part of my creative passions whether or not anyone else hears the songs.

Exploring this newfound interest felt incredibly vulnerable at first. My first steps were to encourage others who were passionate about music to pursue their interests in this genre. Then I had the experiences described in the last chapter, where I started feeling inspired to journal lyrics in my phone and then experienced a profound heart-alive experience in a co-writing session. The delight inspired me to put digital audio workstation software on my laptop and start writing songs by myself that connected to my journey. At times, I would feel uncertain about the process. But I could not deny the profound sense of personal connection and passion I felt in the process. Over time, doors opened for collaboration with others. These moments have become more natural and life-giving, simply by getting more reps.

I used to think that I could only find delight in expressions or activities in which I was highly skilled or experienced. That's a lie. The truth is the opposite: finding the joy and satisfaction in a creative expression can powerfully fuel the practice and repetition that help strengthen skills. I am still nowhere near as experienced or talented as many with whom I collaborate, but that doesn't stop me from recognizing what I can bring to the table and being able to enjoy the process. Deep friendships and community have sprung out of these adventures. Sometimes

CHAPTER 4 | PROCESS UNLOCKED

the value we gain through different stages of the creative process is beyond what we expected. As you continue your journey, consider which aspects of your expressions make your heart come alive. Is it the activity itself or the experience or context that it creates for yourself or with others? The answers may be surprising and can help identify additional intrinsically motivated themes.

Here's to the Wobbles

The keys listed above aren't sequential steps. They're more like a bag of assorted tools to draw on throughout your journey. You may have to build some new goals, tighten the bolts of your foundational mindsets, or hammer out places where discouragement has dented your dreams. If you need to repeat some of these steps again and again—and again— you're not alone. Navigating different creative seasons can feel uncertain, so be kind to yourself in the process. Not only will you make it through difficult periods, but also you will grow through them.

Creative expressions can go through different seasons, just like parts of a garden. There are times for growth, times for fruitfulness, times for harvesting, and times for dormancy. Sometimes plants wither and die and become fertilizer for what is to come. Your current and past creative expressions can provide fuel and guidance for future adventures, if you allow them to. Keep an eye out for the learning you gain even in efforts that don't continue as expected: a greater understanding of your potential, a willingness to try new things, an ability to fail successfully, and appreciation for learning and resilience. You may need to uproot and replant in certain seasons; it is part of the cycle of life. Soil replenishment, sowing seeds, nurturing growth, weeding, harvest— each part has its beauty and plays into what is coming. Just like how tomatoes and strawberries have different growing and harvest seasons, when one of your expressions needs a rest, another might be ready for work or fruitfulness.

I hope that the picture of a baby giraffe wobbling on its crooked, knobbed legs stays firmly planted in your mind as you explore your expressions. May this mental image remind you that it's okay to look, feel, and be imperfect, awkward, uncertain. Your journey can bring greater

CREATIVITY UNLOCKED

joy and connection to your life, in ever-deepening ways, especially as you address barriers related to the topic of our next chapter: healing from past creative pain.

> ### ✒ ONE-STEP ACTIVATION
> Identify which of these keys you need most for your process today. Where are you getting stuck? Journal about how the ideas in this chapter can help you move forward. If you are having trouble picking one, practice experiencing the benefits of limitation. Give yourself a time limit or other constraint for an expression, and start creating.

JESSICA | VISUAL ARTIST

Jessica has been making art ever since she can remember. But her journey to see this passion become more of a career has involved a process, and she continues to take it step by step. Needing income after finishing her Master's in Fine Arts, she took a job as an assistant at a consulting firm. Over seven years, Jessica worked her way up within the company to leading events and other activities for hundreds of employees, as she continued pursuing her passion. Now a professional artist, her time in the corporate world contributed to her development in unexpected ways. "It grew my confidence, communication, problem-solving, and relationship-building skills," Jessica shares, "and through it I was led to my most significant project yet: a nine-month installation and exhibition at the Gates Foundation in Seattle."

For Jessica, the process of creating art is deeply meaningful and personally satisfying. "I get lost in simply mixing colors, which is deeply therapeutic for me. The smell of paint or the sight of a blank canvas does something to my brain. Though my experience is in classical approaches to painting, I love taking on new mediums: sewing, music, street art, sculpture, installation, and more." Jessica finds a natural exhilaration in the fresh challenges and adventures these mediums present. For a while, she questioned whether she should have more of a focus, but now she sees the variety as core to her creative approach and identity. "One of my strengths as a creative being is a comfort with risk," she says. "Short-term failure is never the end."

Jessica very much follows the momentum in her creative process, and her experiences carry attributes of the concept of flow state. "Art is a restful place, where time fades away. My process is spiritual. Art allows me to authentically express important creative themes and interests." A few years ago, Jessica completed a series of thirty-seven street art angels depicted in Renaissance style. She displayed them around the city of Seattle and intentionally picked places frequented by people experiencing homelessness. Placing many of these images under bridges, in alleys, and in areas less frequented by typical gallery visitors aligned with the vision to provide a sense of hope and connection for people. "It's a community I've gotten to know through volunteering, and many of them shared that they often feel unsafe in their surroundings. A street art angel is not the same as a home or shelter, but I hope that it provides a reminder that they are not alone, that they are loved, right where they are."

Art is also a channel through which Jessica can honor and explore her heritage. A sculpture series inspired by her Korean heritage helped with processing the beauty, pain, and confusion she has felt. Another significant project stemmed from an intuitive, unplanned discovery. "During a busy season at my corporate workplace, I started experimenting with making flowers from a mixture of Korean traditional dress fabric and old army uniforms. At the time, I think I was burned-out on critique after undergoing so much during my studies. I would sit down as soon as I returned from work and find refreshment in creating these for hours." Jessica decided to follow this passion and make what brought her joy instead of feeling constrained by assumptions of how others might respond or hindered by comparison. "These flowers, drawn from such disparate materials, brought a sense of intrinsic peace and fulfillment to me personally, regardless of the outcome." Though Jessica had not planned to display them, they eventually led to a public exhibit.

A huge part of Jessica's passion is platforming others. She founded the Seattle Art Post to help elevate emerging artists in her city. It has been a hit: hundreds come to their events, and a good number have received gallery representation. People ask her why she spends so much time on things that have little financial reward. Her response: "Honestly, the work aligns with other creative expressions—serving and empowering others—and my deep passion for art. I postured my heart to serve people in the field that I feel a calling toward, and now lots of opportunities are arising."

HEALING UNLOCKED

Address blockages and pain that hinder your journey. Rediscovering creativity might dredge up difficult moments from your past. In this chapter you will learn to unlock healing that lightens your load and increases freedom for expression and exploration.

Rocks, Rocks, Rocks

It's time to talk about rock. No, not the music genre, the beloved actor, or the *Schoolhouse* video series that educated a generation about government. I'm referring to the hard stuff that makes up a large portion of the world. According to *National Geographic,* rocks are generally classified into three categories: sedimentary, metamorphic, and igneous, based on how they are formed.[20] They are pretty much everywhere. And they provide a great metaphor for the past or present pain that can hinder your creative exploration.

Whether the size of a mountain or a pebble lodged in a shoe, rocks and pain can significantly hinder physical or creative journeys. Both can be formed by fiery moments, battering opposition by external forces, layers of accumulated muck compressed together, or intense pressure. They can turn an otherwise fun adventure into a disaster via an unexpected slip or a surprising collision. Though the characteristics of a rock or pain do impact the wound and specific solutions required, they don't change the fact that something needs to be addressed. A small stone can be just as deadly as a rockslide if experienced in a particular manner. Unresolved pain of any size can affect your creativity.

If finding joy and meaning in your expressions is difficult, there may be an unrecognized reason. Past experiences of difficulty, disappointment, and rejection can impact your present emotions around creativity. When you are facing a seemingly insurmountable wall or being irritated by a minuscule shard, acknowledging the problem is the first step. How often do people metaphorically camp out in front of a barrier or create with a limp or a festering wound because they have not diagnosed or known how to address the pain? You don't have to be a superhero. You have permission to raise your hand and say, "This hurts, and I need support." It's a brave, honest step that can transform your experience of creativity.

The goal of this chapter is simply to start the process of recognizing and addressing pain. We will look at a few places where it might be inhibiting your expressions and then explore tools and approaches for healing. Some of these concepts may be more applicable in future seasons. As we dive into what can be a heavy topic, let this simple analogy of rocks remind you of the baby-steps approach of the previous chapter. Start by addressing the pebbles in your shoes and using tools that can help with minor cuts and scrapes.

You may be facing a big rock that requires support beyond the tools offered in this book. That's okay. Other excavators, surgeons, and healers may be needed, like support groups or counselors and therapists. Take heart: healing is possible. In learning how to navigate the rocks in your creative journey, you just might discover tools and experiences that invigorate your life. At any point, feel free to step away and take a deep breath. Come up for air and connect to healthy forms of comfort and fun as needed. Let the inspiration you have found thus far, and the hope of future growth, encourage you to engage in the healing journey.

CHAPTER 5 | HEALING UNLOCKED

Hitting a Rock

Has it happened to you yet? Has the perfect opportunity to create something run aground on a memory of a painful moment that hinders your momentum and joy? Or have there been heavy "rocks" or scar tissue from past experiences that you suddenly realize you are carrying? Sometimes we don't fully recognize these influences until they are removed, or until a friend points out or triggers a wound that needs healing.

Past pain may have led you to subconsciously limit aspects of your creative identity and expression. Mishaps and difficult situations are a part of being human, and they can continue to affect the way we think, speak, and act long after the moment. Just as a broken bone limits your physical range of motion, so too can unhealed internal pain hinder your creativity. The benefits of expressions may not seem worth the muck with which they became associated in your mind. Resistance or limitations around creative activities often indicate opportunities to experience healing that can add ease and joy to your process.

Blockers can arrive via clearly traumatic experiences and less-overt pain. Even that which seems innocuous to another person can play a significant role. The effects of discouragement from a loved one, perceived failure during a performance, or a general sense of inadequacy can stick with us. Why do varying forms of pain affect us so differently? The sting of memories can stay with us because of how we processed, or did not process, the triggered emotions. A 2007 UCLA study using brain scans showed that simply vocalizing negative emotions experienced can decrease the pain one feels, creating a therapeutic effect.[21] Whole models for healing, including cognitive behavioral therapy, have developed from findings showing the benefits of talking through trauma in a supportive environment that produces a different emotional experience.[22] Whether via minor scrapes or major wounds, unresolved pain affects our sense of safety and identity in ways beyond our conscious awareness. It gets shoved down, hidden from the love and comfort it actually needs. Even when we know something is off, uncertainty about next steps or concern about the process can delay the action that sparks healing.

Some of these places of unprocessed pain may not be directly related to a particular creative expression. The rocks may have formed via seemingly unlinked moments that left behind general residual beliefs rooted in unworthiness, hopelessness, or self-hatred. Your sense of identity and worth impacts your words, voice, actions, desires, tastes, and self-expression. This is not just an intellectual, factual understanding of yourself, but one that is deeply rooted and experienced in your emotions and your beliefs. Difficult points that arise in your creativity often tie back to places where your mindsets and core beliefs about yourself were affected by pain and fear instead of love. Learning to love your creative process and expressions generally flows from learning to love yourself more.

There is good news: pain communicates a need for change. It is a signal, a call, an invitation for something new, for help, for comfort, for healing. Nobody can change the past; however, you can change how you see the past and how it affects you today. Healing from difficult moments identified through your creative process will do more than free up specific expressions. It strengthens your foundational well-being and mindsets that affect every part of life. If you're struggling with an addictive pattern, procrastination, anger, relational dysfunction, stress, or other challenges or destructive behaviors, the roots underneath may be the same ones impeding your creativity. Addressing them could spark positive shifts around these challenges. Resolving pain helps you embrace a greater value for yourself and for others that fuels inspiration and clarity.

Healing is an unfolding journey. The process may look different from what you anticipate or understand. Sometimes, an experience of unexpected joy or meaningful connection can help rapidly transform the pain from sour to sweet. Profound shifts can happen in a moment. Creative expressions can sometimes activate these changes. But, often, it takes intention, time, and support for wounds to heal and new experiences to fully form. Whatever it looks like for you, the process is valuable. You have permission to take joy in aspects of your creativity, where possible, as the healing unfolds.

CHAPTER 5 | HEALING UNLOCKED

Healing and Loving My Voice

Pursuing creative expressions has provided opportunities to taste both the bitter, paralyzing fears that can be triggered and the sweet fruit of restoration in areas of pain. Exploring my passion for electronic music sparked healing for insecurities that resurfaced around my voice. From my teenage years to the age of 29, I hated hearing myself speak. I would almost always leave the room if a recording of myself was played. The sound was too nasally, too mumbly, too high-pitched, at least to my ears. Despite supportive voices early in my childhood musical pursuits, failure in some areas of vocal performance and a perception that it was not enough (oh hey, shame!) contributed to deprioritizing something I loved.

During that first unexpected songwriting opportunity described previously, my new producer friend Tedd strongly encouraged me to sing. Thankfully, I did not realize before the session that this would be necessary or I may not have agreed to take part. Singing into a mic that night for the first time in years felt quite vulnerable. But I could also sense a deep connection and joy in the moment as I shared heartfelt lyrics and a chord progression inspired by the discoveries of the recovery journey over the previous few months.

When the producer played back the demo version of the track, a wave of unexpected delight flowed over me, and it kept growing. I got emotional. It was the first time that I could hear the unique tone of my voice and actually, genuinely enjoy it. Tedd's gifting had taken something that felt broken or "less than" to me and found a beautiful quality within it that supported the heart-felt song. It felt like a divine gift. I remember a thought, a prayer of gratitude that pulsed through my mind. Deep within, for the first time, I knew that if my songwriting and music-making were just for me and the Man Upstairs, that was enough.

I could barely sleep that night. I had been given back a part of myself I didn't know I had lost, something that fear had stolen. And the rest was history—sort of. The intrinsic joy of this Christmas-in-May experience inspired the practical steps shared in the previous chapters. I saw how life-giving creating with others could be and that it was actually possible to enjoy a part of myself that I had seen as so imperfect. My voice is not what most would call the most talented or most trained. Far from it. But that doesn't keep it from being a vehicle for intrinsic joy and meaningful connection for me. These new, personally life-giving moments gave me courage to explore how my sounds and words could bless others via music and beyond.

The process helped me own my voice in other contexts: as a speaker, podcaster, poet, and entrepreneur. This breakthrough moment and those that followed likely would not have happened without the discoveries of the preceding months. Unwinding shame and fear through counseling and recovery support—and some key awakening moments I'll share about in the coming chapters—prepared me to discover new perspectives of expressions that I had considered inadequate. My hair still stands up on my arms when I think about these moments and the possibilities they indicate for new discoveries in creativity.

A Model for Reframing, Re-understanding, and Healing

Let's walk through an example of what it could look like to address pain points in the realm of creativity. I will use my own creative expression as an example, but you can adapt the model to walk through one of yours. If possible, go to a place where you can have some uninterrupted time and grab a journal.

To start, pick an area of creative expression on which you want to focus. Choose one that feels hindered but not too heavy, especially if it's your first time engaging with this process. Some aspects of creative pain are best addressed with help from a professional. Struggling to pick an expression? The following questions may help identify a pain point:

- ❖ What's an area of life where you know you have talent but you feel limited in practicing or experiencing it?
- ❖ What's a creative expression you want to explore but that feels uncomfortable?
- ❖ What's one creative expression that you once loved but don't participate in any longer?

Now, consider if there is a particular moment of pain or discomfort that could be related to your answers from above. There are likely limiting mindsets that have formed related to this expression, but they may have grown from specific experiences. If a flurry of memories come to mind, pick one or a few to focus on for this exercise. It may be the moment when you first believed, "I'm just not that type of person who…" or "I'm not skilled or talented enough to…" Other examples include hurtful insults, harsh feedback, or moments when you embraced limiting, negative beliefs about your creativity.

For me, some of the long-held negativity I felt around my voice stemmed from unresolved fears around my singing, perfectionism, a desire to fit in, and childhood speech difficulties. Moments of perceived failure also played a role, including an unsuccessful audition where I could not perform a run of notes. Hearing others who had more talent or training in their voices added to the sense that my gifting wasn't worthwhile enough to explore or be enjoyed. Comparison and a few experiences of perceived failure diminished my value for personally making music.

Back to your reflection. Consider what negative thoughts, emotions, and judgments are attached to these memories. Write down the feelings that come to mind. Now, consider how those experiences impacted what you believe about yourself. Reflect on how your thoughts and judgments about your expressions are linked to places where you've experienced negative feelings or criticism toward them. These painful moments may have taught you to avoid activities or that certain creative outflows would always include stress or other difficult emotions. The negative lens is valid, in the sense that there's a reason you've learned to think or feel a certain way. Because our brains are in the midst of major development when we're young, our experiences as kids have a significant impact. There's good news: recognizing the presence of negativity and pain indicates opportunities for love to come and clean your lens. No matter how ingrained those experiences are, there are new perspectives to discover that activate more supportive emotions. The negative mindsets are not the highest truth, and they don't have to define your creative development or your life going forward.

Comfort and Forgiveness Bring a Shift

I'm sorry that you have felt what you have felt. I'm sorry that your creativity was diminished, undervalued, squelched, or worse. That is not how you should have been treated. May your heart receive the warmth and love it needs in the midst of the pain it has known. You may need someone in person to speak similar words to you, whether once or again and again.

Our hearts need comfort. They need to be able to experience safety that makes space for authentic expression of what they have experienced. Verifying the specific factual details of moments is not the priority in this personal process. Allowing the subjective, emotional experiences to be expressed is key for healing. And it leads into the tool that will help us move forward in the process: forgiveness.

The practice of forgiveness helps us accept our own imperfect humanity and that of others. It does not lessen the wrong committed or ignore the pain experienced. Forgiveness is an extension of love and mercy in clear view of these realities. It is a letting go that actually frees us from the burdens of resentment, judgment, and guilt. The person who rejected, criticized, hurt, or disappointed you, knowingly or unknowingly, can be forgiven with or without direct communication. Sometimes an individual may hurt you by causing or creating a new wound. At other points, they may have done nothing wrong but their words or actions caused pain by hitting a tender spot, indicating an existing, unhealed wound. Regardless of the source or underlying motive, we can benefit from forgiving and releasing the pain. Sharing this gift does not require staying in a position susceptible to repeated harm. You can forgive *and* put in place practical changes and boundaries that are best for everyone's well-being, including your own. In letting go, it's possible to experience compassion and empathy for someone who may not deserve it.

As we extend this gift, whether to our colleagues, loved ones, friends, or ourselves, we are impacted. Forgiveness is the antidote for the poison of bitterness, which robs our present and future if unaddressed. Love is a more powerful motivator for our creativity than anger or fear, because sooner or later the latter will drain us. A meta-analysis of studies found that decreases in creative capacity are linked to experiences of stress specifically tied to a sense of uncontrollability over a situation or judgment from others.[23] Forgiveness is a tool for addressing these experiences that we cannot change or that have contributed to a sense of shame or diminished identity or value. There are situations that we cannot shift but that we can let go so that they no longer have power over us.

Researchers have also affirmed the practical value of forgiveness for general wellness. A 2014 study found that amongst individuals with high accumulation of lifetime stress via difficult experiences, those with regular practices of forgiveness had fewer mental health symptoms.[24] More frequent experiences of forgiveness are also associated with lower levels of stress. Experts are quick to clarify the definition of forgiveness and that it is not the same as justice or presupposed reconciliation. "Whether I forgive or don't forgive isn't going to affect whether justice is done," according to psychology professor Everett Worthington. "Forgiveness happens inside my skin."[25]

Receiving What We Need to Give

When we have experienced pain, forgiveness is often not the easiest or most natural response. One key for activating greater capacity in this area is to recognize where we have received this gift ourselves. Consider where you have been extended forgiveness in your life. Where have people chosen to love and walk with you when you were behaving poorly? Consider those who see the beauty in you and refuse to define you by your worst moments. This is often a form of grace: undeserved love and connection in the midst of imperfection. Its generous nature can inspire change, and it can empower both deeper self-acceptance and forgiveness toward others. Receiving forgiveness, and the often important act of forgiving ourselves, disempowers the voice of the inner critic that spews negativity toward us and our creativity. These experiences are powerful antidotes to the shame-influenced mindsets we discussed in the second chapter. Forgiveness can eliminate the conscious or subconscious regret that yaps at us and lessens our ability to enjoy what we create.

Grace fuels exploration, believes the best about you, and focuses on your strengths and potential, not your weaknesses or past. Grace enables acceptance not by passively ignoring imperfection but by actively choosing to see the potential for love and healing in the midst of the mess. It strengthens a foundation for knowing your value and worth as you experiment and take risks. Along the way, you're going to make mistakes, in small or big ways. You can't grow any other way! You will need to be able to recognize what needs to change while still accepting and loving yourself. Forgiveness and grace help empower this process. Self-criticism and unforgiveness toward yourself are the fruit of shame and silent assassins against your creativity. But grace defangs negative viewpoints that would hinder your ability to freely explore and express creatively.

Forgiveness can help clear the slate, increase peace, and eventually offer opportunities for redemptive joy in the very places we've been most hurt and afraid. As we begin to acknowledge, forgive, and heal from pain, our hearts need to experience the positive, opposite emotions of what the difficult moments carried. Therapy, affirmations, and faith or spiritual practices can help create experiences of exchange: comfort for disappointment, empathy for pain, acceptance for regret or loneliness, safety for insecurity, hope for despair, connection for shame. These exchanges are essential to the healing process.

The Journey of Healing

The choice to forgive may not be easy. You will not always feel perfect, positive emotions right away. But practicing the continued lifestyle of forgiveness toward others and yourself builds new habits in this area. Recognizing your own imperfections and need for forgiveness can help inspire you to make these difficult choices. The more you can see where you have received undeserved love in the middle of a mess, the easier it becomes to share this gift with others. Over time, you'll taste the sweetness of relief and freedom in places where bitterness and pain once resided. You can also gain more experience in implementing healthy boundaries that reduce the likelihood of similar hurt in the same places. As you progress, you might find yourself needing deeper, more personal experiences of grace.

This process may look and feel different for each of us. For me, personal spiritual experiences, vulnerable conversations with supportive communities, and one-on-one processing with a coach and counselor have all proved very helpful. In addition to the supportive practical resources, I needed an experience with grace and a love greater than me. I did and do not have capacity in my own strength to fully forgive myself or others. I will share more about how this awakening transformed my life and my creativity in the coming chapters. There is no shame in needing help in this area.

If there are areas of your creativity that feel off-limits, intimidating, fear-inducing, or uncomfortable, it just means there are opportunities to heal and grow. Look for support and resources that align with your core values. If what you try initially doesn't produce the desired results, keep exploring. Throughout your journey, there will be choices to remain where you are or to continue forward to discover more of the life of your dreams. Your value doesn't come from your pace or perfection in this process.

Healing will help you embrace your ability and capacity for creativity, whether it's expressed through building family relationships, designing airplanes, fixing plumbing systems, sketching, or developing strategies that save lives. Addressing pain in healthy ways builds momentum and can position you to reap the incredible benefits possible through the topic of the next chapter: creative community.

ONE-STEP ACTIVATION

Pick an area where you have felt creatively stuck or limited. Use the tools in the chapter to explore where past pain might be impacting your process and identify someone who could be supportive in your healing journey.

CREATIVITY STORIES

KENDRA | NURSE

Pediatric nurse Kendra has walked through a deep form of pain that many have not had to face. Her husband passed away at the age of 34 after an eight-year up-and-down battle with cancer. In her grieving process, rediscovering creativity played an unexpected role. "The 'heart-alive' theme in Creativity Unlocked materials resonated with me deeply, perhaps because I have had such an intense experience with death—the death of my beloved, and in many ways, half of me. I dove headlong into exploring the idea of what expressions brought me intrinsic joy." One afternoon, while journaling by the lake about experiences that make her feel fully alive, Kendra had a significant moment. "Suddenly, I felt as if I were looking back at my grief as though it were already behind me. And I found myself asking the grief for the first time, 'Is it okay if I leave you behind?' It was a startling and hope-filled experience that was sparked by exploring my creativity."

In Kendra's words, her outlets have brought joy, purpose, and meaning that help make the pain worth living through. She finds great delight in reading and learning from neuroscience research. Kendra also creates through hospitality by hosting gatherings for friends, exploring nature, and paddle-boarding on lakes near where she and her daughter live. "One of my favorite expressions is facilitating beautiful spaces and experiences for friends to come together. We enjoy carefully crafted food, make space to create with our hands, and have meaningful conversations."

Kendra did not anticipate that rediscovering her creativity would lead into a career shift. She recently left her twenty-year career in nursing to go back to school to pursue a PhD in neuroscience. "I found that the discoveries being made at the intersection of this field and others were pivotal to my grief journey. I can also see the immense potential for neuroscience to impact others. Making the transition has felt daunting at times, but my love for and fascination with what I'm learning makes it all worth it!" As Kendra engages in this multi-year journey, she is discovering ways to activate creative themes along the way, including starting a newsletter with articles linking two of her passions: faith and neuroscience. She also finds that the concepts she is learning often come up in conversations that others find interesting and helpful as well.

"Being involved in the workshop provided the focus, tools, and intentional community that have been so beneficial in my grief and reconstruction journey." Kendra found great value in ongoing encouragement and space to verbalize her process. "Having people who would dare to dream with me, believe in me, hold me accountable, and cheer me on has been pure gold. I took small steps until I was ready to take the leap. Be encouraged! It's never too late to pursue a dream. Your brain has the capacity to grow and learn at any age."

COMMUNITY UNLOCKED

Understand roles for life-giving interactions. People can supercharge your creative progress or undermine it. In this chapter, you will consider how others' involvement can unlock experiences of community that add delight and insight to your expressions.

The Secret to the Most Flavorful Pork Taco

I love food. Really. My family knows that I am happy to finish off plates, dive into leftovers, and recite dishes from favorite menus. I don't need white linen or high-priced cuisine to appreciate culinary excellence. If it's good, I'm good (that includes you, In-N-Out). A delicious meal is a great metaphor for introducing this chapter's topic. Pretend that cooking is an intrinsic joy expression for you, and consider the following question: how would you go about making the most flavorful beef taco? Take a moment to think before you read on.

Some of you might be wondering who gets to define "flavorful." Others are racking your brains for your aunt's tasty tomatillo salsa recipe, Googling ingredients, or considering your level of cooking skill. Meanwhile, a small group of you have already picked the wood chips over which you'll smoke the meat or started chopping garlic for that secret family marinade.

However, the answer I'd like you to consider is broader than these specific logistical details. If you truly, objectively want the best, most flavorful beef taco (if such a designation could exist), you're going to need help. You may have the best carne asada preparation in the world, but you would be missing out if you didn't include your grandma's killer tortillas. Or those perfectly fragrant limes from your cousin's backyard garden.

Here's the point: we are designed to create in community. Others frequently hold the metaphorical ingredients or tools that can increase the joy and excellence of our outflows. Intrinsic motivation for our creativity doesn't have to translate to isolation. The overly self-reliant, "I've got this on my own" attitude around our expressions will not serve us in the long run. Healthy community covers our weaknesses, celebrates our strengths, increases our resilience, and makes the journey so much more fun. But there's a problem many of us must face, related to the previous chapter: most of the painful experiences we have endured around creative expressions involved other people. How can we develop an approach to community that doesn't set us up for more pain or repeat past mistakes?

The Myth of Isolated Creators

In movies and culture, creative genius is often depicted in solitary, elusive individuals who eke out an isolated, pained existence. You know the type: the poet living in an attic, heroically baring their tortured soul on the page. Or there's a brilliant scientist who loves his chemicals and petri dishes more than people. Or the successful singer navigating the ups and downs of fame by coping with drugs or alcohol. These images are emphasized to the point that many associate loneliness, depression, pain, and coping mechanisms like substance use with successful creativity. Sadly, there are many tragic stories of talented but troubled individuals, from Vincent Van Gogh to Amy Winehouse, that emphasize this narrative.

A lack of healthy, supportive community is a reason that the creative process can become unnecessarily difficult. All too often, people turn to numbing behaviors that become damaging and distracting to handle the stress and pain they experience. Fears around collaboration, personal insecurities, or underinvestment in relationships can add to isolation, harmful coping mechanisms, or underlying mental health challenges. The fact that these negative patterns shape perceptions and experiences of creativity doesn't mean that they have to define or dominate your process. Your expressions can be a thriving source of relationship that fuels wellness, instead of a destructive burden.

It's time to take a fresh look at the concept of community and rediscover the delight and support that it can provide. New clarity for the roles of specific people in your process will add to your creative momentum and enrich those around you too.

You Don't Have What It Takes (on Your Own)

I have great news: you do not have all of the ideas, answers, resources, or inspiration needed for many flourishing outflows of your creativity. You are designed to create with others, whether directly or indirectly. Your creativity isn't inferior if it involves partnership or draws inspiration from the artists or makers you appreciate. The outflow of any person is influenced and shaped by the inputs they have experienced. To think that we can somehow create without any attachment to previous works or other people is a bit ludicrous. Who made the paints or tools you're using? Who developed the concepts, spaces, or genres that inspire and enable your expressions?

We get to be part of the perpetually growing sculpture of human creativity. At some point, others will be able to stand on our shoulders. This doesn't mean that we should dishonor artists or disregard trademarks or other legal protections. However, we should remove the pressure to somehow be wholly original, independent, or self-reliant. The unhealthy need to be unique often stems from a false belief system rooted in insecurity and comparison. You already are original. No one has your specific blend of experiences, emotions, and perspectives. Instead of listening to the voice of comparison, you can own and express what brings you intrinsic meaning, joy, and satisfaction.

Whew. Take a deep breath. Let go of the measuring stick, and let the pressure of originality, self-reliance, and perfection roll off your shoulders. *It's not meant to all be on you—it never was.*

Community Is Essential for Thriving

Researchers have shown that community helps human beings have better health and emotional flourishing. The Harvard Study of Adult Development found that long-term relationships were the only factor statistically associated with greater levels of happiness over the participants' lifetimes.[26] This is one of the longest-running studies on happiness, tracking the health and experiences of subjects since 1938. It concluded that relational ties "protect people from life's discontents, help to delay mental and physical decline, and are better predictors of long and happy lives than social class, IQ, or even genes," according to Harvard News.[27] The presence of relationships was more important than fame, success, or money when it came to life satisfaction. In fact, those other factors were not statistically associated with greater happiness.

Creativity offers opportunities for discovering and strengthening life-giving, long-term communities that support your flourishing. Regular interactions in groups with shared passions help incubate relationships, especially where there is alignment in values. Whether you connect via skydiving or student teaching, electric vehicles or emo rock, important intangible needs can be met through the friendships developed. Your creative process can also benefit from the encouragement and wisdom of others. Through these relationships, you can give and receive, listen and be heard, learn and teach, and simply enjoy the company of others.

A creative community is not required to start exploring and enjoying facets of your expressions. Seasons of independence can be important for learning, experimenting, and growing in intrinsically joyful creativity. Some parts of your journey may feel too vulnerable to share initially, especially because relationships and creativity are so personal and potentially complex. Nevertheless, community is valuable for sustaining and strengthening your creative process. Life-giving experiences with others can accelerate your discovery and enjoyment of creativity, both early on and for the long term. Others can help you see problems differently, identify solutions, and navigate the emotional highs and lows of the process. If you're feeling stuck or frustrated, the specific insights and encouragements you need to unlock greater ease and clarity may lie in the people around you.

Defining Creative Community

What is a creative community? At the most basic level, it's the people whom you choose to involve in your journey. Your creativity community extends beyond a single group of people. It is the mixture of friends, family members, colleagues, instructors, clubs, collaborators, meetings, mentors, and others who support your journey. Some you may intentionally invite while others have a more indirect role or may already be part of your process.

Consider this a chance to reflect on both your current and ideal creative community. Whether you are intentionally choosing them or not, you are already being affected by those around you. This is not a suggestion to revisit past pains and frustrations with others, but to simply recognize the importance of those with whom you surround yourself. It's all too easy to take the path of least resistance and settle for who is most accessible, at the cost of what best adds joy and fuel to your passions and growth. Whose words or skills are going to best help shape your expressions and your process? Who are you excited to serve, encourage, or partner with? Different people will hold insights and experiences you need at various stages, depending on your context.

When you can, prioritize people who have not only shared interests but also similar mindsets, especially around areas in which you are seeking growth. At the same time, keep an open mind. Unless you live on a deserted island or in a cave, at times you're going to interact with people who see the world differently. Focus on what you can learn from people who have different goals or philosophies, instead of getting stuck on where you're not aligned. You don't have to agree on everything to benefit from a relationship.

Remember that specific individuals and groups may be appropriate for parts of your journey but not for others. Don't be afraid to maintain boundaries around parts of your expressions that feel particularly tender if an individual does not have the capacity to be supportive, even if they are a family member or close friend. You may find it easier to open up about vulnerable personal dreams or pain points with people less connected to your life. At various points, you will benefit from a community focused on a particular expression, whether it's singing or stock picking, because of their ability to offer specific empathy and guidance. What works for someone else may not work for you. Past experiences with others in your creativity can affect what is most beneficial for you. It's a great place to trial and layer.

A Framework for Building Creative Community

Your creative community will be most life-giving when your needs are aligned with the roles and capacity of individuals, and vice versa. For instance, a newfound passion for visual art would benefit from a different form of community than a desire to explore activities that strengthen relationships with one's teenage children. Finding an appropriate level of skill and time commitment is also important. When you're starting out, resist the pressure to jump into something advanced that could leave you overwhelmed and discouraged. There is no shame in signing up for a beginners group. You can also take a baby-steps approach in the emotional aspects of building trust with your creative community. Just because someone shares your interest in Picasso doesn't mean they're the right person to tell your deepest fears or dreams. The framework below highlights four possible roles for community in your journey, each based on a need that commonly arises around creativity:

❖ *Community for consistency.* Early in exploring a creative expression, find people who encourage you to regularly invest time in your efforts. Who will help you persevere? Ask a loved one, sign up for a workshop or program, join a peer-based group, or simply invite a friend to keep you accountable—whatever helps you. Scheduling time for creative activities will help you prioritize them. This group of people does not have to see the results of your expression or give feedback; they are simply there

CHAPTER 6 | COMMUNITY UNLOCKED

for encouragement and accountability. They can help you build new, healthy routines that support your exploration.

- *Community for processing.* As you creatively explore and progress, the journey will cause fears, insecurities, and negative belief systems to come up. With whom in your life can you honestly process these thoughts and emotions? Who do you trust to be a sounding board for the highs and the lows of the journey? They may share your form of expression, but that is not a requirement. This form of community could be a trusted friend, a mentor, a creative coach, a workshop or class, a support group, a therapist, or a counselor. There is something powerful and freeing in bringing into the light what we're experiencing by sharing with others, even if we don't fully understand it ourselves. The words, listening ears, and presence of community are powerful inputs to our journeys, especially when things appear bleak or emotions are intense.

- *Community for collaboration.* As you grow in consistency, you will likely find people with similar passions and expressions. Partnering with others can expand the depth, range, and excellence of your outflows and can help you weather difficult moments. If your expression were to be represented by the color blue, imagine what could happen when you partner with someone else's yellow. A whole new realm of possibility opens up. You may have the seeds for a field but benefit from the friend who brings the tractor or the plow. When the fit is good, collaboration increases inspiration and momentum. Creative partnerships can help you make decisions about specific expressions and tap into delight throughout your process.

- *Community for feedback.* As you continue in your joy-filled, satisfying expressions, your desire to refine your craft can increase, especially as others experience your outflows. Growth and excellence can be intrinsically meaningful. For some creative pursuits, like those within your job, feedback will happen automatically. For most others, you will need to seek it out. Carefully choose who you ask for input, remembering that not everyone will get your style or aesthetic. Communicate in detail what kind of feedback you're looking for: constructive and blunt, gentle and supportive, or something in between. What people are willing to share is a gift, even if they don't deliver it perfectly. Remember: criticism of your work doesn't lessen who you are as a person or as a creative being. We'll talk more about this aspect of creativity in a later chapter.

As you explore and upgrade your community, you will learn more about the types of people and resources that best support you. Tools like the Meyers-Briggs Personality Test, StrengthsFinder, and the Enneagram can help you understand yourself and others better, which will benefit creative partnerships. Not every person or group you invite into your process will be the right fit for you or be part of your journey forever. Some expressions may not be ready for collaboration or feedback. If you have an awkward conversation or two, you're not alone. It's an ongoing part of the creative process, even when you become more experienced in your expressions. Or you may experiment with a partnership and have it go terribly—that's okay. If one doesn't work out, don't fret! Consider a different individual or approach, and then get back on the horse and try again. Move forward and don't let that experience block future experiences of community. There is great value to be discovered for your creativity, no matter how long it takes to be found.

Better Together

Though I'm extroverted and relationally motivated, I can be prone to leaning too much into independence and self-reliance. Recovery gave me tangible examples of the benefits of inviting other people into parts of my life. I became much more comfortable asking for help and input because I experienced the value of the listening ears, insightful wisdom, and consistent presence of others. These interactions proved transformational in rediscovering creativity. They motivated exploration of key intentional partnerships early in the process that shifted my mindsets around collaboration. Some remain fruitful years later, while others were one-time experiments. In writing fiction, starting organizations, navigating team situations, and strengthening family relationships, the guidance and companionship of others have been crucial. As an external processor, clarity and inspiration for projects often appear via talking it out. My creative expressions would not be where they are today without the support of others. Through the process, I've gained something even more important than the resulting achievements: genuine, life-giving relationships.

When you get intentional about your community, there may be some emotionally uncomfortable parts. But that's part of the learning process. Honest, vulnerable conversations can be needed to clarify expectations and capacity with those involved, especially when you reach the stages of collaboration and feedback. Navigating these situations can help you grow in relationships. You will have the opportunity to learn how to better handle conflict and discover new approaches to communication. Resources like books on healthy relational boundaries can help upgrade the interpersonal parts of your journey.

There can be an inherent tension in inviting others into your journey. Privacy offers more space for personal exploration and intrinsic joy, but staying overly isolated can lead to becoming stagnant and struggling. On the other hand, overemphasizing a healthy desire to involve others can provoke more vulnerability than you are emotionally ready for. Let's say you're considering a career shift. Never telling anyone about it could rob you of encouragement or guidance that can help bring it about. But, immediately proclaiming this dream on social media could add pressure or expectation that overwhelms you and blocks your creative flow. Awareness of the possible dangers at either extreme can help you navigate the steps around community best for you.

If you are struggling to find others who seem interested or able to invest in your creative process, look first for someone you can serve. Find a person who is already working toward a creative vision that inspires you and explore ways to help them. Whether they personally take an interest in your own creativity or not, you will be able to learn from their process and likely meet others with similar passions. Healthy community involves both giving and receiving, though this can take many forms. Whatever you do, don't allow fear to keep you isolated and stuck in the echo chamber of your own mind. The fear of criticism or rejection can be just as costly as the actual experiences.

Like many aspects of your creative journey, you will not be able to fully control or predict the outcome of exploring community. Let the intrinsic joy and satisfaction in your expressions refresh you as you take risks. The relationships you build through creative exploration can benefit multiple areas of life. Human beings are built for meaningful connection with others. Not all interactions with others are this life-giving. The experiences of community are most beneficial when they stem from a deep sense of connection with ourselves and that which is greater than us. This is the secret sauce of creativity, and it just so happens to be our next topic.

🔑 ONE-STEP ACTIVATION

Choose one type of community (consistency, processing, collaboration, feedback) that you need to strengthen around a current expression. Using the examples in this chapter, brainstorm individuals or search online for groups that could aid your process, and pick one to reach out to today.

CREATIVITY STORIES

MAEGAN | THE BAKERMAMA

Maegan Brown did not anticipate where pursuing her creative passions would lead. "I never thought I'd be helping people discover the fun possibilities of meals served on boards. It was all birthed as something that really helped my family navigate life with young kids while staying connected to our love for food and hospitality." Today, she has published multiple cookbooks and helped hundreds of thousands of followers on Instagram incorporate creative approaches into their food routines.

When Maegan and her husband, Brandon, welcomed twins nine years ago, they suddenly had three kids under the age of two. This limited their ability to go out for meals, a way that they loved to connect. But it also sparked a new idea. "We started having date nights at home with mini cheese boards, and then we would get more and more creative about what to put on these platters. I love that the idea for boards developed out of the most important individuals in my life: my family."

Maegan has always loved hosting, whether around sports, holidays, birthday parties, or other events, and she began experimenting with displays on boards that matched artistic fun and yummy food. She had already started posting recipes on a baking blog, but when she started sharing these board ideas, they really resonated with people. The feedback was gratifying and motivating. "People find community around the table," Maegan shares. "What we have created resonates with my passion for helping people gather and enjoy beautiful moments of connection. The BakerMama community is all about enabling others to do the same."

Boards display a whole meal or a certain dish in an artistic way. The BakerMama social media profiles and Maegan's cookbooks, *Beautiful Boards* and *Spectacular Spreads,* showcase how many different meals can be shared in inventive, eye-catching displays: French toast brunches, sandwich nights, tailgate platters, and more. For example, a taco board includes lots of small dishes of protein, salsas, toppings and more, artfully arranged amidst tortillas or chips. The process lessens the load on Maegan's shoulders, or on those of other hosts, as guests can pick and choose what they like. Being able to prepare in advance also makes the gatherings more fun for her as a hostess. "My husband and I get to enjoy the moments more and really connect with our guests."

Maegan and Brandon see the value in boards for their children too. Instead of having to tell them what they are going to eat, their kids start serving themselves, once they are old enough. "We put out healthy options, and it teaches them about balance and independence. The salad board is a favorite, and our meal times are more enjoyable as everyone's hands get involved. They get to take ownership and make choices, and it increases their appreciation for what we have." Maegan has found that the boards save a lot of fuss and the ups-and-downs of family meals, though she and her husband still get to help. "Even better, our kids now love to make their own boards, and it activates their creativity."

Maegan's passion for being a mom inspires her BakerMama work. "I appreciate being able to explore this outlet, and it's something I don't take for granted. I'm very blessed to do it." There's a lot of effort involved, and it takes a dedicated team to help her manage all of the pieces. Collaboration and learning continue to broaden the depth and reach of Maegan's expressions. "All of the pieces of what I do as The BakerMama have activated strategic creativity," she shares. "I wouldn't be able to do it on my own." Maegan acknowledges that the process of making boards can feel different than it did initially because of the practical details and platforms now attached to it. "While it still can be wonderful, I make time to get refreshed or activate joy via spending time with my family and other passions too. It is a gift to be able to bring to life creative ideas every day, and in the end, it's all for my family."

CONNECTION UNLOCKED

Discover the secret sauce of thriving creativity. Meaningful connection is the source for the purpose and joy found in our expressions. In this chapter upgrade ease and delight by unlocking connection that turns your creative activities into heart-alive moments.

The Secret Sauce for Creative Expression

It's in the sympathetic smile of a stranger in a subway station after you have trudged through a downpour and now look like a drowned rat.

It's in scaling unmarked slabs of granite on a hike, surpassing metaphorical walls that once defined your limits, as grandiose views of snow-capped peaks emerge.

It's in the cozy feeling of sipping from a steaming mug of tea as you watch Lord of the Rings on a cold day.

It's in crafting a work of art that sparks ecstatic joy and offers to an unsuspecting world a new, visual representation of the tension between grief and hope.

It's in the poignant vulnerability found in church basements and meeting halls across the world, as individuals in recovery boldly and honestly allow themselves to be known and accepted as they are.

It's in the flash of an idea interrupting your routine and ushering in a creative flow that unfolds solutions for a previously unaddressed challenge.

It's in the waves of beautiful emotion that swell and crest amongst a concert audience, linking together hearts full of wonder via sounds that move the human soul.

Meaningful connection takes many forms, inhabits many channels, and fills our hearts in ways beyond our ability to describe with words. This intangible but oh-so-real quality can spark intense spikes of joy or subtler, profound satisfaction.

Think of a moment when your heart felt truly alive. You know, those times when your skin tingles, colors appear a little brighter, and the world seems full of wonder. Where have you experienced these sensations? What were you doing? Who were you with? Chances are you were creating something, whether a memory, a piece of art, a deeper relationship with someone, a tangible product, or something else. Can you spot any commonalities or themes in experiences with similar feelings? They are part of your creative nature, but what else?

What makes these tangible heart-alive moments special and memorable is the meaningful connection experienced, whether it's with others, aspects of our own selves, or something greater than us. This ingredient can shift creative expressions from difficult and dull to refreshing and motivating. Contrary to the messages that dominate our consumer-driven culture, these moments are not dependent on a social media-worthy setting or an expensive purchase. We do not need legions of fans, the latest fad, or a luxurious lifestyle to find and create moments of fulfillment and joy. There are opportunities around us, every day, for meaningful connection. In both pristine and beautiful settings, or raw and messy ones, this is the secret sauce for flourishing in creativity—and in life itself.

Defining Connection

To aid activation of this powerful quality, let's define meaningful connection. For simplicity's sake, we will use three categories.

CHAPTER 7 | CONNECTION UNLOCKED

A first form of connection is with other people. Noted author and researcher Dr. Brené Brown defines connection as "the energy that exists between people when they feel seen, heard, and valued; when they can give and receive without judgment; and when they derive sustenance and strength from the relationship."[28] Conversations, activities, and spending time together are vehicles through which this quality can be felt. Keep in mind that it's possible, and all too common, to be surrounded by people and even engaged in conversation but still be disconnected. Meaningful connection with another person is developed through vulnerability and acceptance.

A second form of connection is with yourself. This bucket involves elements of self-realization, awareness of one's needs, and individuality. We can apply part of Dr. Brown's definition from above: connection with ourselves is the energy that exists when we can see, hear, and value ourselves, when we can express ourselves and rest without judgment, and when our relationships with ourselves add strength and positive qualities to our lives. This includes recognizing our unique personality, tastes, gifts, and perspectives. Another important part of healthy connection with self is honoring our needs as human beings, physically, emotionally, mentally, spiritually, and relationally.

A third form of connection is with something greater than ourselves. This could be in the form of values, a higher power, nature, spirituality or faith, or a cause that provides a sense of purpose and place in the world. Examples of practical experiences include the satisfaction of contributing to a movement or charitable organization, getting lost in the beauty of the outdoors, expressing kindness to someone needing help, or participating in a faith practice. Grounding ourselves in this broader sense supports meaningful and authentic creativity.

Strengthening connection on one level can reinforce the others. Healthy relationships with friends help us care for and learn more about ourselves, and vice versa. Life-giving experiences around existential questions can shift understanding of our own passions and how we show up for others. Meaningful connection can be experienced nearly anywhere, though you may find that there are settings, people, and activities in which it is easier or more natural. Keep an open mind. Some of the most impactful and memorable experiences of connection occur via shared adversity, messy moments, or even life-and-death situations. Discovering this deeply meaningful quality in the midst of difficulty is one of the most life-transforming aspects of our creative nature.

The Benefits of Connection

Why should we care about connection? There is a growing collection of research that suggests its various forms hold great importance for health and happiness, including the Harvard study mentioned in the previous chapter. In her book *The Gifts of Imperfection*,[29] Dr. Brené Brown presents findings indicating an association between positive life outcomes and people experiencing authentic, healthy, vulnerable connection. A 2018 systematic review of research on mindfulness practices, which focus on connecting to one's needs and experiences without judgment, reported decreased stress, higher resilience, and fewer symptoms of anxiety and depression across the majority of studies.[30] A meta-analysis in 2014 indicated the benefits of spending time outdoors. It shared that "those who are more connected to nature tended to experience more positive affect, vitality, and life satisfaction compared to those less connected to nature."[31] In 2015, researchers at the London School of Economics and the Erasmus University Medical Center found that involvement with a religious group had a significant, positive association on people's well-being and happiness.[32]

In addition to supporting wellness, meaningful connection supercharges creativity. Your heart-alive experiences of expressions have likely involved aspects of this quality, whether or not it was recognized. For instance, those moments could have included an activity rooted in your passions and unique skills, an adventure that sparked friendship, the lasting wisdom of a mentor, an authentic artistic expression, a glorious nature scene, a life-giving spiritual practice, a solution to a complicated problem that affects your customers, or an important cause or community. Intentionally prioritizing meaningful connection in your creativity can shift an activity from average to incredible. It is the special sauce that can make baking cookies, fixing a car, getting lost with a friend, attending a child's soccer game, or pretty much any other activity glisten with delight and significance. As you recognize this quality, you may discover new aspects of intrinsic motivation in your daily life.

I often tell my friends that I've approached life more experimentally since the personal shift that occurred in 2016. The outcome variable I'm seeking to maximize is meaningful connection. So far, the resulting delight, purpose, and creative flow have been far beyond what I imagined. Increased flexibility and connection have spurred heart-alive experiences and initiated new adventures and relationships. Organizations and projects have developed and launched via this approach, and I have found far greater intrinsic joy and meaning in them than in previous seasons of unfulfilling achievement. When meaningful connection is the goal, there is much to be discovered every day whether or not things unfold according to plan, because this quality is possible in any context. It can increase the fulfillment and ease of creativity more than perfection or achievement.

My hypothesis is that prioritization of meaningful connection on each level can unlock greater creative flow. There certainly are similarities between the attributes of flow state and connection. When our relational needs are met and we can be our authentic selves, distracting stressors are reduced and we can be more present in the moment. The sense of security and purpose provided by connection to something greater frees our brain capacity to explore challenges and identify solutions.

"It's a Trap!"

Experiences where connection is lacking further prove its importance. Have you carefully planned something you hoped to be wonderful only for the actual experience to feel hollow and unfulfilling? Disconnection robs us of the delight and fulfillment that creative experiences and adventures can provide. The meal at a great restaurant or the dream vacation may promise enjoyment but leave you dissatisfied when your connection needs are neglected. You can receive a work promotion or buy the latest footwear and have the joy quickly fade or never appear in the first place. Moments of fun or achievement aren't bad, but they can be fleeting and leave us endlessly needing more if we aren't experiencing healthy connection on the levels described above.

Disconnection leads to form without substance, acclaim without authentic joy, productivity without purpose, achievement without fulfillment, performance without peace, and company without true companionship. It's one of the reasons why successful people can find themselves unhappy and lonely even when surrounded by people. Riches or fame while disconnected can actually produce a vicious cycle, where notoriety and money introduce dynamics that hinder the vulnerability and authenticity required for connection. All too quickly, we can find ourselves chained to a treadmill to maintain something while neglecting our needs, lacking authenticity in key relationships, and becoming detached from our values and purpose.

In this state, our creative activities can shift from meaningful to muddy. Think about your own life. That homemade pasta didn't taste quite as good after the unresolved fight with your loved one, did it? Have you worked yourself to the bone in pursuit of financial security only to then pay a price in your health for neglecting your own needs? When was the last time you saw the disappointed look of a person you snubbed for that TV show or that scroll through social media? Sooner or later, the outflows of disconnection pile up. What seems like a minor mess can become a heaping pile of muck.

There's a classic and often memed line from Star Wars: Return of the Jedi that comes to mind as I think about practically making choices to prioritize connection. Fleet commander and all-around hero Admiral Ackbar recognizes an ambush and exclaims the now-infamous line: "It's a trap!" Unfortunately, it's too late to save a number of the good guys' ships from the attack. These words ring through my mind when I really want to go to that party or spend another hour working but recognize the unseen danger of disconnecting from rest or relational responsibilities. The opportunity may be good in and of itself, but it might require a cost that I don't realize in the moment. Even the most altruistic causes or charitable activities can come with this unforeseen downside if we're not careful.

Disconnection may be already affecting your creativity. Can you identify an expression where losing your authentic voice to meet external expectations has left you unsatisfied? Or look for projects where you are struggling to make progress due to not taking care of your own needs or the lack of a greater why. Loneliness and unresolved relational pain can drain you of energy for your favorite creative activities and sour your process. Disconnection is not all or nothing. We can be connected on some level, and even experience great productivity or innovation, but dangerously lack this quality in other parts of life. If any of these examples resonates, today is the perfect time to start exploring this reality (via baby steps, of course). Better now than to wake up years down the road and wish that you had given yourself permission to prioritize this earlier.

Addressing the Roots of Disconnection

Thankfully, there are practical ways that we can rediscover connection at any stage of life, as long as we're willing to acknowledge where we need to grow. Learning to recognize and understand disconnection sets the table for changes that bring fresh experiences of creative joy and flow. The signs can be blatantly clear or quite subtle. Look for small indicators, like the consistent skipping of a wellness practice, poor sleep routines, an edge in conversational tone with a friend, or a sense of pressure or dullness in activities you normally enjoy.

Distraction is a major sign of disconnection. We most often disconnect when we are looking for something that provides comfort or familiarity in an experience of pain or uncertainty. Overused coping mechanisms often indicate that we are experiencing pain or difficulty that we don't know how to handle. Unsure of how the credit card bill is going to be paid? Sure, I'll eat a burger to feel better. Stressed about a relationship or a difficult conversation? Not sure how to communicate feelings or enforce boundaries? I'll zone out with video games for an hour or five, or I'll talk to a half dozen people ad nauseam in an attempt to find some sort of peace. Bored or stuck at work? A twenty-minute social media rabbit hole is just what I need. These distractions can help us feel better in the short term but set us up for longer-term trouble. They are most appealing when we lack the tools or experiences with which to solve a problem or when we feel alone in our situation. It can be a vicious cycle: the consequences of disconnection can fuel more negative emotions that increase the desire to numb.

In our current context, distraction can range from innocuous and seemingly good to more clearly costly. Tech devices, achievement, information overload, and over-awareness of others' lives are just a few of its subtler forms. Video games, shopping, gambling, sex, substances, sports fandom, overwork, and other activities can be experienced in unhealthy ways that become addictive. When overused, they become blockers of the connection that is the secret sauce for creativity.

Another sign of disconnection is fixation. It can manifest in toxic thought cycles, anxious thinking about a situation, over-planning, an inability to rest, or a struggle to block out a certain topic or idea. This over-focus on a problem or situation, whether internal or external, makes it difficult to be present and engaged with the person or task at hand (a necessity for connection). Fixation can be a form of self-protection, a subconscious attempt to prevent future pain or navigate current difficulties. In these situations, one may be trying to find a sense of security in their understanding. However, this can be a losing battle. There are many situations that we cannot control or fully understand. Or one might find themselves seeking clarity in a part of life for which there is not a satisfying answer and become stuck in a cycle of fixation.

What we need in these moments of distraction or fixation is meaningful connection. Yes, there is often a tangible problem that requires a solution. But addressing the deeper need for connection is just as important. This quality provides comfort and the courage to take the next step to address the situation. Recognizing this underlying emotional experience can help us access comfort and peace that enables us to move forward. This is one reason why engaging with the tools of a healing journey is so essential for our creative process. Meaningful connection becomes easier when unresolved pain is addressed. Without recognizing these underlying situations, we can still get pushed back to the forms of comfort or control we know best despite our best efforts to avoid distraction and fixation.

Sometimes what feels like a deficiency in connection is not a sign of neglect but just part of our ongoing growth process. Over time, relationships require an increasing sense of closeness and intimacy to remain healthy and strong. What satisfied your connection needs in a previous season may not be fulfilling anymore. This longing for more can trigger discoveries and growth that change our lives and release new forms of creativity.

Practical Activities to Increase Connection

It's time to upgrade your tool kit for proactively deepening connection on each level. For thriving creativity, the goal is not necessarily to equally balance connection across the three levels described above. At times, you'll need to lean in more to certain aspects while deprioritizing others. For instance, if you start getting overwhelmed with the problems in the world, it can be healthy and refreshing to rest or have a meaningful time with a friend. Or if you become too insular, shifting from a focus on connection with self to finding a greater sense of purpose can spur thriving. Remember: activities that bring us comfort are not bad in themselves. Watching a movie, going to a party, working out, and enjoying delicious food can be helpful and powerful avenues for healthy connection, as long as they're not being used to bypass other needs.

This connection framing is a helpful tool for troubleshooting moments when creativity has become difficult. Recognizing an unaddressed need can unblock a channel for creative flow. Along with individual moments, there may be whole seasons when your context requires being more intentional around a specific form of connection, whether with self, in relationships, or with purpose or intangible aspects of life. The best way to activate connection is simply to pause and take note of your needs and then experiment. Developing your repertoire of connection-increasing activities will help you plug and play as you face new challenges or contexts on your creative journey. Here are examples that can help you regain and deepen connection on each level. Some are short-term solutions while others are longer-term shifts.

Connection with others

- Send a family member an appreciation note
- Schedule a catch-up with a buddy
- Go with a friend to an event they are passionate about

- Attend a support group
- Make space for a conversation with a colleague
- Address offense by apologizing, asking forgiveness, or making amends
- Face the need to have a brave conversation with a loved one
- Call someone with whom you can process through current emotions
- Do something fun with other people
- Join a club or workshop focused on an expression you enjoy
- Go on a getaway with friends
- Enroll in a course on relationships that supports growth
- Make regular time for creating in community
- Ask trusted friends for honest, constructive feedback
- Invest in counseling, therapy, or coaching
- Read books on boundaries or relationships that add to your toolkit
- Get input from trained professionals for your family and work situations

Connection with self

- Journal about your current experiences
- Take a walk that you love
- Sit in your room in silence and breathe deeply
- Express yourself artistically
- Drink water
- Revisit your creativity affirmations
- Vacuum your house in a pattern that makes you smile
- Cook a favorite meal
- Practice self-compassion via mindsets work
- Nap or rest
- Listen to music or watch a movie that brings you joy
- Upgrade your sleep schedule

- Join a gym or workout class that supports your physical health
- Learn healthier dishes to cook
- Take a personality or strengths-finder test
- Take a step toward personally meaningful career or education opportunities
- Calendar out more time for intrinsic joy expressions

Connection with something greater

- Get out in nature; find a beautiful view or sight to take in
- Pray, meditate, or activate another spiritual practice
- Volunteer for a cause
- Complete a random act of kindness
- Give to a cause you care about
- Buy coffee for a stranger without their knowing
- Read a book that transports you somewhere
- Reflect on quotes that inspire
- Journal about a societal challenge you have experienced or care about
- Attend a community gathering that lifts your perspective higher
- Reflect on how your current decisions are aligning with your values and goals
- Share existential questions with a friend or community you trust
- Make a regular commitment to serve in your neighborhood
- Find creative ways to support causes important to you
- Allow a sense of disconnection to inspire artistic exploration
- Go on a travel adventure
- Build more time for spiritual or religious practices or gatherings
- Intentionally explore a new faith community or reflect on your belief systems
- Experiment with conservation efforts by changing your diet or volunteering

Some of these ideas will resonate more than others. As you experiment and learn, try incorporating routines into your schedule that help you regularly strengthen connection.

A Growing, Virtuous Cycle: Connection and Creativity

If and when you recognize disconnection, take heart; don't beat yourself up. These experiences are good information for your growth. You can learn more about yourself and what helps you thrive. If you're struggling and not sure why, look at how your connection needs are being fed—or remaining unmet—across various levels. Remember: each level of connection is important. Our relationships with self, others, and something greater than us have a significant impact on our creativity and our wellness. In the process of completing this book, I walked through an unexpected season when old coping mechanisms surfaced surprisingly, indicating an unrecognized form of disconnection. It was frustrating but also an opportunity to strengthen foundations and adjust priorities to better support my own flourishing. Deepening connection is a lifelong journey that we can take one step at a time.

Your creative nature is how you activate connection. The more you experience the joy and fulfillment that this fulfilling quality brings to activities, the more you will want to prioritize it via your daily activities and long-term dreams. Heart-alive creativity is more than just a practice applied to a few channels; it can become a lifestyle. Increasing experiences of connection in your expressions often does not require drastic shifts to your routine. You can create via small changes to your daily agenda, starting by making space to authentically connect with someone around you. Ask them a question that provokes a response and make time to actually be present and listen. The benefits of meaningful connection will make previously alluring distractions less appetizing and spur more satisfying expressions of your creativity.

I hope these words spark more deep, emotionally resonant experiences of connection, not just a mental understanding. May contexts and relationships that have felt dull or disappointing become full of meaning and possibility. You might be in the process of peeling back the layers of external pressures or pain to connect more deeply with yourself, learning how to be vulnerable in relationships, or navigating past difficult experiences with systems or ideologies that have defined your place in the world. The work of discovering meaningful connection is worthwhile, even if it takes time and intention. May the stories in this book encourage you on this journey. Sometimes we struggle to connect to ourselves or others because we lack a deeper form of purpose, of love, of truth to guide our lives and support our wellness. The next chapter will discuss how spirituality can benefit our connection and creativity journeys in surprising ways.

🗝 ONE STEP ACTIVATION

Choose one level of connection to strengthen via your creativity. Reflect on which aspect could benefit your current expressions or where you have sensed disconnection. Pick an activity from the lists in the chapter and spend at least fifteen minutes strengthening connection with self, with others, or with something greater than us.

CREATIVITY STORIES

RENEE | PSYCHOLOGIST AND EXECUTIVE COACH

"There's a sweet spot when I'm connected to who I am created to be and walking in that to serve and add value to others. It makes my work energizing, motivating, and fun. In this creative element, it's like a light turns on," Dr. Renee St. Jacques shares. As a licensed psychologist and certified executive coach, she helps teams and leaders maximize their business impact by making work more life-giving and invigorating. "I walk in my 'magic' when I help executives and workplaces thrive. This is personally rewarding because I worked in tech for years but felt like a career chameleon, advancing in different roles but looking for a deeper sense of purpose and connection in what I was doing."

Dr. Renee's zones of genius include developing creative trainings and content that elevate the leadership skills and emotional intelligence of professionals. These experiences are focused on unlocking a greater sense of purpose and improving culture in work settings, which also benefit the overall wellness of team members. "This expression is especially meaningful because I've been personally impacted by work cultures and family systems where emotional intelligence was low. Many people do not know how to express their thoughts and feelings in healthy, productive ways. Now I get to create solutions for my clients around the very challenges I experienced."

Dr. Renee spent years as a technical product marketer for a large software company before discovering a new direction. "It's not like my time in the corporate world was negative or unhelpful. I benefited and learned from that work, but it didn't make me fully come alive." A sense that something more was possible inspired Dr. Renee to go back to school and get her PsyD (Doctor of Psychology). She now incorporates these experiences into her programs.

The last few years have offered lots of opportunities for creativity due to shifts to remote work. "Online experience design is a fascinating space, and I'm getting to both learn and create as new specific needs arise. Demand has increased dramatically for these solutions, which spark new opportunities for me to innovate." Dr. Renee has seen the effects of changed workplace patterns and disrupted personal and professional dreams. "When people lose vision," Dr. Renee notes, "they often turn to numbing behaviors or get jaded or depressed. Unhealthy uses of food, alcohol, and other coping mechanisms increase, while productivity decreases. Helping people rediscover their passion and purpose implicitly strengthens their mental health and overall wellbeing."

Dr. Renee finds deep satisfaction in being able to give her best to something she cares about. "It's a personal happiness, a form of connection, that far surpasses the satisfaction of just checking the box for someone else. My work as an executive coach and workplace culture consultant adds passion to my life and helps me show up as a better mom. I have more to give at home because of how fulfilling what I create is through my career." In addition to her work, Dr. Renee loves to create through dance, food, and travel experiences with her husband and kids.

Her words of advice for people exploring this topic: "If you're rediscovering your creativity, knowing your why is important. And it stems from knowing yourself and your values. What drives you? What infuriates you? What makes you come alive?"

SPIRITUALITY UNLOCKED

Connect your creativity to something deeper. Foundational beliefs have the power to spark inspiration and empower a personal creative renaissance. Or they can hinder one's progress. In this chapter, explore how unlocking intangible elements like philosophy, spirituality, or faith can impact your expressions.

A Legacy of Spiritual Creativity

Compared to others in the pantheon of the world's most impactful scientists, the name James Clerk Maxwell is relatively unknown. Born outside Glasgow in 1831, the Scotsman's groundbreaking, imaginative findings changed the world forever. He discovered the relationship between electricity, magnetic fields, and light waves that enables your smartphone and modern technology to function. This concept remains foundational for communications, computing, transportation and pretty much every industry in our digital age. In addition, Maxwell made significant breakthroughs around color and light, the use of statistical distributions in scientific measurement, and the movement and dynamics of gasses. According to author Basil Mahon in the biography *The Man Who Changed Everything*, any single one of these discoveries would have marked an incredible career achievement for a scientist.[33] Albert Einstein notably referenced Maxwell as key for his own Nobel Prize-winning discoveries: "I stand not on the shoulders of [Isaac] Newton, but on the shoulders of James Clerk Maxwell."[34]

Nicknamed "Daffy" by both schoolyard bullies and friends, Maxwell began unraveling concepts of mathematics and physics in his teens.[35] His inherent curiosity and keen observatory gifts brought recognition in his youth and led to studies at both Edinburgh University and Cambridge University. Imagination played a central role in his discoveries, as it would for Einstein decades later. Mental pictures helped Maxwell conceptualize undiscovered theories not easily measurable, in some cases before the tools existed to confirm them. Though he produced noted speeches and lauded studies that brought prominence in the scientific community of mid nineteenth-century Britain, some of his most important hypotheses weren't experimentally proven till after his premature death at the age of 48.

Maxwell's passion, inquisitive nature, and noted kindness toward his colleagues and pupils flowed out of a spiritual foundation. His steadfast value for both faith and science echoed in his work and his writings:

> Those who intend to pursue the study of Theology will also find the benefit of a careful and revert study of the order of Creation. They will learn that though the world we live in, being made by God, displays this power and goodness even to the careless observer, yet that it conceals far more than it displays, and yields its deepest meaning only to patient thought. They will learn that the human mind cannot rest satisfied with the mere phenomena which it contemplates, but is constrained to seek for the principles embodied in the phenomena, and that these elementary principles compel us to admit that the laws of matter and the laws of mind are derived from the same source, the source of all wisdom and truth.[36]

Though raised in a culture shaped by Christianity, it was an experience during Maxwell's years at university that made his faith profoundly personal and spiritual. It became a foundational bedrock for his exploration of the wonders of the universe.

The life of James Clerk Maxwell is an example of how one's worldview and spiritual practices can support creativity, and he is not alone. There are various ways to deepen connection with something greater than us, whether via a cause, a political movement, or nature. But spirituality remains a particularly potent vehicle for fueling our expressions with an intrinsic sense of purpose. From scientists like Maxwell to poets like Rumi and Maya Angelou,[37] moments of transcendent creation have erupted for many from self-described experiences of connection to something beyond themselves. Einstein himself referenced a belief in something greater, in a letter responding to a sixth-grader in 1936: "…a spirit is manifest in the laws of the Universe—a spirit vastly superior to that of man, and one in the face of which we with our modest powers must feel humble."[38]

Perspectives about the intangible, transcendent aspects of existence (or the lack thereof) influence one's creativity. Philosophies and worldviews can strengthen helpful virtues like love, gratitude, and freedom of expression, or stir hopelessness or shame that keeps one discouraged and stuck. Spirituality or religious belief can play an important role in the healing from past pain that fuels creative exploration. Conversely, a sense of detachment on an existential level can rob our energy and hinder our expressions. Similar to mindsets, the specific beliefs we embrace have great importance. Within both religious and nonreligious schools of thought, there are some that better support creativity than others. In this chapter, we will consider creativity's role in refreshing the soul and explore how spirituality can impact, supercharge, and further unlock your expressions.

Spirituality, Science, and Creativity

The Oxford Language Dictionary describes "spirit" as "the nonphysical part of a person which is the seat of emotions and character." By this definition, everyone is spiritual in some sense, and creative expression can be very much a spiritual experience because it is often deeply felt. Spirituality can also encompass our worldview, religion, philosophy, or faith, which also have strong influences on our emotions and creative choices. Dr. Maya Spencer writes that "spirituality involves the recognition of a feeling or sense or belief that there is something greater than myself, something more to being human than sensory experience, and that the greater whole of which we are part is cosmic or divine in nature."[39]

In recent years, there has been an increasing groundswell of interest in approaches to life that are deeply spiritual but detached from traditional structures. Author and researcher Casper ter Kuille notes the rise of new forms of spiritual connection-forming practices in his book *The Power of Ritual*.[40] These range from Crossfit groups to sing-a-longs to dining clubs. Some would describe these experiences of meaningful connection with others via community as spiritual. Mindfulness, yoga, holistic exercise communities, reflective journaling, and other practices have been growing in popularity to meet the natural human need to navigate one's inner and outer worlds. Meanwhile, traditional faith systems and new enunciations of them continue to play a role in the creative processes of billions of individuals.

Over the past few years, I have been surprised at how many people I meet who have had life-impacting incidents they can only explain in spiritual language. People from various worldviews and educational backgrounds have shared these moments of wonder, often after I describe my own outside-the-box experiences. Serendipitous circumstances, occurrences that otherwise have no explanation, events that point to something divine beyond ourselves, miracles, or whatever you want to call them are not as uncommon as I previously thought. They are often just left unshared in Westernized cultures with a high value for logic and reason and a general caution around less scientifically verifiable happenings.

Whether through drawing pictures, fixing cars, climbing mountains, or conversing with friends, there are moments of serendipity, of euphoric creative joy, of meaningful connection, and of beauty that can test the limits of our vocabulary to describe or explain. Yes, there are brain chemicals activating during this delight, but where does that come from? Are improbable meetings and paths serendipitously crossing just chance

CHAPTER 8 | SPIRITUALITY UNLOCKED

or influenced by something greater? Is joy just an evolutionary requirement or the sign of a goodness that transcends the human experience? Are the fragile, complex interlocking systems present in nature and in the human body possible without a Creator?

Maxwell, for one, saw the harmony of natural law and the consistency of scientific principles across many distant parts of the universe as additional evidence for a Creator and a faith that he embraced. Albert Einstein famously celebrated the different roles of faith and science: "Science without religion is lame; religion without science is blind."[41] Of course, other learned members of humanity have taken different stances on these topics, choosing to focus on the material or provable.

Creativity is a meeting point for what is quantifiable and measurable and that which is ethereal and incalculable. Scholars and evidence-based practices have fueled great advances for society and human creativity. Technological innovation has extended the length and creative potential of lives, enabled entirely new fields and industries, revealed aspects of reality previously thought unknowable, and amplified the reach and ease of our expressions. Virtual experiences are transforming opportunities for human interaction. Researchers can use technology to see and impact brain function in real time. Telescopes are capturing distant parts of galaxies never previously seen. Human beings continue to create technology that travels (much) faster than the speed of sound and that can communicate with or map any part of the planet and beyond. Yet, the human experience holds both immense potential and ongoing fragility. The creators of machinery that can destroy the world can still drown in a poorly placed puddle. The wondrous intricacies within bodies and brains that enable powerful expressions are vulnerable and infinitesimally small in the vast scope of the universe.

Sooner or later, you will arrive at a point where your creativity touches questions around beliefs. They may spark from moments of wonder or situations where ethical considerations are important, whether in what you produce or your process. Human expression can release love or fear, light or darkness, beauty or destruction. What you specifically create will be impacted by whether you see humanity as a complex pile of genetic code working through predetermined permutations, an intricately designed electric vehicle holding either a mind or a soul or a spirit (or all three), or something else. Spirituality can play an important role in providing a value system and sense of purpose for your expressions. It can also offer ideas around deeper questions that spark direction and fuel healthier connection. Your creative process will benefit from considering how your beliefs and that which is beyond the strictly quantifiable impact your journey.

The Chicken Burger Problem

There may be barriers that are affecting this exploration. When I was in first grade, I got sick on a Friday night after eating a chicken burger at school lunch. Since no one around me got sick, the food likely wasn't the issue. I probably caught a virus. But for years, memories of that specific type of food made my stomach queasy. A similar case of misattribution occurred later on in life. I had a bad food-poisoning experience with a hamburger while working in Uganda—think an IV, lots of unwanted outflows... I'll stop there. Both experiences made me extra cautious around these dishes for a season. Turns out, there is nothing inherently sickening with chicken sandwiches or hamburgers (vegetarians, you may disagree). They are now two of my favorite meals. But specific negative experiences robbed me of enjoying them for a period of time.

Similarly, we can have negative associations with the topic of beliefs due to previous difficult experiences. There may be spiritual or faith practices that once soured your taste or caused you pain because of their delivery or preparation. You may have an aversion to a belief system or philosophy due to the pain you felt for which no one ever apologized. Or you may have inherited a particular lean from a family member's previous experience. Barriers can also stem from difficult interactions with parents, teachers, or leaders, or your perception of events where it seemed like larger forces in the world, like systems and structures, or even God, failed you or others. Or there may have been an unrelated, co-occurring negative factor that shaped your perception of spirituality, like the stomach bug that ruined chicken burgers for me. There are benefits for your creativity in exploring new recipes, or a different chef, that help you broaden your palate again. Within spiritual, philosophical, or religious views that previously felt painful or spurred misunderstanding, there could be comfort for difficult experiences, inspiration for your expressions, and deeper connection and purpose. In the exploration process, it is worthwhile to consider both the tenets of a worldview or spiritual practice and other factors that may have hindered your previous experiences.

Psychologists tell us that our decision-making around ideas and worldviews is deeply impacted by emotional experiences.[42] Each of us (myself included) can operate with biases that affect exploration of beliefs. Experts like behavioral psychologist Daniel Kahneman have demonstrated that human choices are frequently driven more by feeling, context, and past experiences than an objective consideration of the current situation.[43] Emotional associations can impact our judgment of a worldview more than the quality of the ideas it includes. Human beings are resistant to change and drawn to information that confirms their existing perspectives. Most of us find it less than comfortable to admit a change or to engage with uncertainty. This stubbornness can serve our creative journeys at times, but it may also hold us back from experiences that are transformational. In clinging to an argument or worldview, religious or nonreligious, we can miss the fruitfulness of an alternative view.

Current cultural contexts have added to the vulnerability of communicating or exploring spiritual beliefs. Political polarization and rapid-fire social media debates reduce appetite for conversations that could offer learning and sharpening of ideas. Social pressure to perfectly align in ideology lessens appetite for discussions that could provoke disagreement. Negative perceptions of traditional religious institutions have grown. There has been a particular, understandable focus on examining historical records of persecution, control, and abuse by faith entities that prohibited questioning or tolerance of people with different beliefs. Religion, just like many political ideologies, has been used to justify war, oppression, slavery, and many other terrible things. Many fear being compelled or forcing others into a belief system or have had less than ideal experiences of intersections between personal spiritual worldviews and public life. Others don't want to be painted into a corner by sharing their beliefs and being misunderstood.

Some of these narratives have overshadowed the current and historic benefits of religious and spiritual structures. From religious traditions sprang the investigation of science, the formulation of universal freedoms, and shared moral ethics.[44] Atheist historian Tom Holland charted this influence of religion on Western culture in his book *Dominion*, noting that classical Roman and Greek thought did not emphasize the value for every life, weak or strong, that is foundational to human rights. As described in the previous chapter on connection, spirituality is associated with greater wellness flourishing. What if there are heart-alive moments of connection waiting for you beyond what seems possible now? Spiritual experiences that address existential needs could enrich and unlock your creativity. This is what happened to me.

An Awakening

I would not be writing this book without the outside-the-box personal awakening that interrupted my journey in early 2016. I had no idea how much I needed it. Spiritual matters have been a conscious part of my life since childhood. Growing up as the grandson of a nonreligious chemistry professor on one side and the son of a Jesus-loving, prayer closet-inhabiting mother on the other, I've grappled with belief and unbelief at different stages of my journey. I had positive and profound experiences of faith in my youth and spent years involved in church and ministry. But I also wrestled with periods of spiritual confusion and philosophical quandaries relating to the world around me.

I didn't know what to do with a God who seemed conspicuously absent in the midst of the world's problems or at key moments in my own life. Throughout years of study and faith-related service at Princeton and Harvard, I felt a pressure to have every answer for the beliefs that had impacted my life. Uncertainty arose where what I understood as God's promises had apparently fallen short and where there were no *simpatico* answers. I did not know what to do with questions that caused wrestling; I did not yet have an appreciation for mystery. Somewhere I had learned to find security in my ability to explain or understand God, especially in environments that celebrated reason. There were unrecognized aspects of pain and weariness, stemming from this need for control, that motivated a de-prioritization of faith in my life. Finally, uncertainty stemmed from a scary question: what would this God, if real, require of me?

New experiences of spirituality and creativity arrived unexpectedly in the season of hopelessness and dissatisfaction mentioned in the first chapter. The day after the 2016 Super Bowl, I blacked out after drinking by myself and woke up around midnight on a street corner in San Francisco. Life took a sudden, undeserved turn for the better. A drunken call with a loved one and a ride from an angelic Uber driver helped me get home. The next day, a family member aware of my deepening struggles with alcohol over the previous years drove me to a counseling program to get help. I blacked out again en route after darting into a bodega to guzzle down whiskey. I have faint memories of puking out the window while we crossed the Bay Bridge and then waking up three hours north with my cell phone blaring *The Revenant* soundtrack from under my seat.

Despite these signs of unwellness, I deflected suggestions from a new counselor and my family about what I needed. Both deeper philosophical questions and what this meant practically for my tech career and my living situation played a role in this resistance. Blinded to my own state, the idea of letting go of control seemed impractical and unnecessary. Though I needed help, a form of self-reliance kept me closed up.

That Friday night, an outside-the-box experience changed my life. As I walked into a worship service, I felt a sense of unexpected, tangible peace and joy for the first time in months. It was a sensation that I associated with God's presence and had tasted before during previous years of earnest but tiring efforts at Christianity. Suddenly I began to feel inexplicable hope for situations for which I did not have answers. I didn't know where I would go, what my next step would be, but I knew I wasn't alone. This taste of connection, of goodness, provided the inspiration to let go, to say yes to what my counselor was recommending and to open up on a deeper level. I remember praying—I think I spoke it out loud—"God, if you're real, here's my life; here's everything, including the boxes I have put you in."

This spiritual experience of connection brought a willingness to get honest. I recognized in that moment how my best efforts to navigate and control my life were headed in a destructive direction and how desperately I needed help. All of my efforts to be a good student, to be a good person, to be a good son, to be a good Christian weren't enough. I couldn't forgive or rectify my own mistakes, I couldn't take back the words and actions that hurt others and brought me great shame, and I couldn't stop drinking away the pain. Humpty Dumpty had fallen and couldn't put himself back together again.

Without fully realizing it, I had reached a point beyond my ability to control. In this place, I was finally willing to engage with God on God's terms and surrender responsibility I wasn't meant to carry. I thought I had known what God's love was like before, during my decades in various faith communities; I had no idea how much more there was to experience. The mess in which I found myself provoked an openness for change, and I began to experience a God beyond my understanding. In that auditorium, an overwhelming, tangible sense of joy surrounded me like a cloud, lifting off the heavy load of shame.

Something beyond what I thought possible then happened, just after this surrender. I heard a voice in my mind say, "Chris, I'm going to make this easy for you and heal you and set you free." Though it felt profound and sparked a sense of divine peace and joy, I wasn't sure if it was just a random thought. At the time, I could not be by myself for long without getting hammered. Even though I grew up praying for such divine interventions, I could not be certain if I had ever seen something that miraculous. It made no sense to my logical mind that such a good thing would happen in the midst of the worst choices I had made in my life. I had disqualified myself from love, not realizing that my situation demonstrated both the need for grace and how it is extended. Freely. Undeserved. In full sight of harmful choices.

In the auditorium, these new experiences with God continued to unfold. I knew a lot about Jesus —who obviously is central to the Christian faith I practice—but for the first time the reality of God's nature as a Father hit me in a way I had never known. I began to have pictures in my mind and feel the warm affection of a Father who had seen me in every low point and would never give up on me, no matter how messy I got. A visceral joy and peace embraced me in the midst of all of the uncertainty about life and work, the next steps in recovery, and the poor decisions I had made.

I had no concrete answers for how continuing the healing journey would affect my future. But all of those questions seemed so secondary, because I found what I had always unknowingly been looking for: connection, to realize that I never had to be alone again. It was like I could suddenly see colors again after being stuck in a gray, numb world of fading hope. The simple sweetness of spiritual and relational connection, and this sense of the Creator's presence, was so life-giving that it overwhelmed the shame that had been hanging over my head. It also gave me a sense of hope for the outpatient treatment program I agreed to enter. I could see how all of the self-inflicted messes, and other unfortunate experiences of life, had led to this point: a discovery of surrender, connection, and joy I didn't know possible. It has remained the most important moment of my life.

The Gift of Rediscovery

These spiritual experiences precipitated a shift in how I approached everything, including my faith and creativity. Though I could see how previous religious experiences had brought good, I gained awareness of where misunderstanding had sparked pressure and performance that contributed to the broken, addicted state in which I found myself. The desire to numb with alcohol and sexual behaviors came partially from the exhaustion and pain spurred on by belief systems that needed an upgrade. I had previously learned to associate performance with being loved. In my mind, achievement equaled worthiness. I fed this hunger for recognition and success via a variety of dopamine-releasing activities: sports, educational achievement, career success, religious duties. Exhausted by this pursuit, I would turn to behaviors and substances to find comfort, or at least to numb the pain. I didn't know how to enjoy positive milestones or deal with failure or handle the pain of not living up to (impossibly) high standards. There was always more to do.

I remember walking across a bridge the morning of my graduation from Harvard in 2015, prior to this awakening. Already sloshed, I wondered why others weren't drinking. The fancy degrees that looked like something worth celebrating felt hollow. I think this sense of being adrift deepened the growing addiction to alcohol. Graduate school was the final step I had mapped out on the pathway to "success," or what I hoped would bring fulfillment. When I shifted to Silicon Valley, the next season of a life of financial abundance, I still felt behind in terms of income and career progression. Instead of finding the security and significance I desired, I had more discomforting questions and a gnawing sense of emptiness. I couldn't admit or even fully recognize this reality, because I was both in denial and trying to live up to a certain image.

In a way, the personal gifting, financial abundance, and educational resources I had experienced added unrecognized pressure that contributed to coping cycles. Great opportunity became a great responsibility that I didn't know how to carry. The blessings added a barb, a "more money, more problems" scenario. I hated that I could have all of these things and still be unhappy. But engaging further in these self-destructive cycles only deepened the shame. Where I had felt controlled, I had a desire to control others with whom I would connect.

Subconsciously I had started to believe that if all of these things were not working, I was the hopeless problem. Not only was I failing, but I was a failure, in a way that others wouldn't be if they were in my shoes. This unresolved pain contributed to these destructive cycles.

I had spent a lot of time and energy defending the broken pieces of my heart, my beliefs, and my life, staying in a collapsing sand castle when there was a wonderful house just up the beach waiting for me. A fear of being controlled and punished also served as a roadblock for years. I had seen that happen through religion. I didn't want to become a crazy religious nut job or return to serving a relentless taskmaster. But that is not the God who met me on that February night, and it is not the Jesus I get to live in relationship with each day. Rediscovering the Creator via personal, transformative experiences with love and grace changed my viewpoints of previous questions and pain points. I could see the creative work of God in individual lives and across generations in ways I couldn't see before. In what had felt like absence I could see signs of Presence and the creative possibilities through a love that transforms human hearts.

The Friday night experience described above served as an introduction to a personal faith more exhilarating, personal, and restful than I knew possible. For about two weeks after, I felt a non-stop sense of euphoric joy and spiritual connection. The absence of any desire for alcohol or other unhealthy coping behaviors caused me to actually begin to believe the words I had heard in the auditorium. Six years later, I haven't craved alcohol again. Meanwhile, the healing of unrecognized stress and pain continued through additional spiritual experiences and counseling moments over the next few weeks. These helped me begin to clean up some messes made in my addicted state and strengthen relationships with family members and friends. Continued experiences of goodness motivated a desire to live differently and to shift from old behaviors and ways of thinking into something new, even if I didn't know what that fully meant. A leave of absence from work provided space for this new operating system to develop, removing distractions that previously blocked connection. Experiences with the Creator began to activate creativity, though I didn't have language for it then, from this place of childlike freedom.

My whole life I had unknowingly been looking for connection and belonging in trips and fun experiences, career success, religious striving, and a life of impact and significance. In the early months of recovery, I realized that I could find connection in a support group meeting, or in watching a sunset with a friend, or in a church service or other place for spiritual connection, or in an honest conversation at work (once I returned). I found unexpected joy in simple, authentic interactions, whether on a car ride or while sitting around a campfire. In an unexpected place, I rediscovered life. There have been parts of my growth and healing process that have taken more time and intention—I'll share more about that in the coming chapters. But spiritual and relational experiences of unconditional love, grace, and acceptance gave me the ability to love myself and my creativity. These have been the most important source of positive mindsets that flow into healthier, life-giving experiences of creative expression. I'm all for self-care, self-compassion, and self-forgiveness, but I've found that I need a message and experience of love, grace, and forgiveness greater than what I can offer. Through this spiritual reawakening and exploration, internal alignment increased between my worldview, values, and daily life priorities.

Spiritual connection has brought confidence and delight in my creative expressions and new layers of understanding the "audience of one" we discussed in the third chapter. The phrase now has two meanings: honoring my own unique passions, but first and foremost honoring the Creator through enjoyment and practice of my expressions. This perspective has increased the freedom and joy I feel in creating what I love *and* deepened my connection with God. A sense of calling, satisfaction, and presence has breathed life and joyful persistence into parts of the process that otherwise would be much more difficult—the editing, the revising, the feedback, the times when no one shows up. There are times when building a new organization, choosing the high road in a relationship, or simply doing the next right thing can feel difficult or overwhelming. But, in these moments, I can return my focus to simply being a child of God, secure in value and significance, and know that I will never be alone, no matter what happens. Every step can become a place for connection, gratitude, and worship.

An Approach to Exploring Your Spiritual Beliefs and Creativity

No matter your worldview, I hope this chapter invites you to kick the tires on your beliefs and explore how they are impacting your creativity. The experiences described above opened the door for an intertwining of spirituality and creativity that continues to surpass my wildest dreams. As you've heard, re-examination of past experiences and ideas has unlocked incredible fruit.

Not everything we associate with certain ideologies, belief systems, or faith traditions is actually core to its message or truth. There are many with whom I share a religion but with whom I have profound disagreements on various topics, whether politics or interpretation of specific doctrines. But our faith tradition makes space for that process. We can see people with whom we disagree and still love one another and work to see the outflows of our shared faith resemble the virtues we celebrate. Many places that used to hold pain, disappointment, and unanswered questions within my faith experience have become places of discovery.

Misapplications of philosophical, spiritual, or religious beliefs can leave a distaste or cause significant damage. Medicines can become toxic if given in the wrong dose or formulation. The friend who hands you Ex-

Lax for a headache because it helped his constipated body "feel better" is not actually helping. It's not the fault of the medicine itself. Sadly, these unnecessary consequences can cause us to wall ourselves off from the very solutions that we need to unlock flourishing in our many forms of creativity. Wrongly writing off a philosophical, spiritual, or religious belief because of improper use or misdiagnosis could lead us to a day when we won't have the metaphorical Ex-Lax we need to get unstuck.

Might there be discoveries possible within your tradition or from another source that better serve your process? Truth is not afraid of questions, and love walks with us in the journey of discovery. There might be components within current or new belief systems that transform and fire up your creative engine. When our belief systems are strongly influenced by fear or pain, even for very real and justifiable reasons, there is a cost to our experiences of life. We may be robbing not only our ability for connection with each other but our creativity as well. Examining the fruit of your current roots is worthwhile. Of course, for many spiritual traditions, including my own, belief is an initiating action. As I've shared, learning to let go and trust first unlocked experiences and benefits of faith I had not found before, while I was holding back. But there were still a range of baby steps and experiences of hope, goodness, and beauty that fueled growing trust and deeper surrender.

If you are open to exploration, here are a few questions to consider:

- *What would you describe as your current worldview or values in a spiritual, religious, or philosophical sense?* This could be a specific tradition, a loosely formed set of ideas, or conscious choice to believe in very little or the pointlessness of these questions.
- *Where can you see these fundamental beliefs shaping your experience of creativity?* How do ideals and practices of your beliefs inspire your expressions or inform your voice? Can you see any places where a belief or existential question hinders your process?
- *Are the core values of your beliefs helping you thrive personally and relationally?* Reflect on which ones support your wellness and strengthen relationships. Do they add to your sense of hope, capacity for love, peace, or other personal values?

- *What aspects of your philosophy or spirituality could be further explored or deepened?* Are there places where your experience of a worldview isn't producing the fruits that you are seeking? These can indicate opportunities for discovery.
- *What are the values and beliefs of the people who inspire you?* Is there something you could glean from those who carry the attributes you admire? Consider not just their success but also their values and worldviews.
- *Are there places where aspects of belief systems or spiritual practices have been soured by past or present pain?* Has your journey of addressing past difficulties impacted your openness to exploring spirituality or philosophy?
- *How does your belief system help you navigate ethical or values-based tensions in your creative expressions?* For those difficult moments that present moral quandaries, what guides your choices? Is it producing the clarity and fruit you want?

You can take an experimental approach and see if implementing new aspects of spirituality, faith, or philosophy improve your creative journey and your broader experience of life. Whether or not you take me up on that invitation, take time periodically to consider your core values and how they are serving, or not serving, your goals. What's the harm in asking questions, even if you don't consider yourself a spiritual person? Exploring new concepts and ideas can feel vulnerable and uncomfortable at times, so give yourself permission to be "in process." Try not to throw the baby out with the bathwater. Human beings are imperfect and may present a very limited or even contradictory view of truths and belief systems that in healthy contexts provide positive experiences.

The Continuing Journey

Albert Einstein offered these wise words: "The important thing is not to stop questioning. Curiosity has its own reason for existing. One cannot help but be in awe when [one] contemplates the mysteries of eternity, of life, of the marvelous structure of reality. It is enough if one tries merely to comprehend a little of this mystery every day. Never lose a holy curiosity."

CHAPTER 8 | SPIRITUALITY UNLOCKED

I hope that this chapter sparks exploration and adventures around these intangible aspects of life and creativity. No matter your worldview, there could be places where pain or disappointment have limited your experience of the benefits of this channel for connection.

What could your life look like if you could wake up and start again with a clean slate, free from regret and bitterness and aware of the creative possibilities ahead of you? How would you create if the places of deepest pain and disappointment could receive a comfort that goes beyond words and concepts? What would your expressions look like if you knew, in your heart and not just in your mind, that you are deeply and personally loved? Imagine how you could create. Imagine how you could live. Imagine what you could explore from this place of freedom. Something new and beautiful can grow in place of fears, pain, and shame from the hardest moments of your life, whether or not they were tied to religion. We will engage with the redemptive aspects of creativity in the coming chapters. There are shifts possible for parts of your heart and story that have been hurt and scarred, whether by your own actions and or the pain or trauma inflicted upon you.

Our time on this planet is limited. Keep searching until you find lasting hope, peace, and fulfillment. Let the beautiful interwoven nature of spirituality and creativity empower you to write the book you dream of, build the marriage you long for, pursue the career of purpose and meaning that feels impossible, and create from places of joy and authenticity. In addition to aiding your creativity, a childlike approach can be incredibly helpful in your search for truth and life-giving spirituality. Curiosity, exploration, and willingness to learn and grow are strengths in this process. In the next chapter, we'll look at how rediscovering childlikeness can help us create what we love, and we'll discuss the barriers that keep us from these experiences.

🎸 ONE STEP ACTIVATION

Start a regular spiritual, faith, mindfulness, or service practice. Make space to strengthen existing connection or explore this topic in a new way. Pick a daily or weekly time for reflection, reading, volunteering, journaling, or prayer. Take a step forward, even if it feels outside the box for you.

CREATIVITY STORIES

MIKHAIL | HOSPITALITY ENTREPRENEUR

"It was a winter day and I was in a setting with wonderful natural light," entrepreneur Mikhail shares. "In my hands, fragrant Wush Wush coffee steamed from a textured Norwegian-made vessel. I lifted it to my lips and literally started crying. The ambience, the flavor, the moment were so special." It was at this moment that he was reminded of how worthwhile his last few years of pursuing creative excellence had been.

Mikhail's creative passions include aesthetic space design, craftsmanship, service, fashion, and hospitality. They are expressed through the Seattle-based coffee shop, Santo, he runs with his wife. Spiritual experiences have played a key role in his process. "Moments of engaging with my creativity bring me to places of deep gratitude and wonder. When the space is beautiful, the beverage well-crafted, the music and ambience just right, I feel connected to God and to my passions. It's all so perfect. I don't cry much, but these are the times I do."

A passion for detail and excellence of craft marks Mikhail's gratitude-infused approach. "It is hard to believe that I get to enjoy such beauty: the potent flavors, the craft of making a pour-over, the feel of a perfectly weighted cup in my hands. The rush of joy and the emotional highs in those moments are hard to describe and they bring me back to an awareness of the gift that life is."

Detail-orientation and perseverance have been visible throughout Mikhail's life, starting with interests in working on cars and other handy projects in his youth. His expressions in food and beverage are a relatively new application for these themes. A faith awakening caused Mikhail to start taking notice of the little things in nature, like flavors and aesthetics, on a whole new level. "The goodness, the beauty all around me are constant reminders of God. There's something I love about taking a simple thing and elevating it to a level that is memorable."

While Mikhail developed his craft, he worked as a mail deliverer for five years. There have been starts and stops in his journey. Throughout this time, Mikhail and his wife explored their passion for hospitality and the opportunity for deeper connection through moments that surprise and delight others. "We like to invite people over informally and go over the top with our menu and dishes, simply because the excellence brings us joy." These experiences helped initiate the model of creative service and quality that Mikhail strives to replicate at Santo.

Community has been crucial for Mikhail's creative endeavors. He loves empowering people to step into their creative passions. A specific focus is helping them translate dreams into sustainable structures, as others have played a key role in his process. "We are designed to take creative risks and to explore beauty. But a lot of people struggle to move forward. Most of us need people cheering in our corner, supporting our goals, and helping us take the leap. I'm honored that I get to help people do just that, because others have believed in my creative dreams and passions." Mikhail points to the business partners who came alongside him at just the right time to make the coffee shop possible.

This entrepreneur offers these words of encouragement: "We are all creative, but it can take a lot of work to make dreams reality. Keep going, keep pursuing, keep growing in what brings you life. I love my creative passions for food and drink, but I am excited to keep exploring the themes and passions that make my heart come alive, even as I savor the gifts in my hands today."

CHILDLIKENESS UNLOCKED

Experience the benefits of a lighthearted approach. Wonder, playfulness, and confidence fuel joy and ease in authentic expression. New environments and tools can help unlock these fruits of a childlike process and fuel your creativity.

A Landmark Discovery

In 1985, Dr. Vincent Felitti could not figure out what was happening. At least 50 percent of the patients in his innovative obesity program were dropping out, even though all were successfully losing weight.[45] Frustrated, he began to investigate. After hundreds of interviews, a slip of the tongue revealed a startling and consequential answer. A woman shared about the linkage between her rapid-weight gain, food behaviors, and repeated trauma that started as a child and involved her father. Subsequent conversations with other patients indicated a potential pattern linking abuse with obesity and other non-ideal health outcomes. It was the first step toward a new understanding of the role of trauma in human health and development that is still transforming the world of medicine today.

Though some practitioners initially resisted this idea, Dr. Felitti partnered with the CDC to conduct research at the Kaiser Permanente program in Southern California where he was based.[46] In 1998, its findings were released in a landmark study that indicated strong associations between adverse childhood experiences (ACEs) and much higher rates of alcoholism, depression, severe obesity, smoking, and other poor health measures. Those who had experienced four or more types of ACEs—such as abuse, living with an incarcerated parent, or having an addicted family member—were four-to-twelve times more likely to attempt suicide and two-to-four times more likely to have a sexually transmitted disease or have poor self-rated health as adults.[47] Further research has substantiated the longer-term effects of ACEs. People with these experiences often have "difficulty forming healthy and stable relationships…, unstable work histories as adults, and [struggles] with finances, jobs, and depression."[48] Sadly, these experiences are common: 61 percent of Americans report at least one ACE in their past.[49]

In light of these findings, researchers identified a range of important factors for supporting healthy childhood development, which is now recognized as a foundation for flourishing in life. Pain and abuse, or the fear of it, activate the fight-or-flight mechanism in a way that diminishes other aspects of important brain function needed for problem-solving, emotional control, and decision-making. Today, a whole range of programs, practices, and professions are working to reduce the prevalence of ACEs and proactively provide what kids need to grow and thrive. Children who receive these inputs are more likely to have stronger relationships, better physical health, higher income, and other positive well-being indicators as adults.

How does early childhood development relate to unlocking our expressions? Children are superheroes when it comes to creativity. Rediscovering childlikeness is rocket fuel for our process. Healthy kids possess imagination, permission for self-expression, and ease in accessing joy that would benefit many adults. Several decades ago, NASA partnered with researchers to measure the creativity of prospective astronauts. The developers of this test decided to also study

CHAPTER 9 | CHILDLIKENESS UNLOCKED

this quality across different age groups and found that young kids naturally exhibit incredibly high levels of creativity. However, it appears to sharply diminish as they get older—98 percent of five-year-old children scored highly on their measure, but that percentage decreased to only 30 percent of ten-year-olds, 12 percent of fifteen-year-olds, and 2 percent of adults.[50] Now, this is a more limited definition of creativity than what we're using, focused on idea generation and outside-the-box thinking, but the broader truth still holds. Unlocking creativity is rediscovering a part of ourselves that has always existed but has been forgotten over time.

Understanding how kids healthily develop can offer ideas for rediscovering childlikeness in our creativity. Each of us has had difficult past experiences that limit this quality in our adulthood, and some more than others, by virtue of living in an imperfect, broken world. But the journey to rediscovering childlikeness is worthwhile, and it has already begun via the chapters you have read thus far. Surprise! Upgrading mindsets, exploring joy-filled expressions, healing from past creative pain, developing meaningful connection, finding our sense of place in the world—these are all part of returning to a childlike approach. This is one of the most important keys for unlocking creativity and increasing joy and meaningful connection in our lives.

Why Childlikeness Can Supercharge Your Creativity

How often do you hear the words "This is just how I am" or "This is just how it goes," whether from your own lips or from a friend? You may not verbalize these sentiments out loud, but you probably have at least a couple creative expressions where this mindset has taken root. Childlikeness counters these limitations by providing permission to grow. It's an antidote that empowers exploration. Kids' daily experiences of school and play are consistent reminders that they have permission to keep developing and discovering in multiple aspects of life.

The brain's neuroplasticity is a scientific basis for our potential for change, no matter our age. We are developing patterns continually, whether it's reinforcing existing ones or intentionally learning new ones that better serve our journey. As the ACE research shows, it's true that many hindrances that adults wrestle with were set in motion in their younger years. But these cycles, and the neural networks underneath, are not permanent. Researchers have found that disorder or degeneration in one's brain does not prevent creative activity.[51] Dr. Anna Abraham, author of the book *Creativity and Neuroscience,* has noted that brain structures that develop deficiencies in some areas of function may have advantages in others.

It's important to clarify that childlikeness is not the same as childishness. This is not an encouragement to become selfish and petty or to only think about one's own problems. You may have already run into people who create childishly: throwing tantrums, refusing to share, name-calling, the list goes on. On the contrary, the positive qualities we admire in healthy children unlock creativity in ways that benefit themselves and others. Childishness is stubborn and uncomfortable when new ideas conflict with theirs. Childlikeness, on the other hand, is enabled by a sense of security that allows curiosity, flexibility, and imagination. Childishness thinks it knows best and must have what it wants *right now*. Childlikeness is built through experiences of love that encourage kindness and generosity. Childishness erupts emotionally when insecure or lacking. Childlikeness is strength and tenderness rooted in an expectation of something good. It requires neither the powerlessness nor defensiveness that develop through pain and trauma.

In a world that offers many reasons for fear and cynicism, rediscovering childlikeness requires intention. Before we explore how to strengthen this quality, let's dive further into its benefits. Here are eight reasons to develop greater childlikeness in your creativity:

1. *Joy capital.* Children delight in their creativity at most every stage of the process. Can you imagine the momentum your expressions would gain if you smiled as broadly when tackling something new as a five-year-old holding up their drawing to a parent? Kids have fewer limitations in place around feeling and expressing their emotions. Childlikeness increases capacity for laughter and supports development of joy capital that strengthens resilience and growth. You'll spend more time creating if you delight in your expressions. Plus, this joy is good for your health. Research has shown that laughter is associated

CHAPTER 9 | CHILDLIKENESS UNLOCKED

   with lower stress and depression and improved cardiovascular and immune system function.[52]
2. *Flexibility and resourcefulness.* Kids are better at embracing new information. Studies have shown that they naturally exhibit greater *distributed attention* than adults, who employ *select attention* that aids focus but causes them to be more likely to miss fresh information.[53] A study by researchers Nathaniel Blanco and Vladimir Sloutsky measured greater "costs" to adults versus children in situations where key additional ideas appeared as a process unfolded.[54] The natural tendency of kids to stay open to new information fuels creativity. Childlikeness involves learning how to navigate change in situations where one does not have control. This can aid you in the unknowns, challenges, and potentially awkward situations that are part of the creativity journey.
3. *Confidence to dream.* Astronauts, police officers, scientists, professional athletes, adventurers, superheroes—children in supportive environments know they have permission to dream about their futures. Embracing childlikeness will naturally increase vision for your creativity. It does not matter how old you are; there is time to embrace dreams for yourself and for those who come after you. Designer Vera Wang did not launch her first collection of gowns until age 40;[55] Julia Child's first cookbook was published at age 50;[56] artist Grandma Moses painted the first of her 1,500 paintings at age 77.[57] Childlikeness proactively resists the voice of cynicism and trumps the negativity that sees challenge instead of potential. Your dreams may not feel significant right now, but they matter. Where we go collectively depends on individual dreams and choices made in our families, our communities, and our societies.
4. *Experimentation and outside-the-box thinking.* Children create whole worlds and imaginative stories with simple cardboard boxes. They develop detailed characters from socks and rocks. Kids see new possibilities in what adults overlook and have a lens that sparkles with wonder. What areas of your creative expression could benefit from a fresh perspective or from an

imaginative repurposing of something already in your life? This aspect of childlikeness can breathe fresh inspiration and excitement into your art, your problem-solving, your relationships, and other expressions.

5. *Fun, play, and spontaneity.* Research has substantiated the benefits of play for adults, including greater emotional stability, increased divergent thinking, and freer creative expression.[58] In children, play contributes to brain development, activates new competencies, and aids in overcoming limiting fears.[59] Kids can make up a game in any context; regular tasks can be opportunities for spontaneous ideas. Childlikeness gives us permission to have fun throughout our journeys. We are on this planet not just to be problem-solvers but also to be fully alive human beings. Fun is a powerful source of refreshment, especially when our creativity involves addressing heavy problems in the world.

6. *Permission for learning and mystery.* "Where are we going?" "Why are we doing this?" "Is the moon made of cheese?" Children *know* that they do not have all the answers and they're very willing to ask questions. How many times have you shakily faked it through a task, palms sweating, simply because you didn't want to look foolish by admitting you didn't know how? Thinking we know everything cuts us off from one of the greatest creative superpowers: the permission to learn. Becoming childlike means that we feel comfortable going on a journey of discovery and accepting that there are aspects of our lives that we don't fully understand. Comfort with mystery is crucial for creative exploration, because there are many points where we will not have a full understanding of the finished product or our next steps. Mystery is far less uncomfortable when we know we're not alone.

7. *Abundance thinking and generosity.* Healthy children are used to having their needs met. Kindness and generosity flow from a sense of safety. Kids love to be a part of something bigger than themselves and can cheer on others. They celebrate others' victories and support them in difficult times. This openhandedness

can also fuel better connection with others around creativity. Productive interactions and sharing of ideas are easier when one feels secure in their value and has an abundance-based perspective that their needs will be met. Collaboration becomes more life-giving and less scary. This can free up creative possibilities as one cares about an overall result or goal and not just one's own role or recognition. Kindness and selflessness can help accelerate the creative process.

8. *Resilience and perseverance.* Childlikeness reduces the pressure for perfection and increases adaptability. A missed homework assignment, falling off the bike, learning how to ask for help—they're all a part of growing up. Healthy kids recognize their permission to not have it all together and are quick to cry out for help when trouble arises. Difficulties don't keep them down. Children learn to reframe failure as opportunity for growth and seize chances to try again. Kids raised in supportive environments know that they will keep progressing and advancing despite their momentary struggles.

Unlocking Childlikeness

How do we proactively increase childlikeness for our expressions? We can loosely apply best practices from early childhood development to our creativity. When kids are protected, nourished physically and emotionally, cared for, educated, encouraged, and given healthy correction and guidance, they develop confidence, security, skills, and the motivation to pursue their dreams. Here are five practical ways you can strengthen childlikeness in your creativity:

1. *Improve your external environment.* Where do you find yourself at rest with a sense of emotional and physical safety? Stress triggers can siphon away brain capacity or lead to distracting coping mechanisms via technology, sex, food, or other substances. Find a place where you can go that helps you experience peace and focus. It might include art, inspiring music, pleasant scents, comfortable seating, or other elements that are energizing for you. Sometimes the physical space matters less than the people whom

you are around. Are there places where people who are part of your creative community gather? Once you have found a space, set specific time periods in which you eliminate distractions. If needed, turn off your smartphone or disable internet access. For example, I will frequently write via my laptop in my parked car, whether in the In-N-Out lot or at a scenic viewpoint, because I find myself less distracted than when connected to WiFi.

2. *Make space for free expression.* Over-structuring can hinder our natural creative flow and joy. Are you making time and feeling permission to create without the weight of task lists, responsibilities, pressure, or even tangible outcomes? Activities and expressions for which there is no clear tangible "so what" can benefit our well-being by more easily enabling connection and joy. Investing in these moments requires intentional effort, especially when external validation and reward for expressions increase. Proactively make time to express your creativity in playful ways, especially if you sense stress increasing and ease decreasing. Resist the pressure to judge your journey solely by a specific outcome, and stay connected to the delight of your expressions.

3. *Try new creative experiments.* How do kids develop new skill sets and increase their dexterity? Well, it's not by sitting around and rehearsing negative thoughts about their abilities. They grow by taking on new tasks, going after challenges, involving themselves in learning environments. From wobbly grasps on spoonfuls of mashed carrots to throwing basketballs through mini-hoops to that first time getting behind the wheel with sweaty palms, activities provide great opportunities for learning. New activities or contexts provide children opportunities to experiment. Making space for continued exploration will help us maintain a childlike approach to creativity and fend off the pride that robs us of new discoveries.

4. *Stay creatively nourished.* Children don't grow without nutrients. Exercise and play matter, but if kids aren't being fed, the results are disastrous. What are you consuming creatively? Do you get refreshed via viewing art or film, having fun experiences with friends, getting out in nature, or enjoying introvert time in

your room? Just like with food, not everything that we consume creatively provides the same nutrients. Some may hold more resonant, encouraging messages or themes, while others include a bunch of junk that feels great in the moment but does not benefit your journey. You don't have to go on a crazy creative intake program. Have fun with it. But recognize that what you take in will impact your outflow and your process.

5. *Strengthen your internal environment.* In addition to having a positive external context, greater childlikeness requires a more life-giving internal world. You may need to address specific hindrances that have limited your ability to embody this quality in your creativity. Continue your journey with mindsets and healing from past pain. This can bring even deeper experiences of safety and peace that spur childlikeness. Add affirmations about playfulness, spontaneity, and fun to your ongoing list, and revisit relevant earlier tools as necessary.

Dreaming About Unlocked Creativity

What would our communities look like if more of us started creating with the joy and confidence found in childlikeness? How could greater flexibility and resilience fuel your expressions and inspire full-sized dreams? What challenges would you take on if you knew that success is simply saying yes? I get giddy thinking about the life-altering, world-changing possibilities, whether you are developing incredible technological innovation, diving deep into artistic projects, serving youth in your community, or parenting your children well and unleashing their creative potential.

Have you ever seen one person suddenly shift an environment through their choice to do something childlike? It can look like a buttoned-up, over-serious party becoming lighthearted and fun through an individual's expression of joy or playfulness. Or, the asking of an honest question opens needed dialogue and vulnerability in a meeting. The choice of one person to ask for help and embark on a healing journey can end generational patterns and create a new future for their family. Your creativity and your journey toward childlikeness can directly impact people *and* indirectly give permission for others to experience its benefits. The more that people experience the joy and goodness possible via their expressions, the more emotional capacity they have to share with their loved ones. Embracing this approach to life may even help reduce the frequency of ACEs in the next generation.

If the idea of childlikeness in creativity is provocative or still seemingly far from your current state, that's okay. The attributes of this quality may look different within your unique approach to life, but none of them are exclusive to certain personality types. Laying a foundation of childlikeness is the perfect lead-in for our next chapter, where we will delve into the power of narrative and the possibilities for re-examining and re-creating our stories.

ONE STEP ACTIVATION

Let's have some fun. Set aside 20 minutes for creative "play." If it helps you relax, pick a new format or medium, where there is no pressure for a certain outcome. You have permission to get silly. Make up a game with household items, use kitchen ingredients to make art, cook a new dish, or venture to a park or neighborhood you enjoy, just for the sake of it. Start your play time with affirmations that support a childlike approach to creativity.

JOY | MUSICIAN AND TEACHER

"Comparison shuts down creativity," says Joy, a New York-based musician and English teacher. Educated at Princeton and NYU, she has at times felt the pressure to simply check the box and take expected career steps based on her background. "We live our lives so influenced by tradition. It's important to ask questions. What if there's a better way? A deeper way? In the letting go, in the seeking of what is most important, I'm finding more than I could ever give away."

Better known by her artist name, Elysse, Joy has embraced her creative nature in discovering a meaningful career path that blends art and education. Her journey into heart-alive creativity has enabled her to rediscover and enjoy passions that she has held since childhood and to see her expressions weave together in unexpected ways. "All aspects of life can be creative. In my work as an English teacher, I saw how applying training and practices from my love for jazz could bring something special into the classroom. The techniques I use as a musician, like intentional listening, improvisation, vulnerability, surrendering to the moment, and commanding a stage, informed the dynamic of my teaching. Students started opening up to me because they felt like a human being, not just a test score. They even started a group chat where they could ask me about life."

A passion for service has infused Joy's teaching. "The question for me became, how could I help nurture the people entrusted to me as a teacher? Acknowledging the human being in front of me enables me to engage in deeper and more supportive ways." Joy structures coursework so that her students can approach lessons as collective creative challenges. She loves to pose the question of how they can together get through a test, a deadline, or a project so that it becomes an opportunity to creatively problem-solve.

New discoveries have helped Joy embrace her lifelong passion for music. "As I've continued on my journey, I've realized that music is my primary calling for this season. It's something I can't shut down within." For Joy, living authentically is essential. "Success isn't selling a certain number of copies or a certain level of income; it's creating with conviction. Songwriting for me always starts with the germ of an idea. I'll sense an idea that has greater weight, and *ding!* It just resonates differently."

Joy has developed a process that helps her enter into the flow during times of artistic expression. She is intentional about both her internal and external environments. "Going for a walk, communing with nature, enjoying a long shower, finding an inward sense of peace with diffusers and candles—it all helps me prepare. I will spend time in prayer and meditation, inviting divine inspiration. When my mental state is flowing with joy, lush and lavish, creativity is easy. Once I find inspiration, I let it flow like water. I become a channel, a vessel through which soundscapes can be released."

Joy's process is full of childlike appreciation for the unexpected. "I am very interested in the element of surprise in my work. Understanding the landscape of lyric, melody, and structure helps me explore what I can add to the current musical discourse that's new. I want to push the boundaries around song and inspire people to express themselves."

There is a clear linkage between everyday life and artistic and non-artistic pursuits for Joy. "I think it's important to live as curiously as I can. Much of my art comes from synthesizing experiences and processing life. If you're going through a rough patch, explore those accompanying thoughts and feelings. There is catharsis in being able to connect to deep emotions, and sad songs have helped me in different seasons. Recognizing the possibilities for creativity in mundane parts of life continues to add delight and meaning."

10

NARRATIVE UNLOCKED

Expand possibilities by rewriting your own story. Your creativity is profoundly impacted by narratives that influence how you understand yourself and your expressions. In this chapter, you will learn techniques rooted in neuroscience to help reframe your story and unlock greater clarity and momentum.

Social Media and the Power of Echo Chambers

In 1997, Andrew Weinreich gave a talk that would have far-reaching consequences for humanity. At a gathering in downtown Manhattan, he announced the launch of the Six Degrees platform, the world's first online social network. Named after the popular "six degrees of separation" theory developed by researcher Stanley Milgram and popularized thanks to actor Kevin Bacon, the website suddenly allowed individuals to create digital profiles and connect online with others via email addresses and mutual friendships. "We all went home," Weinreich remembered in a 2014 interview, "and then over the next couple of days we had these moments of, 'Is anybody going to join this thing?'"[60] The platform did not take off right away. Its initial half dozen participants were joined by more, but that growth plateaued for a period at around fifty people per day.

The world looked different back then. Most Americans did not have an email address or access to digital photography. Smartphones would not arrive for a decade. People's profiles only held text, and the Six Degrees team debated the pros and cons of having participants send in photographs to be scanned and uploaded (it proved too cost intensive).[61] The company stuck with it and soon the power of an online social network became clear, even when based purely on text and information. Six Degrees entered a period of rapid growth, and the business got purchased by a larger company for hundreds of millions of dollars. As a predecessor of MySpace, Instagram, TikTok, and, yes, Facebook, it laid the foundation for the world-changing reality of online social networking.

This forerunning social media platform initiated profound shifts in how we connect to each other and are influenced by information. People began to have more access to details about the lives of individuals than ever before. The ongoing evolution of social media continues, creating whole new ways to consume news, opinions, and content. These platforms are reshaping the narratives of individuals, communities, and whole societies in ways both consequential and concerning. The 2020 documentary *The Social Dilemma* explored the psychological reasons behind this danger. Echo chambers can develop when the algorithms that determine the content displayed in an individual's feed are set to maximize engagement. Emotions drive clicks. Confirmation bias, a common psychological fallacy, causes people to seek out and prefer ideas or opinions that align with their existing beliefs, leading to a habitual reinforcement of them. This is a reality that happens regardless of whether or not an idea or narrative is true. Our trust in certain groups or voices can make us susceptible to embracing information that is unhelpful and even factually inaccurate, whether about distant global events or our own lives.

CHAPTER 10 | NARRATIVE UNLOCKED

The Importance of Narrative

What are the narratives shaping your experience of creativity? Have you found yourself in echo chambers that dictate how you see parts of yourself and your expressions? This chapter's purpose is not to bemoan the risks of technology. Rather, my goal is to help you recognize that the same principles that shape viewpoints via social media might be at work in your life regardless of your technology use. We can be prone to confirmation bias that sustains self-limiting narratives when we anchor to information at work, school, or home simply because it is most accessible or familiar. Our past and present experiences convey ideas that shape our narratives. Some are true and helpful, while others are not and hinder our creativity. What we do with the information that enters our minds will create the stories we believe about ourselves and our expressions. These perspectives are not permanent. In fact, our ability to rewrite our stories is a core aspect of our creative potential.

Social media is not the first channel to profoundly influence narrative. Throughout history, media, religion, politics, propaganda, protest movements, and art have played powerful roles in shaping perceptions of one's self, capabilities, and place in the world. We all are prone to potential blindspots based on our contexts. Healthy and clear vision about one aspect of our lives doesn't eliminate the potential for missing something in another. If you were at a basketball game and could only read part of the scoreboard, you could have very accurate information about one quarter but be detached from the final result. The game might look like a loss when you're actually ahead, or vice versa. There may be more time to play than immediately apparent. The same is true for our creativity. We may be only seeing a portion of the picture, and thus find ourselves unnecessarily frustrated or disappointed, harried or complacent. Think about the new ideas and expressions that you have uncovered through this book already. Let the joy and satisfaction from these discoveries inspire excitement for what else you can uncover in your personal narrative.

If your life was a movie, what is the story that it is telling today? Or, more importantly, what narrative do *you* hear about it? Are there scenes or chapters that make you proud and inspired? Are there other parts that leave you feeling embarrassed, fearful, or guilty? The story you're agreeing with in your mind is as important as the objective facts of your life. There can be both similarities and tremendous gaps between your perceptions of key events, the reality of them, and what your heart experienced in the moment. The childlike approach and healthy connection you are discovering provide a good foundation from which to explore your narrative. You can celebrate your progress as you remain open to new discoveries.

The problems you have encountered are not insurmountable barriers to a life of purpose and joy. Rather, they indicate that you are designed to overcome adversity. Author Joseph Campbell famously studied and articulated the hero's journey. This is a framework for narrative extremely common in mythology that shapes most all stories we hear today. Fictional stories with this structure resonate deeply with audiences because they are parallel to the human experience. Whether crafted by Shakespeare or Disney, every hero we celebrate faces challenges and goes on a journey of discovery that involves friends and foes, mentors and mystery. Woody in *Toy Story* is battling irrelevance and a changing role in his most important relationship. The Little Mermaid is searching for her place in the world and fighting for a voice crippled by an ill-conceived partnership. Mulan is overcoming fossilized perceptions of strength and prowess that trivialize the capabilities she has to offer the world. Who they become through their adventures is as important as what they accomplish, and in each story there is a rejection of an old narrative in order to embrace the new.

Pick a problem that you have faced in your life. Can you see where it may indicate possibilities for your own heroic potential? There are heart-alive, creative adventures waiting for you. The narrative that sees you as a hero on a journey is as true as any lens through which you have seen yourself previously.

Rewriting Your Story

As previously discussed, your mind powerfully creates through its thoughts and mindsets. New beliefs can also be created that reshape your story, as you have experiences that counter what you have known in the past. Rewriting narratives about your life can benefit your creativity, whether by granting permission to explore, bringing greater purpose and peace to the process, or solidifying your strengths and sources of inspiration. In his book *Social Intelligence,* clinical psychologist Dr. Daniel Goleman quotes other researchers in explaining how one can intentionally alter the story that has been created about their past.[62]

> Whenever we retrieve a memory, the brain rewrites it a bit, updating the past according to our present concerns and understanding. At the cellular level, LeDoux explains, retrieving a memory means it will be "reconsolidated," slightly altered chemically by a new protein synthesis that will help store it anew after being updated. Thus each time we bring a memory to mind, we adjust its very chemistry... The specifics of the new consolidation depend on what we learn as we recall it. If we merely have a flare-up of the same fear, we deepen our fearfulness. But the high road can bring reason to the low. If at the time of the fear we tell ourselves something that eases its grip, then the same memory becomes reencoded with less power over us. Gradually, we can bring the once-feared memory to mind without feeling the rush of distress all over again. In such a case, says LeDoux, the cells in our amygdala reprogram so that we lose the original fear conditioning. One goal of therapy, then, can be seen as gradually altering the neurons for learned fear.

As Dr. Goleman shares, memories are impacted by the emotions and viewpoints through which they are seen. Our present experiences of past difficulties can change when we see them via a different narrative. Experiences of acceptance and authentic connection can help us partner with new perspectives and actually change the neural networks in our brains, which can impact our creative process.

There are new ways to understand yourself and your expressions. The narratives surrounding moments of your life and experiences of creativity could shift and become supportive of your goals. Weaknesses become opportunities for growth, problems become invitations for innovation, pain indicates a need for healing. What if the challenges you have experienced aren't just something to survive but the dragons you're meant to slay, the wounds you are made to heal, the treasure you're meant to unlock? The story of your creative process can be as poignant and beautiful as your specific outflows.

As you explore the power of narrative, the thoughts you choose are paramount. Dr. David Burns, psychiatrist and pioneer in the development of cognitive therapy, affirms the importance of intentional thinking in shifting emotional experiences of life events in his book *Feeling Great*:[63]

> It is your thoughts, and not the circumstances of your life, that create all of your feelings... Sometimes, though, we think about ourselves and our lives in ways that are pretty illogical and even unfair to ourselves. We make interpretations about what's happening that are twisted and misleading, but we don't realize it. That is what cognitive distortions are: a highly misleading way of thinking about yourself and the world. It's a way of fooling yourself.

Discovering a new story about your creativity often involves addressing negativity or painful moments via a different narrative. Neuroscientist Dr. Mark Noble describes how simply recognizing and choosing new thoughts can actually be a form of "microneurosurgery" that transforms not only your thinking but also your feelings:[64]

> Neuronal networks are also the physical units that underlie your thoughts, feelings, and behaviors, and they change whenever you learn something new... Whenever you learn, you are modifying groups of nerve cells that work in a coordinated manner... In learning you've reached into your own brain and conducted microneurosurgery—modifying specific networks in your brain. And you're doing this with a level of specificity that is completely out of reach of any other approach to modifying brain function... The distorted thoughts that trigger these [negative] feelings can be fairly easily challenged. The negative thoughts are the neuronal networks we [need to] target for modification.

There are more hope-filled, life-giving perspectives about your expressions and your creative journey waiting to be embraced. Your current narratives may feel very real and seemingly unshakeable. But these experiences are not necessarily permanent. The stories we perceive about ourselves and our expressions are more subjective than realized.

CHAPTER 10 | NARRATIVE UNLOCKED

There are ways to re-experience events that align with a higher truth and better serve our creative journeys. Thoughts, desires, and feelings can all change over time, thanks to the brain's neuroplastic quality.

A community, mentor, therapist, or counselor who cares about you *and* is willing to provide honest feedback can be helpful for building new narratives. If you find yourself wondering if getting help is for you, take the step! As you consider who to work with, look for someone with values, life experiences, and qualifications that resonate with your journey and needs. These professionals and others around us in daily life can help us identify possible blindspots. However, while others can play an important role, you must engage with the work to shift into new, authentic, hope-filled stories about your life and creativity. No matter how many people share an encouraging thought or narrative with you, it must take root in your inner reality to be most fruitful.

Blindly embracing an optimistic viewpoint completely detached from reality can be counterproductive, as can maintaining narratives rooted solely in pain, shame, or punishment that become oppressive. Growth is found in the tension between the aspirational and the actual. An honest narrative does not have to be detached from difficulties or be overly dour and punishing. Many of us have developed lenses too shaded with the negative or critical and could lean into more redemptive, positive narratives that inspire the change we seek. Hope is the powerful motivator we need and it can coexist with hard realities. It is the bridge that brings us from brokenness to healing.

Shifting My Narrative

Re-understanding my own story revved up my creative engine and fueled a new experience of life. One of the most freeing, unexpected benefits of recovery for me was the realization that many patterns of thoughts and emotions I had experienced for years weren't actually hard-coded or permanent. Narratives influenced by perfectionism, chemical dependency, stress, and performance began to shift. They're not the truest form of myself.

Until I started my own healing journey, I did not see how the ambition and performance that brought me to Harvard and Silicon

CREATIVITY UNLOCKED

Valley linked to underlying perspectives about myself rooted in shame. The pressure to perform, succeed, and somehow be "enough" came from a deep sense of being unworthy or disconnected from love. Later events (hello confirmation bias!) exacerbated these cycles and discouraged creativity. I found temporary comfort in numbing the reels of shame and fear that played in my mind, whether about current uncertainties or one of the worst moments of my adult life. Unhelpful mindsets and beliefs had influenced the story I told myself around it, and these cycles of coping deepened into addiction. I didn't know what to do with the guilt or fear it triggered. For years, I tried to forcibly stuff down events. Fears of judgment and rejection delayed experiences of the grace and unconditional love that I actually needed in those moments.

The spiritual experiences described earlier marked a dramatic shift in my journey. But there was also a process of healing and narrative shift that unfolded over time. Opening up to trusted supporters enabled me to share and reconsider the stories I believed about me and my worst moments. Through this sense of connection, I began to experience comfort and have more hope-filled perspectives around the parts of my journey that had been hardest. The moments of great shame and pain became an invitation to experience grace. I could experience a love that hadn't left me in the mess. The process was bumpy and not always easy, because the narratives influenced by fear, judgment, and performance were so familiar and deeply ingrained into my thought processes. I had to let go of my attempts to minimize and hide, but I also got to let go of the horribly self-critical, exaggerated stories that had haunted me for years. The process forced me to learn how to receive grace more deeply and to let go of the self-reliance I had carried. The reality of this undeserved love and forgiveness felt so foreign at first that it was hard to believe. But, bit by bit, experiences of compassion and connection helped shift the stories in my mind.

A previously unseen array of creative possibilities began unlocking in this process, both for practical expressions and for broader life vision. The kinder narrative relieved pressure and allowed greater childlikeness, which fueled greater risk-taking and enjoyment in my expressions. I could write with authenticity and joy, no longer beholden to the lie that it was useless, pointless, or not good enough. Life-giving changes in

CHAPTER 10 | NARRATIVE UNLOCKED

my hobbies and career priorities inspired me to explore what else could shift. I began to see *and* experience a different story for my journey that changed my sense of self and identity. Moments of deep intrinsic joy and meaningful connection via my creativity highlighted a new understanding of purpose in places of pain. This all stemmed from a healing journey that set me free creatively, emotionally, and spiritually.

The journey of narrative refinement continues daily. On a regular basis, there are opportunities to recognize and upgrade aspects of the story shaping my perceptions. Moments of exhaustion, failure, poor choices, and stumbles can occur, but there is now a trajectory of hope. In fact, some of the greatest growth I've experienced came through some of the biggest messes I've made since the transformative shift in 2016. They provided a fresh opportunity to experience the gift of grace. While the consequences for poor choices are far from ideal, they also provided experiences of transformative, unconditional love that have deepened the healing my heart needed. Failures have helped me access tools and make practical changes that are aiding and sustaining my creative journey. One example is exchanging passivity for intention in personal growth and discovering the power of affirmations. I am still learning and developing a prioritization of rest, which has been an ongoing journey throughout my life.

Experimenting with New Narratives

The scientist in me would say that the results of this experimental approach of a new story have been a massive success. Joy, peace, and experiences of meaningful connection are my daily norm. Healing from my own unrecognized pain helps me see the actions of others that used to infuriate or offend me as an outflow of their unhealed pain. Kindness, self-discipline, and generosity have strengthened through experiences of grace, not weakened (though my friends will tell you I'm still a work in progress). Some of the very topics and channels that proved most isolating and destructive for me are now the very avenues in which I get to create, build connection, and share the love and hope I have experienced. The redemptive delight of seeing life grow out of the broken cracks gets me so pumped up I want to swear.

I started writing this chapter two years before this book was finished. As I now make final edits, it is wild to read these words and see how much my narrative has changed since starting the writing process. There are whole creative endeavors and roles I've stepped into that I had no vision for back then. And there have been deeper levels of shift around the greatest wounds in my life, including both self-inflicted ones and others over which I had no control. I see now how these moments have enabled me to better sit with others in their pain, to extend grace that helps people change their lives, and to create solutions that enable people to avoid the messes and pain I have experienced.

Your failures do not have to be the defining factor of your identity. Rejection by people or organizations does not mean you are a reject. Addiction to a substance or behavior or feeling does not make your ultimate identity an addict. Moments of personal failing do not indicate that you a failure. You are a human being, created in love, by love, for love. You are so much more than any challenge or disorder you experience, whether it is a recent occurrence or a long-term battle. The story you are perceiving and writing with your life each day can hold plot swings and scene shifts that surprise you in a good way.

Shifting Your Story

Reframing is a powerful tool for discovering new narratives about your creativity and yourself that fuel hope and growth. Weaknesses and failures often stem from places where strengths have been overextended or where valid needs have gone unmet. Applying a compassionate, creative lens to your story can help you find unexpected strengths and unmet needs in these painful parts of life. Granted, there are some traumatic experiences that might be difficult to reframe, especially initially. That's okay. Reframing a narrative does not change the past, eliminate consequences, or erase the need to feel and validate pain. When used in healthy ways, this powerful tool will enable you to embrace the present and future aspects of your creativity. Exploring new narratives for past events or ongoing struggles will strengthen your ability to reframe, and rewrite, your story. Photographers exemplify the skill of discovering something striking, original, or beautiful in imperfect contexts.

CHAPTER 10 | NARRATIVE UNLOCKED

Recognizing root issues, needs, and even potential strengths shifts the narrative from one of failure to one emphasizing hope and growth. Shifting these stories can motivate and sustain change in the very places where limiting or self-destructive behaviors are present. Read through the list below and journal about any that resonate with your journey. Note over-extended strengths and see whether possible underlying needs might be present. (Hint: they often indicate a need for connection on some level.) A similar reframing could be made of other challenges.

- *Overwork* is an **unhealthy extension** of the gifts of diligence and persistence, and an **indicator** of the potential for healing from shame.
- *People-pleasing* that is overly apologetic and diminishes one's own voice is an **overextension** of awareness and sensitivity to others' needs, and an **indicator** of the potential for greater boldness.
- *Guilt* is an **indicator** of the potential for healing and forgiveness, a need for grace. It also demonstrates a sensitivity to justice and an awareness of right and wrong.
- *Stress, anxiety, and worry* are **indicators** of the potential for discovery of greater peace and rest, and an **overextension** of healthy desires to help, protect, or provide for oneself or others.
- *Loneliness and never-fitting-in* may be both an **overextension** of independence and an **indicator** of present or potential uniqueness, outside-the-box perspectives, and bridge-building gifts.
- *Challenges around healthy body image* are often an **overextension** of a life-giving appreciation for beauty and a valid need for health.
- *Hypochondria* is an **overextension** of a healthy desire to protect one's physical well-being.
- *Experiencing a trigger from past trauma* is an **indicator** of potential for healing and a valid need for comfort and empathy.
- *False responsibility* can be an **overextension** of compassion and a healthy desire to help, and an **indicator** of a need for comfort and connection.

- *Co-dependency* and *sexually compulsive behaviors* are often **indicators** of valid needs for healthy connection.
- *Self-hatred* is an **indicator** of the potential for healing and radical self-acceptance and love. It often stems from self-criticism, which can be an **overextension** of strengths in excellence and craft.
- *Bitterness* is an **indicator** of the potential for forgiveness and healing. It can be an indicator of a high-value for fairness or justice, or the fruit of an **overextension** of a healthy desire to be safe.

You can utilize, and go deeper, with this reframing technique as you continue your journey. Start practicing this tool by seeing opportunities for growth or hidden strengths instead of beating yourself up. Validating your intentions or needs reduces the paralyzing sting from past mistakes, and it can help you identify new strategies for the challenges undermining your creative purpose and joy.

When Grace Is Your Narrator

The reframing section above draws from a previous key referenced in the chapter on forgiveness (chapter 5, "Healing Unlocked"). Grace can play a significant role in shifting long-held narratives. Growth requires an honest recognition of weakness and failure and the stories they have developed. Yet, without connection and love we often lack the capacity and hope to change. Grace is rocket fuel for exploring and strengthening new narratives because it offers a bridge between present reality and future possibility. It sees us through a lens that is more than the sum of our current parts or behaviors and offers a story better than what appears deserved. Grace is a gift, an unearned love that fuels our becoming. It can provide the atmosphere our hearts need to be honest and express what has been wrong. Grace is not afraid of messy situations. Acknowledging pain and failure is a necessary part of rewriting our stories.

There can be unresolved conflicts and messy situations that inhibit our narrative shift and our creative processes. A foundation of grace provides motivation to seek restoration, flowing from the love received, not the voice of self-hatred. Treat others like you would want them to treat you in the process. If you were in their shoes and would have liked an apology or other form of restitution, do your best to do so. If you're constantly bothered by perfectionistic questions about the need to go back to find the classmate you said a cross word to in the third grade, you may be overthinking it. For some mistakes in our lives, we can go back, apologize, and make amends. For others, this isn't possible. But you can still receive grace in these areas. For me, the situations or mistakes I couldn't correct or apologize for remind me of my need for unmerited, undeserved grace. The words of a friend help remind me of this powerful concept: "Grace is for those areas where we cannot forgive ourselves."

When you let grace be the narrator of your story, your daily expressions will be infused with greater empathy, compassion, and love for people because you will have greater empathy, compassion, and love for yourself. Our own experiences of grace in places of brokenness can give us a profound empathy for others, especially those who find themselves trapped in destructive practices. I've seen enough of the consequences of addiction to know that it can take anyone down a dark path. Children do not set out to become adults who cause pain or even do monstrous things. But the absence of the connection and love we are wired for can have costly consequences. That is where far too many end up. There is a solution for them, and for each of us, in whatever messy areas our lives present, and it's called grace. In the midst of the horrendous things perpetuated in the world, grace sees humanity, the broken inner child, within the people involved—but it also doesn't turn a blind eye to what is wrong. Grace offers hope that brings healing, empowers change, and leads to whole new creative possibilities.

Many of us are aware of a need for greater kindness and compassion in our journeys, whether toward others, ourselves, or our creative processes. Experiencing the depths of grace, of proactive acceptance and love, enables it to become more a part of our nature. Think about it: if every day you took a bath in a tub full of your favorite fragrance, whether perfume or nutella, you would carry that scent with you throughout your schedule. Compassion, kindness, and grace are powerful gifts that we can offer others via our daily activities. But first we must receive them ourselves. You're not going to be able to put on or serve your guests any *eau de nutella* until you have a supply at your house.

The Daily Narrative Journey

Rewriting your story is a daily adventure. A supportive community can be incredibly helpful in this process. The perspectives of others can help you recognize and shift the stories you believe. Remember: narratives are influenced by our environments. That scroll through a social media echo chamber, an offhand conversation with a friend, or the latest office gossip can either fortify a new, positive narrative or strengthen a negative story.

For me, hindering thoughts or emotions around the creative process typically indicate disconnection from the new stories I choose to embrace. Old narratives rooted in fear, failure, disconnection, self-hatred, or other unhelpful thoughts sprout most quickly if I'm not intentional about receiving the nutrients I need. Personally, it is helpful to have periods of time away from social media, especially when I don't want to spend energy pushing back on comparison or other hindering narratives. Negativity toward oneself or one's creative projects can grow through seemingly harmless information. Researchers have found that social media use can affect self-esteem. Practical boundaries with technology and emotional boundaries in relationships have helped strengthen my creative process and my emotional health.

Science is still discovering facets of how we are affected mentally, emotionally, and physically by all sorts of influences, from the food we eat to the people we're around. Studies have demonstrated the concept of "emotional contagion," through which people start have similar feelings or moods as others in their community.[65] Direct and indirect interactions can both trigger common experiences, e.g., neurological synchronization. Depression, for instance, can "spread" through social connection.[66] Simply spending time with people with certain emotional states or behaviors can affect your own. I write this not to underemphasize your responsibility to shape your new narrative but to draw attention to possible influences. If you, like me, are someone who is able to read people well and can be sensitive to what is happening around you, there may be forms of communication that are operating without your awareness. Past pain may also contribute to being hyper aware of others' emotions as a form of self-protection. Whether these effects are due to behavior mirroring, trauma responses, or some form of deeper, spiritual connection (shout-out to the empaths out there), we can be affected in ways that we do not see.

I have had several spiritually poignant moments that are harder to quantify. Multiple times I have walked into coffee shops or events in the midst of a good day and been hit by a deluge of self-hating, negative thoughts that are otherwise inexplicable. After these moments, I have then met strangers in that context who I learn through conversation have been dealing with similar specific thoughts and feelings. Each time, there has been an opportunity to connect, to encourage, to serve that has been life-giving. These outside-the-box moments have played a positive role in the examination of my narratives and exploring what shapes them.

Recognizing the possible sources of narrative in our daily lives empowers us to create something new for ourselves and others. The moments described above in the coffee shops became opportunities for meaningful connection with two new friends, one a veteran going through a difficult season, and one a young woman working in mental-health tech due to her own challenges. Proactively building your own narrative can help you offer encouragement and hope to others who are in the process of rediscovering their stories too. This is the type of daily, redemptive creativity that the next chapter will explore. Within life's messes are nutrients for meaningful, joy-filled expression.

🗝 ONE-STEP ACTIVATION

Choose one area of personal growth where you have a weakness that you can reframe as a strength. Think about how it can play a role in a narrative that supports your heroic journey.

CREATIVITY STORIES

CHRISTIAN | THERAPIST

"Spoken word provided the space to wrestle with questions and tell stories as part of my healing journey," shares Christian, a Seattle-based psychotherapist. "Creativity has always helped me process emotions. Initially, it provided catharsis for challenging moments from my upbringing involving my father and mother. I drew more from pain back then. Now I have learned how to connect and create via childlike joy, inspired by the curiosity and wonder of my own kids. Intentional inner work has also enabled this shift."

Creativity has fueled personal growth for Christian. "Expressing myself through the arts played a major role in helping me find my voice. These activities provided a unique form of satisfaction and support for the journey of re-understanding my own story that has shaped my fatherhood." He values the role of creativity for helping enable connection to a full range of emotions. "Sometimes I had a significant moment via a whispered verse. At other points, I needed to scream out truth."

Christian also activates his creative nature via his work. "Each person's story is a tapestry that is unfolding and being knit together all at once. I need to be nimble, aware, and thinking in the abstract to help my clients find pathways and keys that unlock a new narrative. It is meaningful work that helps me stay aware and humble in my own ongoing journey. Therapy involves thinking about the past, present, and future in new ways. Different models, whether based on Carl Jung's work or otherwise, involve a reframing that is creative in nature."

Christian appreciates opportunities to help people process grief and trauma and discover something new as they experience integration. "When I hold space for a client's story, there's an element of imagining with them what's possible. Hindering ideas and beliefs about their lives may need to die so that new possibilities can be born."

Given what his career requires, Christian keeps his creative tank full by connecting to things that are expansive and perspective-broadening. "Spending time in nature helps bring me to a different vantage point. I love to travel. Making memories with my wife and children in new locations and cultures brings me a lot of joy. In fact, interacting with my kids is one of my favorite ways I get to be creative. I appreciate being able to invest my time and energy into their lives as their personalities and giftings develop."

In his professional and personal life, Christian remains focused on the inputs fueling his creativity. "I think of an old Cherokee legend about human nature that involves two battling wolves. One represents the broken aspects of humanity that we can engage with: greed, selfishness, hate. The other represents goodness, kindness, and other positive qualities. In the story, a grandfather reveals to his grandson that the wolf that wins is the one that gets fed."

The creative tension between structure and freedom fascinates Christian. "We need to be able to roam and explore, to breathe deeply in the rush of wind that takes us to unexpected places. We also need intention, like with any aspect of life." He offers these encouraging words to people who are in process of rewriting their narratives: "Every person's story holds possibility, and there is something sublime and beautiful to discover within it. Just because the good is not visible yet doesn't mean that it doesn't exist. Don't give up on your potential; you may just need another set of eyes to help you see it."

REDEMPTION UNLOCKED

Uncover treasures amidst daily pains and difficulties. Challenges can become opportunities for life-giving creativity. In this chapter you will discover unexpected benefits by unlocking the redemptive possibilities of your expressions.

Poop: The Hidden Treasure

Creative possibilities can be found in the most unexpected places, starting with excrement. Did you know that human waste has helped multiple civilizations throughout history feed and sustain their growing populations? Yes, you read that right. Though smelly and messy—I'll stop there; you're probably familiar—excrement contains minerals crucial for agricultural productivity. For centuries, the potassium, nitrogen, and phosphorus in poop helped restore and replenish the sandy soil of Japan and other countries, keeping it from becoming nutrient-deprived. In fact, human and animal waste played such an important role in multiple cultures that "night soil" became a prized commodity.

Today, startups are developing the means to grab hold of the value within these messy and common outflows. Their technology turns biosolids, the polite term for treated human waste, into energy-providing briquettes that serve as fuel in developing countries. A growing movement is supporting the role of biosolids in helping agricultural lands remain nutrient-rich—pending addressal of concerns around pathogens and other undesirable chemicals that can be found within human waste. Herein lies a tension: if not properly treated, waste on its own can become incredibly toxic. Having the right systems in place is essential to transform the mess into magic.

There is value waiting to be discovered in what has been messy, imperfect, and even stinky in your expressions and your life. Within your daily routine and your dream projects, there is unexpectedly sweet and nourishing fruit that can grow from turning the crap you experience into fertilizer for your expressions. In the moment, the messes that have impacted you may not carry anything you want to smell, let alone utilize. But in the right context, the nutrients within these materials can help accelerate joy and meaning in your daily expressions.

Making Fertilizer from Pain and Difficulty

A creative lifestyle can help you turn crap into fertilizer. Whether the mess is self-inflicted or the proverbial doggy doo is accidentally stepped in, difficulties can trigger life-giving moments that unlock new outflows for yourself and others. This chapter presents two broad categories of redemptive rediscoveries for your exploration: creative moments within your normal routine and longer-term expressions and projects that draw from the challenges you have faced.

The silver linings in the midst of the clouds you encounter don't negate the reality of the storms themselves. Redemptive creativity does not mean downplaying trauma or treating challenges or hardships flippantly. It's not healthy or wise to ignore pain, stay in abusive situations, or deny that dangerous things are present. Untreated crap will make you sick. Fertilizer still stinks. Your well-being and safety are priorities. You would not want to lie down in a vat of crap or live with fertilizer in your house. But awareness of the creative discoveries possible can bring hope, comfort, and even joy in the midst of processing pain.

The muck we experience—the tragedies, challenges, poor choices, and difficulties—hold unseen nutrients for creativity, starting with inspiration, empathy for others, and chances for connection. Whether you express via the arts, family relationships, problem-solving, your career, or your daily interactions with others, hard experiences will arise. They are inevitable in an imperfect world. But new processes can help us navigate crap in life-giving ways. First we need to be willing to look at messes and stop pretending that our process is perfect. Reaching out when we need help keeps the muck from overwhelming our lives. No one enjoys a faulty plumbing system.

Your body is already doing this every day. It is searching for the proteins, carbohydrates, fats, and minerals it can find within both the healthy items and the junk food you consume. Multiple processes strip out the value from what you take in, while certain things you consume contribute more to the waste. For valid reasons, humanity has created whole systems to quickly, cleanly deal with the outflows of the body, though they still contain elements useful in other contexts. Sometimes one can want difficult situations or unexpected occurrences whisked away as rapidly as possible because they are messy and painful, not realizing the potential they carry.

How Difficulty Provides Inspiration for Expressions

In your creative exploration, there is *nothing* off-limits from serving as a source of inspiration or motivation for your outflows. This includes both the sweet and sour. Much of the art and entertainment we consume comes out of the heartbreak, grief, anger, disconnection, or loss that their creators have experienced, whether directly or indirectly. J.R.R. Tolkien's fantastical storytelling skills, which led to *The Lord of the Rings*, developed as a means to cope with tragic losses in his youth. Maya Angelou's seminal writing flowed from painful experiences of hardship and injustice. These are just two of countless examples. Many world-changing pieces of creativity, whether art, inventions, technological solutions, or organizations, were birthed out of challenges that confronted their maker.

Along with joy-filled passions, the difficulties you have walked through can influence what you want to build, make, or design. Hard moments frequently tie into themes that provide intrinsic motivation because it can be satisfying to express oneself or create solutions around difficulties one has personally experienced. For instance, current uncertainty about your future relationships can become a song from your heart. Challenges in accessing education or work opportunities can inspire new organizations and solutions. The regret over loss or past choices can flow into your poetry. Seasons of loneliness and isolation can inspire intentional gatherings with people and meaningful connection. The experiences you have each day—the painful, ridiculous, painfully ridiculous, or ridiculously painful—can become source material for short stories, screenplays, choreography, spoken word, and more.

This principle is true for both the minor inconveniences and the major difficulties that shape your everyday experiences. From a spat with friends to broken family relationships, from a short-term sickness to major health limitations, from a missed opportunity for fun to a permanent loss, there is creative fuel to be discovered. Start by applying these concepts to adversity that won't overwhelm your emotional capacity. If you are earlier in the healing process, it can be more difficult to perceive and identify some of the redemptive treasures for places of pain, especially major ones. One indicator of healing is the ability to be able to talk about or experience situations that once triggered fear or anguish without feeling overwhelmed or sliding into despair. If thinking about a past situation brings back a loop of heavy thoughts, pick something smaller with which to explore this concept. More time or healing may be needed before mining certain difficulties for gold. That is totally okay. In the words of a dear mentor from my youth, "Love where you are, and grow from there." Start with what you can.

Translating Crap into Creativity

What are the specific benefits of this redemptive approach to creativity? Here are a few of the hidden treasures that you can uncover in the messes you encounter. I've added a few examples from my journey and those of friends to help make the concepts more tangible.

CHAPTER 11 | REDEMPTION UNLOCKED

Meaningful connection. Opportunities for the secret sauce for creativity can arise from daily challenges, long term adversity, and other why-is-this-happening experiences. It might look like providing encouragement to a weary employee doing their best, an unexpected chance to find writing inspiration via the person sitting next to you, sharing a laugh with a stranger in a ridiculous situation, or a relationship strengthened through taking on a problem. Delayed or disrupted plans may allow space to connect with yourself via rest or time for expression that brings joy. More substantial difficulties can encourage you to get in touch with wellness needs or something greater than yourself. The challenges you can't handle on your own are opportunities for the vulnerability that fuels connection. Shared adversity can deepen and add meaning to relationships. Recovery groups and military units are just two examples where strong bonds can be built through difficult situations. Connection can be a hidden treasure found in crappy situations.

- Spilling a salad all over the carpeted floor at a public event sparked deeper connection with a friend who graciously helped and a story to laugh about after.
- Travel trouble around a wedding initiated a chain of events that led to a serendipitous meeting and building of a new friendship, as well as extra time with the groom.
- Sickness, mental health challenges, addiction, or loss have initiated new experiences of community and discovery of creative passions for many.
- Delayed filming of OneStepHope's first feature documentary led to far better weather for filming and access to facilities that were not possible or even feasible in the initial window.
- Being left off the invite list for events has provided more space for artistic expression or needed rest.

Learning. Difficulties offer opportunities to discover a different way of doing things, especially for the crappy situations that arise out of our own choices. You might uncover a new way to communicate with others, better processes to complete tasks, different resources that support your own wellness or goals, or tools and solutions you didn't know existed. Inventor extraordinaire Thomas Edison's quote about failure is a helpful encouragement: "I haven't failed. I have just found 10,000 ways that won't work."[67] Keep that in mind the next time you end up with egg on your face or feel like you have stepped in metaphorical doggy doo. Whether in your career, your relationships, your hobbies, or your family context, there are helpful opportunities to gain knowledge and wisdom in the midst of hard circumstances.

- A failed baking experiment—mixing the ingredients in the wrong order—provided a learning opportunity for techniques for future meals.
- Discovering that jobs or specific educational degrees were not providing the long-term purpose or compensation desired have informed next steps at school or work.
- Awkward, painful conversations with a significant other have led to discovering better techniques for expressing oneself.
- Burn-out and unhealthy coping mechanisms have presented opportunities to learn how to better take care of physical, emotional, and mental needs.

Expertise. The knowledge you discover via walking through a challenge can develop beyond just personal learning. It can deepen your understanding of contexts that enable you to create with more authority and insight in ways that serve others. Progressing through problems increases understanding of both solutions themselves and the experiences of activating them in real life. Your personal journey also strengthens credibility and confidence for sharing this information. From health challenges, to family situations, to headaches at work, to artistic exploration, to moving house, to changing jobs, the wisdom and skills you build can benefit the journeys of others. This simple reality has inspired many creators to develop impactful inventions and organizations by discovering the parts of their journey that can be generalized to serve many.

CHAPTER 11 | REDEMPTION UNLOCKED

- A challenging season at work led to a team change and a product-design project that added a skillset and empowered a future nonprofit's services.
- Personal experiences of the demanding college preparation process built insights shareable with others needing advice.
- Frustrations of working in traditional finance inspired startup ideas that brought a more purposeful career and new lucrative solutions
- Researching and supporting a loved one's mental-health journey increases knowledge that aids other families in similar situations.
- Rejection in a personal relationship has motivated new discoveries around communication, emotional health, and self-care that have been shared with others.

Empathy. The challenges you have faced can spark compassion and love for people with similar experiences. You can find yourself caring for issues and communities you never have before. The emotional depth of relationships built in the midst of unique challenges—from marriage support groups to cancer-survivor communities—are particularly strong. Empathy activated for a specific group of people can increase this quality throughout your life, whether it's for the person bussing dishes from your table or the parent managing a screaming infant in the grocery store. It's a key ingredient for deepening meaningful connection via relationship as it motivates listening and acceptance. If you think about your life for long enough, you will see where adversity has already deepened understanding of and care for others' journeys.

- Experiencing addiction recovery personally or supporting someone struggling with a substance use disorder can fuel greater compassion and love for those struggling.
- Completing a hands-on task outside of one's wheelhouse has given deeper appreciation for people doing this work every day.

- Pursuing new education, looking for housing, becoming a parent, or being treated unjustly increases your capacity to listen to and support those walking through similar situations.

Inspiration and motivation. Necessity is the mother of invention. The challenges you're feeling can inspire complex, powerful art or a whole range of practical solutions or actions. Difficulties or deadlines can fuel change and discovery for ourselves or for others in similar situations. A quickly diminishing bank account can motivate entrepreneurial experimentation and diligence. Negative emotions and problems can inspire art that helps you process or that speaks to others navigating similar feelings. The systemic challenges you recognize can increase desire to donate to, work at, or serve organizations tackling these issues. Urgency helps bring clarity to priorities for one's time, energy, and money.

- Feeling fed up by the lack of after-school opportunities has inspired the development of a farm that provides healthy community, practical skills, and emotional support for youth.
- Painting, dancing, weaving, and other art forms have flowed from swirls of disappointment and loss.
- Frustration with a social challenge has motivated letter-writing campaigns, advocacy work, creation of petitions, or volunteering with an organization addressing that issue.
- Unpleasant personal experiences and emotions have informed storylines, character arcs, customer personas, and product designs.

As you continue to recognize and enjoy unexpected benefits hidden within messy situations, it's possible to actually build patterns of anticipating something good. When the flight is canceled, the lasagna burns, the event is rescheduled, the questions become, what can I discover or experience now? What can I create in the midst of these hard moments? You still may need to process through disappointment and frustration. Remember that reframing difficulty is not stuffing down negative emotions or pretending they don't exist. But, in those moments, you can begin to make intentional choices to create, and new thoughts and tangible actions can shift your experience and your feelings.

There is something powerful that happens when we can flip the script and see opportunity in the midst of challenge. Creativity shines as a superpower in these moments. Personal experiences of loneliness inspire gatherings that help others know that they're not alone. Sending a simple text message or a heartfelt greeting reminds someone that they have more to live for. Struggles with negative self-talk or insecurity inspire sharing encouragement that brightens the days of the giver and the receiver. Changes in one's geographical or technological context spark innovation around connecting via digital experiences, events, or workplaces.

We *all* are facing problems that affect us and many others. We *all* are wired for connection. We *all* need that extra push at times to create, to step into the arena, to serve. The challenges you face right now, as you read these words, may be the birthplace for outflows of creativity that brighten your journey and impact many others. You may not feel like you have much to give. That's okay. Take it one step at a time. By making connection and intrinsic joy your primary goals, you can enjoy the process. Big trees start with small seeds. The challenge you face might be the spark that fuels whole new aspects of your creative identity.

Funky Thanksgiving

I can't tell you how many times I've seen a tough day or a crappy thought or emotion redeemed through the inspiration of a creative idea. One of my favorite personal examples comes from early in my recovery. The week of my first sober Thanksgiving proved an unexpectedly difficult time mentally, emotionally, and spiritually. Though I found myself around positive, supportive people, heaviness, fear, and uncertainty unexpectedly overwhelmed me, like a fog I couldn't escape. Phone calls with friends helped me process through the moments, but the emotions didn't shift right away.

That Sunday, as I was having a spiritual moment of expressing gratitude, I felt a sense of peace and joy. Suddenly I began to see how what I had experienced the previous week was perfect insight and inspiration for the protagonist in a writing project I had been working on for months. Ideas flowed and key concepts for this work appeared with a clarity and poignant spiritual connection. Positive emotions overwhelmed me as I began to see the redemptive possibilities of that week's pain and confusion. What had been a difficult time of disconnection became a source for learning and inspiration.

Several years later, the idea that emerged on that Sunday is still one of the best sections of the whole project. I return to this memory often for encouragement when I find myself in the midst of difficulty. There's a running list of other examples that I keep: friendships that sprang out of wrongly booked flights, chance introductions through delayed appointments, and song inspiration arriving through moments of failure and difficult emotions. Heck, this whole journey around creativity sprang out of experiencing addiction and getting help and healing that transformed my life.

Finding Connection in the Mundane

One of my favorite aspects of redemptive creativity is how it can transform the seemingly mundane or unimportant parts of life. There are opportunities within your errands, chores, work situations, physical fitness, and beyond to spark fresh joy and meaning. The following steps will help you make your life even more of a canvas for meaningful connection, inspiration, and creativity:

1. *Make a list of difficult or mundane experiences.* Think through the parts of your weekly routine that take the longest to complete or that feel like places of boredom or wastes of time. Examples include cleaning around the house, running errands, long work commutes, feedback conversations with loved ones that are important but unpleasant. The less the likelihood of enjoying the activity, the greater the benefits of creative discovery can be.

2. *Brainstorm connection or inspiration opportunities.* How could you turn a commute, a chore, or a different, seemingly dull, experience into something that brings joy via connection? Maybe the activity becomes an opportunity to connect to yourself through a podcast or music you love. These moments could also offer space for deeper connection through prayer or reflection or enjoyment of the views around you. There could be opportunities to offer kindness to someone you meet along the way, whether via an action or an encouragement. Or you might seize the moment to catch up with a friend via a call. Finally, run through your current list of creative expressions and consider whether there might be inspiration for them waiting in difficult or mundane parts of your days. Your emotional experience could inform a character's feelings in a story, the details of a customer intake flow for a company, or a point of empathy in relationships with others.

3. *Find the channel for connection that works for you.* Don't write off your potential for experiences of connection due to your personality type. You don't have to start by talking to strangers or suddenly transforming into an extrovert. Take small steps as you find how you enjoy building connection. Incorporate your gifting, style, and passions. Preparation and openness can be helpful keys for these new experiences. For instance, if you are more reserved but want to create moments of encouragement and kindness for others, you could carry materials in your car to write a note for someone or to leave a gift or packaged food for a person in need. These moments can be profoundly meaningful when rooted in intrinsic motivation and can be fun whether or not you see the outcome.

4. *Add margin to your schedule.* How you manage your days affects your ability to enjoy positive, spontaneous aspects of creativity and connection. If you're running from appointment to appointment, it's hard to be emotionally open for the unexpected moments of connection that can occur. It may not always be possible, but, when you can, try adding little buffers in between your scheduled events. Doing so can help you seize moments for spontaneous, fun, meaningful creativity without becoming an emotional wreck.

Redemptive Creativity

The treasures in the muck waiting to be discovered may not be obvious at the moment, but they will continue to become apparent as you step forward in your creative journey. It's a virtuous loop: when you start finding more of these nuggets in your own life, it becomes easier to recognize them everywhere. In both our long-term narratives and our daily expressions, repetition is powerful. Activating the redemptive possibilities of creativity builds metaphorical muscle memory that will serve you and others in the future when difficulties arise.

Creative experiences rooted in connection and joy help reinforce the intention and persistence needed to embrace these opportunities. Celebrating your capacity for redemptive creative experimentation today will help you grow. As you activate this key, new narratives can form about past or present circumstances, even if they take time. Your brain's pattern-recognition capacity will begin to see opportunities in the midst of difficulty, and hope will naturally increase. Can you imagine what life could look like if every painful experience or daunting challenge became the fertilizer from which something lovely can blossom? The world contains both great brokenness and stunning beauty. Opportunities to turn more of the former into the latter can provide a deep sense of purpose and satisfaction in one's creative journey.

The end of this chapter marks the conclusion of the first section of this book. It has been focused on the linkages between creativity, one's internal reality, and unlocking intrinsic joy and meaningful connection. As you move forward, remember that creative inspiration is not solely found in pain and difficulty. Your expressions are powerful tools for experiencing gratitude and celebrating the many beautiful parts of life. In this chapter, I have focused on pain and difficulty because their potential for inspiration is counterintuitive. Plus, as previously discussed, exploring creativity can reveal barriers, challenges, or situations where healing is needed. You do not need to stay rooted or largely focused on the negative in order to be creative. Experiences of joy and connection will increase, and they can fuel your creative growth too. The next few chapters will focus on external aspects of our expressions: developing a

CHAPTER 11 | REDEMPTION UNLOCKED

life-giving approach for refinement rooted in intrinsic motivation, sharing with audiences, sustaining a long-term process that helps you thrive, and the impact of creativity beyond our lifetimes.

> **ONE-STEP ACTIVATION**
>
> Choose a challenge that you have experienced this week and draw inspiration from it for a creative expression. Be intentional: can the occurrence provide meaningful connection? An idea for a solution? An emotional canvas for your art? Celebrate the shift from pain into progress as you create.

CREATIVITY STORIES

KARA | NONPROFIT EXECUTIVE AND CHANGE-MAKER

"When I was in my lowest moments, I did not think that I would one day be an executive in a pioneering healthcare organization or helping leaders shape restorative policies around the criminal legal system." Today, the hardest points of Kara Nelson's life have become the seedbed from which she gets to create redemptive solutions for change. "My healing process enabled strengths to emerge around the challenges I experienced, a picture of grace that continues to inspire my work. The cycles of trauma, incarceration, and substance misuse shifted, and new things started emerging in my life when I experienced an unconditional love beyond what I could ever deserve."

Born and raised in Alaska, Kara is Director of Development and Public Relations at True North Recovery, a behavioral health nonprofit that has seen hundreds of individuals and families who have been affected by addiction experience restoration. Their innovative approach is rooted in the evidence-backed peer-based recovery model. "I am a voice for those who aren't being heard, a protector, a hope dealer," Kara shares. "I am a woman in recovery who spent almost two decades in active addiction and in and out of prison. But, before all that, I am first a fierce mama, a sister, a daughter. I am passionate about changing the way people see those with stories like mine. Before I am a testimony, I am a human being, and I believe that seeing the humanity in each and every person transforms the world."

What Kara values most today are the family relationships that have been restored with loved ones, especially her kids. "Our connection was strained and difficult for years. But today we are so much closer. Restoring these relationships is better than any accolade or career success I could experience. Each step of healing with my kids matters more to me than everything else."

CREATIVITY STORIES

Kara's journey exemplifies the redemptive aspects of creativity, and specifically how difficulties can lead to greater empathy and expertise. "Early in recovery, I started attending city and state legislative hearings around issues close to my heart. I was dismayed to hear that decision-makers weren't hearing from people who were directly impacted by their policies." Kara continued to show up, stand up, and speak up, and encouraged others to do so. "My passion for these issues came from lived experience. I knew how individuals and their families would be impacted by sentences and policies that didn't help people heal. Consequences matter, but we can all too easily allow the cycles of poverty, incarceration, and addiction to repeat across generations if we miss the opportunity to help people find another path and invest in them with compassion."

A few serendipitous introductions around the time that Kara started speaking up led to helping start and run a restorative home for women with these experiences. "We began to see lives transformed, families healed, and policies enacted that better support human flourishing as we recognized the power of our voices. Like any creative process, there were ups and downs, challenges and solutions, but I wouldn't trade it for the world." Kara's journey has involved many meaningful interactions with fellow changemakers in these fields. "It takes a village to shift these paradigms, and we are seeing the recovery community recognize this more across different pathways."

At the core of Kara's transformation were experiences that provided new mindsets and beliefs. "Radical experiences of unconditional love and grace brought lasting freedom from the cycles of shame and despair that had kept me numbing for decades. I went from everything being about trying to get these unmet needs filled to being able to serve, make, build, and lead." Along the way, she has rediscovered her creative nature. "I didn't realize how creative I was until taking the Creativity Unlocked workshop. It was like, 'Holy moly, I'm really creative! And so is my work!' All of my life I had seen myself as not creative. This shift in my thought process

CREATIVITY STORIES

has added understanding to the intentional connection-focused approach I take to my work. Now I get to be part of helping people who have been impacted by addiction and incarceration recognize and activate their creative potential. One by one, we are changing the world."

REFINEMENT UNLOCKED

Upgrade your expressions from a place of love and rest. As delight and connection increase in your creativity, opportunities for refinement will naturally arise. In this chapter, find keys for unlocking the excellence that feedback can ignite, while staying rooted in intrinsic motivation.

Appreciating the Journey

Whew. Take a second to pause and celebrate what you've experienced thus far. You have strengthened understanding of your creative nature, discovered and activated expressions that bring intrinsic joy and satisfaction, and learned about healing in places where shame and pain have hindered your process. You have received an invitation to explore narratives and discover outflows that make your heart alive in everyday life. You have explored new approaches to community and discovered the secret sauce of creativity: connection. That is *a lot*. As we shift focus to how an intrinsically motivated process intersects with external aspects of creativity, keep celebrating and practicing what you have discovered thus far, especially in imperfect parts of your journey.

It's possible to stay rooted in a childlike approach that prioritizes joy and authenticity as you engage with external feedback and audiences. Over the next few chapters, we'll activate keys for different parts of your creative journey. A connection-filled approach to your expressions can fuel refinement of your craft, sharing with audiences, a life-giving process for the long term, and broader potential impact. These topics are intentionally placed at the end of the book so that a foundation of intrinsic motivation and connection could be built first. You will find that aspects of outward creativity that have held difficulty or disappointment can be experienced in a more enjoyable and fruitful way.

Growing in excellence by refining your expressions can be a powerful source of intrinsic motivation. Feedback can help you explore and increase the skill and delight that your creativity provides, first as a gift to yourself and then as a natural overflow that impacts others. Loving your creativity often motivates refinement. The growth process can become a vehicle for deepening connection with your own creative identity, with others, and with a cause or purpose. When you enjoy what you create, at any stage of the process, growth happens more naturally.

However, the process of refinement can bring up external considerations that may feel in tension with the priorities you have learned thus far. Tension is not your enemy. It's an opportunity to discover how you weigh important internal and external considerations. The more secure you are in your intrinsic value and in the joy of your work, the easier feedback and learning are to experience. The greater the confidence in your creative identity, the more freedom you will feel in exploring new ways to authentically create without losing your voice and satisfaction. Remember: you get to develop an approach to refinement that fits your specific goals and needs, and you don't have to do it alone. Read on to see how the learning and feedback process can be more life-giving than it may seem.

A Healthy Approach to Feedback

Refinement helps expressions remain meaningful and fresh. Sometimes creative activities feel stale because growth is needed; it's no longer new. Think of a baby: there is sheer delight found in learning to walk or speak.

CHAPTER 12 | REFINEMENT UNLOCKED

But these poignant discoveries are designed to grow into more complex experiences that provide continued joy and satisfaction. We don't typically find great significance or meaning in a teenager saying a word or taking a step unless there is a special circumstance. The initial expressions of movement and communication provide the pathway to new skills and experiences that require learning and feedback, whether racing dirt bikes, crafting arguments in speeches, or building a home. This is why we can deeply appreciate both the stick-figure drawing of a four-year-old and the exquisite paintings of artists. It's also the reason that adrenaline-loving adults have traded in their big-wheel tricycles for other vehicles—at least until they have kids.

Think of an expression that brings you intrinsic joy. Chances are there has been some sort of development of skill or context that helps keep it interesting and rewarding. The law of diminishing returns applies in a sense to our creativity: staying in a similar place may not provide sustained emotional benefits. But there is a natural progression, rooted in love and not in pressure, that provides both joy and growth. Early on in songwriting, I delighted in recording scratchy, off-pitch voice notes with ideas. I still do. But now the development of these pieces into well-crafted, polished tunes sparks a different aspect of joy that adds fuel to my process.

Refinement can help activate the redemptive aspects of creativity discussed earlier. Asking people for input or investing in your skill set can help you better translate your creativity into experiences that people can access or digest. Whether or not you share your expressions with others, there is value in the process of engaging with feedback. Many a gifting goes under-appreciated or gets stale because of missed opportunities to refine, repackage, or modify the expression. In fact, a fear of feedback or the editing process keeps many from experiencing fresh joy and connection around their creativity, whether in their careers, their hobbies, or their relationships. Refinement will deepen your satisfaction by enhancing excellence and unlocking new possibilities. It's healthy to take on fresh challenges that stretch but don't overwhelm your capacity.

Intentionally pursuing feedback for your expressions also provides opportunity to strengthen belief systems and community. Constructive feedback can be tough to swallow, but it forces us to remain rooted in our own inherent value and worth, instead of needing perfection or someone else's validation. Inviting and implementing feedback can be humbling. Remember: though others' perspectives can be incredibly helpful gifts, your value, worth, and creative potential aren't based on the opinions of others. Constructive feedback also does not change the value of your work. The sculptor Michelangelo once said, "I saw the angel in the marble and carved it until I set him free."[68] Beauty is in the eye of the beholder and in the creative idea you envision in your own proverbial marble block. There is treasure and value in every stage of the process. Suggestions of what could be improved or cut out can be helpful, but they are not authoritative truth. Difference of opinion or disagreement does not have to undermine your significance or authority as a creative being. Engaging with these honest conversations can actually help you keep strengthening healthy mindsets.

In creativity, there is a difference between subjective taste and objective truth. Most expressions benefit from helpful, basic feedback that is more objective, like if the beat isn't consistently in rhythm or the vocals are out of tune in a song. Other pieces of input will be far more subjective. These viewpoints can also carry value but should be evaluated. If you share a song with an individual who does not like that style of music, or who is outside of the audience you're targeting, you may get negative feedback on something that would be seen as good by others. Ask yourself whether you think it's objective or subjective and based on that person's taste. Scour the ideas shared for any wisdom you can glean, even if a lot of the feedback doesn't resonate. As you consider feedback, you will find ideas that are either immediately helpful, best to put on the shelf and see if they resonate later on, or something you should politely dump.

Let's return to the pork taco example from the chapter on community (chapter 6: "Community Unlocked"). Your aunt's feedback on your salsa recipe or your friend's better technique for roasting peppers may take your outflow to another level. There is a natural delight and satisfaction in experiencing an increase in beauty and flavor. Your expression may take a leap in goodness when you add in the seasoning of someone else's wisdom or gifting. Suddenly it's blowing your mind with flavor and scrumptiousness. Cue the food truck, the cookbook, the TV show—

CHAPTER 12 | REFINEMENT UNLOCKED

all of which can be created from a foundation of intrinsic motivation and connection, instead of the fickle tastes of others. Whatever your expression of creativity, other people may have important expertise or perspective that you need.

Keys to Improving Your Refinement Process

Have you ever felt someone's reaction to your expression stab you like a knife or knock the metaphorical wind from your chest? Me too! Feedback can be this painful, but it does *not* have to be. Instead of blindly walking forward, there are practical keys for your approach that can prevent unnecessary pain. The following concepts will help you navigate the refinement process:

- *Clarify your goals.* Understand your personal why for your expression. What values and goals do you want to shape your process? Enunciating these will help you make decisions, navigate emotions, and communicate to others involved in feedback. What will you prioritize when your perspective conflicts with that of another? How much are you willing to compromise personal preference to align with external standards? How important is your unfiltered creative voice versus incorporation of feedback that could broaden appeal? Are there future goals you have that might require specific formats or conditions? Whether in the workplace, artistic expression, or relationships, solidifying your priorities will help you navigate these tensions, shake off unhealthy expectations, and strengthen internal stability when people express different viewpoints.
- *Start with self-refinement.* Leave space to experience and reflect on your own expressions first. You can save yourself unnecessary awkwardness in feedback by taking time to review your own outflows. Sometimes taking a break and then returning will make it easier to catch simple mistakes and identify opportunities for growth. Practically, this can look like reading your writing aloud or watching a recording of your performance. Or journal your thoughts about what is going well and what

you would like to modify in your career or at home. Value the internal feedback that arises, but be careful to not spiral into self-criticism or shame. Timing for self-reflection is key. Remember the importance of not critiquing yourself right after a vulnerable expression. Wait until after you have had a chance to rest. If you find yourself getting overly negative, intentionally celebrate your growth by restating positive affirmations about your creativity from the earlier chapters.

- *Invite specific input from trusted sources.* Feedback is a gift. We all have our blindspots, so we need input from others to help us grow. It's okay to be selective in who you invite into this process. Your trusted friends, advisors, creative collaborators, or others may have helpful wisdom or ideas for your expression. Remember that they do not have to align with your style or be more skilled than you to offer feedback. Be mindful of their context and background as you consider their thoughts. Provide specific questions that set boundaries; otherwise, they might share opinions that are off-topic or unhelpful or that create unnecessary tension. Getting feedback from multiple people will help you see themes and common perspectives. Not every idea you hear is worth implementing. When you're emotionally ready for blunt honesty, intentionally invite people to give it. This may be easier for people who are less close to you relationally. Sometimes those we know best struggle most to share honest, constructive thoughts. We all need people who are willing to tell us the truth.

- *Pursue learning from others more skilled or excellent than you.* Feedback from a range of sources is helpful. But to accelerate your growth, assistance from others more skilled or experienced is needed. Don't shy away from seeking out those who are experts in your areas of creative expression. You may not be able to access your dream mentor, but don't let that keep you from exploring the opportunities that stretch you. We also live in a time of incredible access to learning resources and experts. Check out YouTube, look for reputable books or coaches, or find a digital or local community that can help upgrade your skills. Remember that this does not only apply for artistic endeavors. There are experts who can support your journey in your career, family, and other creative forms. As discussed in the chapter on community (chapter 6), doors for mentorship and feedback from experts may open if you first approach them willing to serve.

- *Digest feedback over time.* Opinions that don't resonate with you initially may still have great value and wisdom. New ideas, even good ones, often feel foreign or uncomfortable at first. Don't overreact or immediately write off feedback, even if it feels off. Give space for it to breathe. Don't judge the value of suggestions solely on the influence or following of the feedback giver. Honor those who support in any way. Resist any initial fears that would inhibit you from receiving feedback or assistance, whether it appears as discomfort with change or another form. Try not to let offense or poor delivery rob you of the gold it may hold. There can be great treasure found even in badly wrapped packages. Ongoing feedback partnerships can be very helpful, as connection, trust, and communication grow over time.

- *Don't force the feedback process.* Creativity is complex. Sometimes it is hard to predict when you have most capacity for refinement versus ideation. For instance, you may not always have capacity to edit a work, which can require a different type of thinking than drafting or brainstorming. If you hit a snag or task where you feel stuck, you can shift your focus elsewhere. Keep creating. Don't be afraid to pause what you think you have to do in order to follow where you are finding flow. Being flexible may stir fears of not finishing or of being misjudged. Connect to comfort, community, and compassion in those times. Holding projects with an open hand enables you to not carry their full weight and to remain encouraged in times of delay. Sometimes it's in letting go or putting aside an expression for a period of time that we find the distance needed to see it more objectively and understand our next steps. Your novel may turn into a short story or shift to another character focus. Your attempt to hold a family Olympics may devolve into a laughter-filled water fight.

Your outdoor adventure could transform into singing songs in the car on a rainy day. The end outcome matters, but there are opportunities for connection and creative joy in many forms along the way. Remember: you don't need to achieve perfection or finish your dream project to prove your value.

- *Commit to investing in your growth.* Change often requires intention and effort. When you find what helps you learn and grow, commit the resources and time needed. I'm not talking about irresponsible spending choices; you can take it in small steps. Don't hold back your refinement because you don't believe you're good enough yet. That mentality is a vicious cycle that will keep you believing you never are worthy. Leave it behind today. As you upgrade your expressions, reassign resources, energy, or time that you previously spent on a less fulfilling activity to follow your passion. Exchange some of your Netflix watching or time at boring parties for experimentation and refinement. Who knows? You might discover what you were born for. Put practical structure in place if need be: use calendar reminders, limit your technology use, or ask a friend to keep you accountable. Where resources appear as a limitation, brainstorm simple ideas on how you can refine your creative expression in your daily life. You may not be able to afford all the tools you desire now, but there are likely more affordable or free options to discover that can provide value.

- *Maintain outlets for rest, creative fun and joy.* Continued delight experienced through your creative nature will help you navigate the vulnerable parts and any discomfort that arises in the feedback process. Be aware that as your expression increases in excellence, external recognition and rewards may increase. This can make it easier to detach from the foundation of intrinsic joy that you have been developing. Many professional artists attest to the challenges of navigating this tension, where the stress of improvement or external perspectives adds pressure that lessens the joy of simple expression. If you find yourself in a similar situation, intentionally make time for rest and for creative expressions

CHAPTER 12 | REFINEMENT UNLOCKED

that make your heart come alive *and* are detached from current sources of validation or income. Find new expressions for which there are low stakes. Make sure it's something you find fun. Focusing too much on one creative outlet can tap you dry, which adds stress and fear to the growth process. If a free-flowing, joy-filled expression begins to feel heavy and high-stakes, especially during refinement, allow it to rest. Take a break and do something new: paint, play a new sport, organize a room, get outside, brainstorm a product or service. The joy of these new discoveries will be fuel for your other activities.

- *Set healthy expectations.* Be patient and kind to yourself in the process. Rome wasn't built in a day. Many masterpieces take far longer than anticipated. A lot of time and resource has almost always been invested beforehand to develop the skills needed to operate at that level. Remember that everybody was an amateur once, so allow yourself permission to practice and progress without being perfect. Leave space for your creative expressions to breathe, as necessary. You may not have had the lived experience you need yet to bring the song, novel, family gathering, company, or other outflow to the form you believe it can reach. There may be people you need to meet first because they hold a key insight or skill for the project. Finally, remember that your creative journey does not have to prioritize the end result. The process of creating is a gift in itself, and one that at various points you will be able to share with others.

Developing healthy refinement practices can feel a bit like eating one's less tasty vegetables or implementing a new exercise regimen. But these short-term, less comfortable decisions will help you maintain and increase the joy and connection in your expressions. I can't stress enough how valuable the refinement stage of the creative journey has been for me. Whether in music, business, writing, or organizational leadership, making space for intentional feedback and encouragement has upgraded projects and increased the joy and connection I experience. In fact, I could have benefited from starting these practices sooner. Learning to receive constructive feedback has been a process.

Sometimes refinement looks like a broader shift in career or life priorities. Remaining open to change can lead to powerful discoveries. I did not understand that moments of uncertainty could provide space to consider job shifts that would become the incubator for dream entrepreneurial and artistic projects. Each instance required holding something good with an open hand and being willing to let go of what had been great for a past season but was actually part of the pathway to something greater. What you have experienced and created in past seasons will serve your future expressions in unexpected ways.

The Power of Pruning

Most creative expressions benefit from some form of the concept "less is more." Computer programmers seek to develop the simplest and thus fastest ways for code to complete functions. Restraint in the quantity of furniture or artwork, appropriate for the design aesthetic, gives spaces a welcoming feel. Architects and builders seek to maximize the functionality and aesthetics of a structure while minimizing the resources used. Writing often is more pleasing and effective when editing has reduced text-heavy drafts into cleaner, simpler prose. Through development of your Resonance Map and exploration, you may have a long list of possible and current expressions. Pruning is important not just within expressions but also between them.

Technology has greatly increased opportunity for expressions. The evolution of social media alone provides infinite opportunities to express through video, imagery, comments, conversations, even emojis. With it has arrived a potentially overwhelming range of possibilities that can easily contribute to distraction and a lack of focus. While these channels and tools can enable life-giving, positive creativity, they can also siphon energy away from deeper joy and purpose in our expressions. We can literally always be posting, sharing, creating. Even if social media is not a pitfall for you, this idea can appear in other parts of life, from relationships to experiences to hobbies. There are many potential sources of distraction that can serve as invitations for reflection: are we spending our creative energy on what brings connection and intrinsic joy (not reliant on a response), whether in real life or via technology?

CHAPTER 12 | REFINEMENT UNLOCKED

Pruning is an essential part of the creative process. In agriculture, reducing the number of branches or vines on a plant helps focus the nutrient density for the remaining ones, and thus leads to stronger, riper, larger fruit. As you discover what expressions bring greater joy and more meaningful connection for both current and future seasons, you will need to focus on certain activities and commitments at the expense of others. Pruning can increase excellence, whether you are revising an artistic work, developing an automation that simplifies a job, decluttering a house or space, or investing more deeply in a few key more relationships or social settings. This aspect of refinement requires powerful choices and brave communication, but it will help you step into new elements of and confidence in your creative identity. The steps above, like clarifying your goals and investing in expressions aligned with joy and purpose, will help. We'll return to this important concept in chapter 14: "Longevity Unlocked."

Your voice matters. As you engage with refinement, stay aware of your authentic perspective. Look for where common themes intersect with your resonance and joy. What you believe about and do with the feedback is as important as collecting it. The process of refinement holds value in itself. If unsure of the input, don't worry. Give yourself permission to come back to it later. Don't get stuck in the mud of overthinking. Return to your creative motivations rooted in love. At the end of the day, your journey gets to be your own. Life is full of tension, and refinement holds one that we get to engage with in our creativity as we discover what brings heart-alive experiences. The next chapter will dive into practical tools that help us navigate a related topic: maintaining joy and fulfillment when sharing your expression with new audiences.

🖌 ONE-STEP ACTIVATION

Learning is an impactful part of the creative process. Engage with your next step in refinement for an expression today. Choose a friend or collaborator to ask for feedback, or pick a YouTube expert or course from which you can glean insights that will help you upgrade your craft.

CREATIVITY STORIES

TOPHER | RECORDING ARTIST AND LABEL CEO

"When I make music, I come alive. I feel like I'm doing what I was born to do. It's deep and life-giving at the same time. But there are still questions I and many others have to navigate as an artist. Will I choose to speak into the world instead of just reflecting what's already out there? Or does the audience dictate my creativity?"

Topher Jones is a recording artist (aka King Topher), producer, and owner of electronic music label Bring the Kingdom. His passion for excellence and authenticity in his creative expressions reflects a healthy perspective on the refinement process. "With my art, I never feel like I've fully arrived. There are always ways to grow as I enjoy what I'm making in a given season, whether it's in shaping frequencies and sound waves or experimenting with new vocal styles and themes. Receiving constructive feedback is such an important part of the process. But I'm selective with whom I'll invite to share their thoughts." Topher listens to those he trusts and who are willing to walk with him on the journey. "I highly appreciate feedback and don't mind receiving it, because I recognize that my identity is not defined by what I make."

Exploring sounds, revising songs, and growing as an artist have been part of his journey. His music is his full-time profession, but his career in the arts has had peaks and valleys. "There have been times when I'm playing the biggest stages in the world and when tens of millions of people are hearing what I create. And there have been seasons when a label that has now released a bunch of my tracks rejected thirteen of my submissions in a row, after a period of success." Topher points to using this feedback as motivation for growth and as key in his process. "I could have sunk into frustration. But that's not helpful. Discipline and perseverance are difference-makers, and it helps that I love creating music."

As a musician, Topher experiences a tension felt in the creative process. "Since this artistic expression is tied to my income and profession, I have to navigate both what brings me personal joy and what will serve the audience we're trying to reach. Regardless, it is an honor to get to create and share something that helps people find joy and experience the world differently." He maintains a passion for bringing something fresh and new in his art, even if it's riskier than delivering a sound more familiar to listeners. "This internal alignment between my creativity and who I am is fulfilling and important for me."

Topher identifies family time and other hobbies as essential for fueling and refreshing his creative process. "I don't believe that artists have to be tortured to create beautifully or powerfully. Creativity does not have to be miserable. Many people who are struggling with insecurity and stress end up sacrificing their well-being for art, and it's tragic. When I need to refresh, I take breaks. I spend time with my wife and son—that's a whole different type of joy."

AUDIENCE UNLOCKED

Share your expressions and enjoy the process. Inviting others to experience your creativity can feel wonderful and vulnerable, exhilarating and awkward, especially if external validation has driven your process in the past. In this chapter, you will explore how to unlock a new, life-giving approach for engaging with audiences.

Leaving the Safety of Being Unseen

If you were to look through photos in family albums from my childhood, you would often see a pair of eyes peeking out from behind a set of legs or a skirt. I thought I could escape the intrusive glare of the camera by tucking myself behind a family member and covering my face. Whether in front of a monument, by the beach, or with extended family, little Chris was unsuccessfully doing his best to not be seen.

Over the years, I have had many experiences of sharing creative expressions that felt like this. Torn by a desire for acceptance from an audience and a discomfort with being seen, the delivery often felt forced and dissatisfying, because part of me wanted to hide. Some of this emotional experience may have stemmed from an unusual childhood quirk. From the ages of two to six, I ran around without my upper two front teeth. All I wanted for Christmas indeed. My baby ones required removal several years before my adult teeth had scheduled their arrival. The unusual look brought a difficulty in pronouncing certain sounds and words, making *R*s, *L*s, and *W*s particularly difficult and nearly interchangeable. Without these important assets, being seen or heard felt awkward. During those same years, experiences in other countries brought occasions where my different look drew an overwhelming amount of attention, which I did not know how to process.

My friends today, aware of my extroverted, talkative personality, chuckle when I recount my childhood shyness. I actually was held back for a year in preschool for extra social development. Every recess, I would faithfully take my tricycle for a spin on the blacktop, pretend to be a police officer, and pull over every speeder and rule-breaker I saw. Of course, they were all of the invisible variety. There was an endless supply of targets in my imagination. I don't remember talking to another kid that whole year. I laugh at these memories now, but I also see how they may have introduced limitations around self-expression and engaging with others. Throughout grade school, my shyness receded, but discomfort with sharing remained. I competed in speech meets, shared at assemblies, and spoke in class, but the process remained more uncomfortable than it appeared.

Fast-forward to today. Color me surprised that in the summer before the completion of this book I would find myself not only launching but *enjoying* the process of recording and sharing videos about creativity on social media. Developing the @yourcreativityguide accounts on TikTok and Instagram has been both part and proof of a shift I've experienced around engaging with an audience (shameless plug alert). The notion of being in front of a camera so much, especially as a thirty-something influencer, was not only something I have resisted but actually would have felt like a nightmare for a good chunk of my life. My delight in this new aspect of expression is a personal reminder of how much one's capacity for sharing creativity can change.

What has caused this shift? It has felt like a natural next step in the process described throughout these pages. Finding deep joy, rediscovering childlikeness, and a revamp of personal narratives around creativity all played a role. So has embracing refinement and building a life-giving community. Greater awareness of my needs and capacity has enabled a step-by-step process. But at the core, what transformed my ability to share expressions is connection: spiritual, emotional, relational, personal. The vulnerability of sharing feels different when it's about something so linked to an authentic passion. I could talk all day about rediscovering expressions, which is one reason I've written this book. Even when listeners aren't in the room, I get fired up about unlocking creativity because I honestly believe that these keys can transform lives, and through them, the world. This intrinsic passion has helped make what felt costly something I do willingly. Sharing the fruit of these concepts with others has inspired wobbly baby steps (thankfully not baby teeth) that continue to grow into bigger leaps. There are whole new versions of myself I am discovering—and I think there are more expressions of yourself to find too.

A huge part of this connection has been personal: embracing my favorite creative expressions and ultimately myself. On social media, I feel permission to blend together terrible dad jokes, my fervor for history, and a love for communicating heartfelt, pastoral messages in an outflow that is authentic. I am more comfortable sharing both failures and strengths today than in previous seasons when that felt unsafe. Growing up, I held back in my studies at times because I did not want to be rejected by certain friend groups. I did not want to offend people or come across as full of myself, though I'm sure I probably did anyway. Healing from self-rejection continues to help me overcome fears about being misunderstood or judged by others.

There is a need for and beauty in seasons of not being visible. I still find great joy in anonymity and supporting others behind the scenes. But I also celebrate that I am stepping into greater creative freedom and joy in sharing my outflows every day.

The Feeling of the Unknown

Let's return to the tree example from chapter 3 "Expressions Unlocked." New creative expressions are like saplings that, watered by joy and connection, will grow in height and fruitfulness. Visibility will increase and branches will naturally develop fruit or cones that offer sustenance and covering for external audiences . Whether in developing your skills at work, hosting parties, painting landscapes, or volunteering at a school, growth in your intrinsically motivated expressions will attract eyes and ears while offering benefit to others. At times this greater exposure will stem from your choice, and in other moments it will be outside of your control. The process can involve different external winds and test your foundational roots. But it is also a key part of natural creative growth.

When was the last time you felt yourself on the verge of stepping out? Was it on top of a steep ski slope, just before asking a difficult question in front of colleagues, preparing to perform a poem or song, or getting ready to tell someone how you truly feel? Can you remember the emotions you felt? There was probably some mixture of excitement, hope, anxiety, concern, fear, or adrenaline-fueled delight. If you're like me, then there may have been anxious flashes of worst-case scenarios mixed with an anticipation for the moment.

Having others partake of your expressions contains risks and rewards. Sharing with people can spark joyful, satisfying experiences of connection with parts of your own creative identity. It is gratifying to see others enjoy or benefit from what you have brought forth. But the process can also be painful. You likely have had experiences like mine where expressing yourself led to being misunderstood and rejected. The emotions experienced are real and common. But they don't have to hinder your progress forever or keep you bottled up. Your healing journey and your foundation in intrinsic motivations and connection can help you navigate the exploration of your audiences (i.e., anyone who is impacted by one of your expressions). There is a pathway discoverable between two unhelpful extremes: being paralyzed by fear, and oversharing out of a need for approval. It's possible to recognize and appreciate responses from others without becoming dependent upon them.

Remember that the process of sharing your expressions or having a specific response does not make you a more valuable human being. It can be fun, but it may not be as satisfying or meaningful as anticipated. Similarly, keeping things personal or unseen does not make you less valuable. You can make decisions to release or conceal your expressions from a place of freedom, security, and love. There can be intrinsic joy

CHAPTER 13 | AUDIENCE UNLOCKED

and meaning in either approach. The five tips below will help you healthily navigate the tradeoffs involved with sharing your expressions in alignment with your goals and values.

Tip 1: Recognize Your Motivations and Capacity

Before you start sharing an expression, reflect on your motivations and take note of your capacity for vulnerability. The practical details matter. How you share, when you share, and with whom you share will greatly affect both the outcome and the feelings of the process. Clarifying your goals will help you pick timing and format. They will also provide a foundation to which you can return if the response experienced is not what you envisioned. If you take a swing and miss with an audience, you can still celebrate your intention.

Often, the decisions around sharing are less about right and wrong and more about tradeoffs. Whether you're releasing a book or organizing a gathering, stepping into a new job or taking a family member on a trip, think through the possible range of responses from a particular person or audience. Are you willing and able to handle the consequences if it doesn't go like you hope? Ask yourself these questions:

- ❖ If people misunderstand or reject my expression, or another worst-case scenario happens, will I be okay?
- ❖ Who will I lean on to process through any messy parts of the journey?
- ❖ Would I prefer for them to engage with my expression now or at a more fully formed stage?
- ❖ Am I sharing because I'm feeling a deficiency of value and worth, or is it because I'm taking a healthy risk from a place of security?

Many of us do not spend enough time actually enunciating or owning what we truly want in a given situation. Or we live with unstated expectations that may or may not be realistic. These can set us up for spirals of disappointment when even a small piece of criticism or rejection arises.

It's easier to see this reality via a specific, albeit extreme, example. If someone is writing a screenplay or script for the first time, it probably won't get signed by a major studio. Though a wonderful long-term dream, this goal isn't very realistic or helpful for their current stage. However, if having a screen play signed is subconsciously motivating their writing process but is not honestly recognized, any response less than a deal could feel discouraging and even paralyzing. Desires or expectations that we don't enunciate can still powerfully impact our process.

In this example, one would benefit from setting achievable goals for sharing with a new audience, like sending to a writers critique group or completing five submissions to possible partners. These are process-related instead of outcome-dependent. Not sure if unhelpful expectations are present around an expression? Check whether the next time you share you feel the sting of things that didn't happen more than the celebration of what did occur. If so, there are likely expectations to review. If you can be honest with yourself by choosing and stating your goals, then you can ride the waves of various forms of responses instead of being hit in the face by a wall of perceived criticism or rejection.

Tip 2: Take a Staged Approach that Honors Your Process

You don't have to rush your sharing journey. Sometimes you may feel excitement or pressure to reach further or faster than you have emotional or practical capacity for. Many a creative voyage has been shipwrecked by people taking a big risk, having it not go as intended, and then getting stuck in disappointment or other unintended consequences. Learning to take this process one step at a time, based on your context, will fuel your journey over the long haul and ultimately make you unstoppable.

What does this look like practically? Think about potential audiences for a given expression as a series of stages increasing in size. Reflect on who is experiencing it currently. Is it just you, your loved ones, another part of your creative community, or your social media friends? As you explore expanding your audience, invest in the refinement and feedback tools from the previous chapter. When sharing a new expression or in a new context, consider what channels best align with your goals and current stage of growth. It could be wise to start intentionally with a smaller audience instead of blasting out to the whole planet all at once. When I started making electronic music, I intentionally did not tell anyone about the process for several years, other than a few key friends. Meanwhile, sharing about my recovery journey had different timing, because I found an ease and joy in being more public about parts of it early on. As you reflect and experiment, take note of your emotions. You may not realize how the process of sharing will affect you until after you try.

Lean into childlikeness. You have permission both to take joyful risks and to go slow and not be an expert. The more personally vulnerable the expression, the more thoughtfulness you should use. People may have different reactions based as much on their own past experiences as on what you create. Sharing personally vulnerable details with others could lead to responses, or a lack of them, that feel painful. If you're unsure about your next step, ask a trusted friend or mentor for their input. Maintain a healthy intake of experiences, thoughts, and activities that activate fun and remind you of your worth, as sharing can bring unexpected emotional swings.

Today, I can love sharing expressions and vulnerable aspects of my story because I have learned to embrace the process. As much as I enjoy celebrating the power of story, I do not allow obligation or fear to motivate sharing. Instead, I make conscious choices inspired by freedom and love for those around me. There are still parts of my story I'm not ready to share. Experiences of connection, joy, and redemptive possibilities have marked this approach to vulnerability, rooted in love. My definition of success in sharing isn't determined by the response I get or the people I impact; it's by staying personally rooted in connection with myself, with others, and with something greater.

In unlocking my own creativity the past few years, I definitely have taken steps that I would redo, whether in sharing my story, sending samples of writing to others, or communicating work endeavors. Heck, I even sent out a premature announcement of this book's launch, only for it to take an additional five months to finish. There have been times when, looking back, I would move faster and other moments when I would now slow down. That's part of the process! I celebrate the growth that has occurred. This low-and-slow approach has enabled me to take and share more intrinsically motivated creative risks in the past five years than I did in the decade before, while still loving my creativity.

Tip 3: Develop Strength by Stepping into Opportunities for Rejection

There will be moments of sharing your expressions with external audiences when the next healthy steps feel uncertain and uncomfortable because of the possibility for rejection. Take the steps anyway. When aligned with your goals and capacity, these are opportunities for growth, even if the response is negative. Sooner or later, you will be misunderstood or misperceived by someone, even if you do everything in the most ideal way. Not everyone will appreciate your style, your taste, your skills, or your passion. Repeat this truth to yourself as needed: "It is impossible to please everyone. It's okay that not everyone will understand my expression or my journey."

Experiences of perceived failure are perfect opportunities to strengthen your foundational core beliefs and lean into connection. Processing through these non-ideal experiences in healthy ways can actually lessen the sting of rejection over time. What was once painful can become more enjoyable. Failure and imperfection will be part of your process—you're human! When we have a healthy, supportive community that offers connection, there is no slip-up or fault too big to handle. Mistakes become opportunities for growth and fresh ideas. Experiencing compassion and connection in these vulnerable moments will empower you to keep taking steps forward in sharing your expressions and other areas of life.

If it's more natural for you to focus on the pressure to succeed or the possibility of failure or rejection, then you will need to be intentional about your mindsets and your affirmations through the process of sharing. Fear is not your friend. In fact, over-focusing on what you're afraid of may make it more likely to occur. Have you ever been so determined to not fall falling while bicycling, snowboarding, or skateboarding that you threw yourself off-balance, leading to a spill? Fear-focused viewpoints can lead to halfhearted approaches, distractions, nerves, and timidity that decrease your ability to function well, whether in your golf swing, your art, your leadership, or in the sharing of a new venture.

Your creative freedom can grow as you progress through situations where others respond in less-than-ideal ways. Navigating these uncomfortable situations will demonstrate that you can express yourself without old constraints. The more you love yourself and your expression, the easier the sharing process gets. As you continue taking healthy risks, situations that once felt vulnerable will become more comfortable.

Tip 4: See Vulnerability as an Act of Generosity

If you've taken the thoughtful approach to sharing your expressions described above and are still battling nerves, try embracing and reframing those feelings instead of resisting them. In economic theory, the value of something is determined both by the cost to the giver and benefit to the receiver, where supply meets demand. What if the awkwardness or discomfort you feel in the sharing process—extending an invitation for an event, presenting one's artwork, speaking in front of others, launching a new project at your job—is just part of the cost of the gift that you are offering? The depth of feeling and uncertainty may simply indicate the great value of what you are giving.

Your vulnerability in inviting others to experience your creativity is a beautiful, generous gift. The possibility of rejection or criticism and the doubts you face when you step out are what you are paying for these opportunities for connection. You've probably tasted the fruit of the creative vulnerability of others in the past, via their performance, event, encouragement, or other expression. This gift of vulnerability can be experienced in many forms: when someone speaks up for what is right, goes out of their way to help a stranger, takes a financial risk to pursue a job that has more meaningful impact, or shares gritty details in a support group that gives permission for others to be honest and accepted.

Reframing the uncertain feelings of sharing can help you enjoy and appreciate the journey more. The next time your palms begin to sweat, think of how this gift of vulnerability can benefit your process or the lives of others. It could be through an experience of beauty or ingenuity, a helpful solution, greater self-acceptance, an opportunity to be known and loved, or the building of a foundation that helps one show up as a better parent or spouse. Each time you present the gift of your creativity, you are offering the chance for connection to yourself and others.

Remember, a positive response is not required for your generosity to be beautiful and powerful. Sometimes the gift we give is a seed that takes time to sprout and bear fruit.

Tip 5: Adjust Your Measurement System

The current cultural narrative commonly advertises that success is determined by the quantity of likes, followers, sales, and other external returns. It values noteworthy, well-styled portrayals of "the good life." There can be pressure to have audiences react or respond to the experiences and expressions that you share. While there is value in aspects of external feedback, overemphasis on these aspects of serving audiences can undermine the meaningful connection and joy of your creativity. The hustle and the game that define much of modern life aren't always the most fulfilling. If you live for this type of recognition and "success," you'll also die for it.

Be intentional about defining success for yourself when you share. Recognize the external and internal metrics that matter for you. Celebrate the current stage, honor your process, and utilize a healthy approach aligned with your personal values. Remember that you can only do so much to influence peoples' responses. Seeing your expression as an offering will reduce your attempts to control the reactions of others and save you unnecessary stress.

The most important audiences are those closest to you, starting with yourself. Consider how sharing an expression could affect your loved ones. As we have discussed, what actually brings lasting fulfillment in creativity is different from that for which culture salivates. Every day there are examples of people taking unhealthy risks and violating their own wellness for what they believe will fill the hole inside. But much of what is found in these endeavors is less satisfying than desired. Fulfilling creativity is about so much more than a quick response on social media or living to check the boxes of what other people recognize or accept. Your creativity is designed to be a source of deep, authentic connection and beauty, and there's no prize greater than for your heart to be full of joy and fulfillment. It's better to have fewer days full of creative delight and freedom than thousands trapped in cycles of exhaustion and stress. Find what makes *you* come alive, and share from that place. And if that process has ups and downs, or failures, or delays, they will add to the story. Let go of trying to please or prove yourself to some invisible "audience" of critics that judges the perfection of every move. People aren't paying that much attention anyway. What you can discover on the journey is worth it.

One Step at a Time

The changing context of your life will help you evolve and grow in how and what you share. This includes your personal journey and the environments in which you find yourself. There may be whole channels and communities beyond what seems fun or possible now. Have you ever seen someone who said they would never in a million years sing in front of an audience then break into a song for their kids? Why is that? The context provides an audience that they are eager to bless, a gift they want to give, and listeners who will love them all the same. The situation is supportive for their sharing, and they are ready to step into that arena, as the opportunity for connection provides motivation to experiment.

No matter your specific expressions, you will find new opportunities to explore this aspect of the creative journey. Learning how to navigate audiences is not a one-time process. As you experiment, continue to replace negative comparison with positive thoughts, celebrate your victories, and resist perfectionism. Your creative journey is not a race; feel free to give yourself time to pause or rest, especially after taking uncomfortable steps forward. Remember that growth in vulnerability is what can lead to deeper connection and more fulfilling experiences of life. The important thing is to keep progressing. Over time, as you grow in sharing parts of yourself that you never thought you could, the flavor and reach of your generous expressions can also evolve and add fresh joy and inspiration.

Honor the areas of your creative exploration that feel too vulnerable to share right now. We all have them. There is no pressure to be further along. Even the most seemingly polished person—confident, engaging, personable, put-together—has places where they are legitimately afraid.

Sometimes people who seem most outgoing, bold, or loud are using that to mask places where deep anxieties persist. There's something encouraging about the recognition that every person faces obstacles to sharing their gifts with the world. You have the power to move forward at a speed that is life-giving for you, and you don't have to do it alone. A healthy pace for all parts of your creative journey is the topic of the next chapter.

> 🗝 **ONE-STEP ACTIVATION**
> Using the keys from this chapter and awareness of your own emotional capacity, identify and take your next step in sharing an outflow of your expression. If you choose to use an online channel, feel free to use #creativityunlockedchallenge; we would love to celebrate with you.

CREATIVITY STORIES

REBEKAH | POET AND HISTORIAN

From Scottish trading companies to South Asian labor networks to racial justice and activism, historian Rebekah's unconventional academic journey has included unique combinations. Pursuing her passions has helped her navigate a career path that requires longevity and flexibility. "The sense of discovery and ingenuity in research can often be an extension of one's way of seeing the world. The joy of bringing ideas together in a new way or, in my case, uncovering underutilized archival sources helps fuel my continuing work." One memorable instance involved finding a new, creative use for company records in Glasgow that shed light on an area of focus: workers' rights in the Indian subcontinent.

Rebekah recognizes that her variety of fields may seem incongruous at first glance. She holds a PhD in history but has previously earned degrees in anthropology, theology, and regional studies in Asia. "I have been the only one with my focus in certain degree programs and, at times, the only one who looks like me in gathering places of similar academic expertise." Rebekah celebrates her uniqueness. Each period of study has been tied to passions that fuel her longer-term goals. "I have found a calling and a deep sense of resonance in each unexpected turn of my journey, as well as ways to share the process with others. As I've continued to step forward, I have discovered how these passions can overlap and touch topics around which I am passionate: justice, protection for the most vulnerable, race, and cross-cultural learning."

Rebekah is currently engaged in a new project that examines histories of social activism across national borders. She has a longer-term dream of helping students with limited opportunity experience and learn from other parts of the world. Rebekah credits her multi-disciplinary studies for helping activate an expression that is personally meaningful and academically beneficial: travel. "A sense of adventure arises when in an unfamiliar place, surrounded by people, languages, foods, and settings that are new. Travel has helped connect me to history and heritage while I help build solutions in different locations." Rebekah highlights the importance of understanding one's personal story for empowerment to make change. "For me, revisiting my own history continues to help me shape and inform my work in powerful ways."

The idea of supporting others and leaving a legacy marks Rebekah's journey. "I sometimes view myself as a pathfinder—one who tries to make it a bit easier for those who may follow behind me. My experiences traveling abroad as a black woman have also informed my ability to help others push past uncomfortable situations, do what has felt difficult or unattainable in the past, and find joy in everyday encounters." Rebekah credits the creative tools that help her mark the path that she is making, even when the steps may not work together neatly or the path is not easily understood by others.

Artistic creativity has also been a significant part of Rebekah's process. She has written poetry since childhood. "I value this expression most for how it helps me process life and the things that I experience. It was especially beneficial when I lost my dad at the age of eleven and in the years following." Rebekah processed much of her grieving through poetry. "Crafting words over the years, both academically and privately in journals, has contributed to a profound sense of spiritual meaning; writing is a recurring expression that provides a canvas for the ideas and themes near to my heart."

Rebekah offers these words of wisdom to those who are self-conscious about the resurgence of long-abandoned or forgotten creative skills: "It is okay if all of your creative expressions are not active at the same time. My writing can ebb and flow, depending on the season. Sometimes the complexity that we desire to convey in a particular expression grows in our stillness—or while we build in other areas of our lives. Recently, I have returned to videography and other visual mediums that I hadn't explored since high school." Rebekah celebrates how years of poetry writing and historical study have now strengthened her narrative-building and storytelling for these other expressions, which are becoming tools for her academic and artistic projects.

One key for Rebekah's creative journey has been the "… presence of people who support creative growth. I have benefited from being a part of creative collectives and groups of diverse, impassioned academics, and I've learned significantly from those who occupy both spaces. The *Creativity Unlocked* workshop provided a community that helped me think more about the long process or lifestyle of creativity—including the refinement and enhancement of craft." Rebekah describes a greater sense of freedom found for her creative expressions. "I am now able to be more open to critical feedback—even on things that are close to my heart. Both the course and experiences I've had since with family and friends have reminded me that I have an incredible heritage inspired by creativity. They have also inspired me to leave a legacy of the same."

LONGEVITY UNLOCKED

Choose pacing and priorities that allow you to flourish. There are too many tragic stories that highlight the challenging tension between pursuing creative passions and finding a sustainable approach. In this chapter, reduce your chance of burnout by adding structure that unlocks longevity for your many expressions.

A Hidden Danger

A word of caution: the powerful joy and motivation that creativity can activate represent a good news/bad news scenario. The good news: this passion builds momentum for expressions, strengthens emotional health, and adds purpose to daily life. The bad news: it is possible to overindulge in particular outflows at the expense of other important life priorities. Whether driven by internal or external motivators, spending too much time and energy in certain aspects of creativity can negatively impact personal wellness, relationships with loved ones, and even one's favorite activities and dream projects. Like many good things, more of a specific expression is not always better. Intention around your pacing and priorities is essential so that your creative rocket ship doesn't explode or run out of gas in the middle of the cold and dark of space.

Longevity isn't just playing defense. Building a sustainable approach to your creativity can help you achieve your creative dreams. Meaningful, excellent creative projects can involve a journey that requires months, years, or even decades. Whether your dreams are for your next season or your future, take a moment to consider what's possible. Imagine an artistic vision fully realized and funded, a thriving relationship with your loved one, a career that is purposeful and activating intrinsic joy, a personally meaningful change in your community. Let these glimpses fuel intention around sustainability, even as you read about potential pitfalls.

Newspapers and history books are littered with tragic stories displaying a hidden danger: talented artists who loved their craft but became isolated and unstable, impactful inventors who had major deficiencies as parents, well-intentioned social-justice or religious leaders embroiled in secret lives that conflicted with their values, successful entrepreneurs with broken family relationships. Too many of the most impactful, creative individuals, who rightfully are honored for incredible contributions to society, had significant points of failure in their leadership or personal lives. Or, in a moment of great pressure, they capitulated to compromising their values, brought unnecessary pain to others, and tarnished both their own joy and their impact on the world. The pain of broken trust and poor choices ripples through families and communities.

I write this not in judgment but with empathy. No one is perfect. In my own, limited settings, I have had seasons of joyful, creative accomplishment that also held unexpected mess and behavior inconsistent with my values. I have experienced multiple levels of burnout, including a mini version during this writing process, where I personally needed to adjust my pace and priorities and return to some foundational practices. Longevity is not about perfection, and past or present struggles do not disqualify you from meaningful, impactful, joy-filled creativity. But discovering an approach that helps you navigate changing contexts and pressures around expressions can save you unnecessary pain and delay. There are keys that can prevent the metaphorical blown engine and address the wear and tear that develop over time.

CHAPTER 14 | LONGEVITY UNLOCKED

People rarely wake up one day and suddenly decide to embezzle money, cheat on their taxes, break trust with their children, violate their core principles, or be unfaithful to their spouse. Small compromises, often in response to unmet needs, move people closer to crossing these lines. Pressure, stress, anxiety, untreated mental or emotional challenges, unhealed trauma, destructive belief systems, shame, and a lack of community can be contributing factors that motivate unhealthy coping mechanisms. These can grow in their destructive capacity. Pride—and the isolation and self-reliance it promotes—truly can lead to a fall. I write this not to add shame or fear around failure. There are amazing redemptive possibilities for *any* low point, no matter how broken. But cleaning up unnecessary, avoidable messes costs us time, energy, and trust with those who matter most.

If you don't think this topic is relevant for you, you may want to read it twice. There are structures you can put in place today that reduce the chances that your pursuit of purpose and joy via creativity will swallow you whole. Think of them as maintenance routines and guardrails that will help you progress—and thrive—holistically. Adding these approaches to your journey will sustain growth and deepen delight across your multiple creative roles: as a friend, a spouse, a significant other, a parent, a leader, a colleague, or a creative collaborator. Recognizing your range of expressions and identities will help you keep the fire you are sparking in your metaphorical workshop from burning down the house. Your future choices may never become newsworthy, but your ability to create with longevity via intentional pace and priorities will significantly benefit your life, your family, and your community.

Why We Overindulge

Researchers have shown that the human brain is wired to seek that which most easily brings pleasure or safety.[69] When we find something that offers joy or comfort, we are prone to utilize it at an ever-increasing rate. Thus, as we unlock delightful, purpose-providing creativity, we can over-prioritize certain activities at the expense of other important needs. The neural pathways providing delight through a particular expression, whether in sculpture, cryptocurrency trading, or skiing, become superhighways. Meanwhile, others that could spur joy through meaningful connection are not firing as frequently and can become further neglected. Our brains gravitate toward the path of least resistance, and suddenly we are on the sixth episode of a bingeable TV show or the fourth hour of painting. Overindulgence has the potential to hinder expressions tied to important responsibilities, whether around personal wellness, financial stewardship, or family relationships. When our brains are full of endorphins from life-giving expression, it can be harder to note these deficiencies until they provoke consequences.

We are more likely to overemphasize expressions that provide comfort when other aspects of life that could provide connection are unstable. For instance, it can take more intentional energy to experience joy-filled connection in a difficult family relationship than a video game if neural pathways have formed that prioritize the latter. Ongoing pain and uncertainty can further motivate overindulgence. When we are having a hard time connecting with ourselves, others, or something greater, that Netflix drama, sports game, or bowl of ice cream becomes more appealing. Though the delight of expressions can be powerfully motivating, longevity for our favorite passions requires staying aware of how we are showing up in other aspects of life.

Compulsive behaviors showcase the darker potential for this creative aspect of our brains. As discussed earlier, disconnection and unresolved pain motivate numbing and comfort-seeking behavior, whether via alcohol, television, sex, food, gambling, prescription drugs, or other sources. These actions can reprogram the neural networks in the brain. The pathway to quick comfort overwhelms the more difficult challenge of resolving conflict and experiencing connection, even when longer-term consequences are recognized. Other pitfalls of overindulgence can lurk in unexpected places. The pursuit of a cause, especially one that we deem righteous, can all too easily be used to justify destructive compromises. Passion for your expressions—designed to be sources of joy—can become pressure requiring perfection or adding stressful, heavy burdens. As I've shared, even positive goals like achievement, recognition, and impact can contribute to vicious cycles when used to crowd out needs for healthier connection.

CHAPTER 14 | LONGEVITY UNLOCKED

Increasing validation and reward from creative expressions can actually add to the weight that individuals feel and motivate overindulgence. Many do not see the potential consequences of success until it's too late. Shifts in expectations, perceived responsibilities, and relationships can contribute to disconnection and pressure that ultimately rob us of the childlike joy and meaning of creativity. These changes are not inevitable. But intention and tools are needed to navigate these journeys and maintain connection. Increasing opportunity or privilege can reveal the cracks in foundations around mindsets, creative identity, and community.

There is hope: moments of weakness or wobbling can actually be a gift. They invite us to discover new approaches that support wellness or new sources of physical, mental, emotional, or spiritual strength. This conversation parallels what we discussed regarding fixation and connection in chapter 7. There are real motivations underneath the healthy or unhealthy behaviors from which we seek comfort. The problem is often not rooted in the behavior or action but in the unmet need underneath. Building practices that help us stay aware of these needs will help us avoid burnout and thrive in our expressions and beyond.

Three Essentials for Longevity

How can we reduce the chances that we hurt ourselves or those around us and still love and enjoy our creative expressions? Here are three keys that can help you flourish emotionally and avoid overindulgence:

1. *Embrace your multifaceted creative nature.* You are creating in dozens of contexts every month: via relationships, hobbies, work, service, nature adventures, or other experiences. Recognizing and strengthening meaningful connection and delight in multiple types of expressions can provide additional sources of joy and purpose. These become especially helpful in times when there are delays or uncertainty in your primary creative outlets. Limited capacity or progress around an expression is most painful when you are overly dependent on it for joy and connection, or when you can't see purpose in the change. A red stoplight or a closed road may not be desired at an intersection, but it's preferable to rolling your car into a sinkhole or getting hit by cross traffic.

It might take more intentional effort to find the joy and satisfaction in some parts of life, especially if they have held pain or disconnection. But the work is worth it. As you take small steps to unlock creativity and deepen different aspects of connection, you will find seemingly unrelated passions merging together into projects, experiences, work opportunities, communities, or other outflows that bring increasing amounts of delight. If there is an area of life that feels difficult and dormant for creativity, invest in tools that support growth in that specific area.

2. *Intentionally set your pace.* Timing is everything. Finding a rhythm that is designed for the long term is crucial for experiencing sustainable peace, joy, and wellness. Your pace may vary by season, but when you're mindful of this aspect of your process, you can make adjustments as you go. There are two main ditches to avoid. *Rush* is rooted in fear and shame and drives you to compromise on your values, cut corners, neglect your wellness and key relationships, and push action over doing it right. Rush often tells you to keep going faster in order to prove yourself, to show you're not a failure, or to keep up with others. This unhealthy pace can cause you to miss the treasures available throughout your creative journey and will leave you depleted physically, emotionally, and spiritually. In an always-plugged-in, ambitious society, it is easy to justify rush, even when it is both unnecessary and surprisingly costly. Does that email really *need* to be sent? Is that turnaround time for the next draft of a project really providing space that supports wellness and excellence? Does the choice you're making to finish a task now violate connection with yourself, others, or something greater that will incur greater consequences?

The other ditch that threatens longevity is the combination of *passivity and procrastination.* Also often rooted in shame, this state is frequently sparked by the possibility of perceived failure, the fear of rejection or getting it wrong, or a sense of swirling futility. Signs include overthinking and difficulty accomplishing normally doable tasks. Procrastination feels like stepping on the brakes and the gas pedal at the same time. You either want or feel obligated to move forward but are discouraged that nothing is happening. Passivity says that there's no point in trying. It whispers that you're not good enough, capable enough, resourced enough, or worthy enough of moving forward. Perfectionism can fuel passivity, as the pressure to get everything right further slows down the process. Staying in this ditch lowers the likelihood of continuing with creative dreams over the long haul.

Prioritizing connection across all three levels—self, others, and something greater—will help you set a healthier pace that avoids these ditches. You will need, at times, to make a powerful decision to choose rest when everything inside of you wants to rush. At other moments, you will need to bravely step into action propelled by your goals, dreams, and visions, resisting the pressure to stay stuck. Experiences of meaningful connection can help us slow down or move forward, depending on our needs. Interestingly, periods spent operating in one unhealthy ditch can push us into the other. Sometimes what needs to shift is not the speed at which we are advancing but the posture with which we do. Sprints can have an invigorating, positive role in your creative growth in certain seasons. But moving fast with a limp or poor form, or without rest periods, is painful and leads to long-term damage. There's a big difference between an elegant, well-formed run and an anxious, unbalanced gait. Taking note of the fruit your pace is producing will help you adjust the speed and posture of your movement.

3. *Set strong priorities within your creative outflows.* Just because you are creating in multiple ways each day doesn't mean they each need equal attention. The enemy of your experiences of wellness, joy, excellence, and inspiration can be too much of a good thing. Overloading your plate with responsibility, even around activities that bring you life, can wear you down physically, emotionally, and mentally. Intentional focus and an ability to powerfully say no to opportunities are crucial for longevity. If you are someone gifted in ideation or are extroverted, prioritization may be as appealing as that vegetable you disliked as a kid. But it's worth it!

Your priorities naturally change as you grow. You may become aware of different sources of significance and joy as interests evolve and as you view life through a different lens. Throughout your creative journey, think about what you might value most in the future, especially when it conflicts with priorities today. Consider what people near the ends of their lives appreciate most. Often, it is their relationships with loved ones, other sources of larger purpose, and their impact on others. As you set strong priorities, remember to recognize the multiple forms of connection you're wired for. It is the source of fuel and fulfillment that will help you build a well-rounded, sustainable creative life.

Building a Burnout-Prevention Plan

There are no set rules on pace or priorities that will guide your path to longevity in every context. Life is constantly full of change. Success is less about getting it right all the time and more about developing processes and community that can help you make adjustments as you move forward, fail, and learn. Building practices that prevent burnout into your process now will serve you over the long haul by protecting your creative longevity and helping you thrive across different aspects of life. Here are a few keys to implement:

Recognize your vulnerabilities. Which of the pitfalls have you stumbled into before? Are you neglecting your own health or relationships due to overindulging in expressions? You might be someone who is prone to rushing or getting stuck in procrastination—or both. In the words of philosopher General Sun Tzu, "If you know the enemy and know yourself, you need not fear the result of a hundred battles." Self-awareness is a powerful tool for recognizing and adjusting your pace and process over the long haul.

Accept that you do not need it all to be fulfilled. There is always more that we *could* do: sales to make, paintings to finish, national parks to visit, promotions to achieve, parties to attend. Practicing contentment with ourselves, our relationships, and our place in the world helps us savor the beauty and delight in our current situations and new adventures instead of being driven by pressure and a lack of fulfillment into overextending ourselves.

Take action around neglected aspects of your creative nature. Diversify where you find joy through your creative nature. Pursue new sources of delight and connection in different areas of life. If you're spending large amounts of time and energy in your art or in your work, make sure to maintain space for meaningful relationships. If prioritizing social connection is natural and easy for you, take note of possible needs to emphasize rest, explore personal growth in physical exercise or spiritual practice, or find creative expressions that offer deeper purpose.

Establish a regular self-check practice. This might be the most important key in this whole chapter: build a routine that allows you to become aware of your mind, body, and emotions before unmet needs spiral into mess. Take note of when signs of irritation, stress, or exhaustion appear. Pitfalls around pace can be difficult to spot because they're subtle and culturally accepted—and even celebrated. Participate in a community where you are able to emotionally process your week, make a regular time for reflective journaling, or use our Warning Light tool in the Creativity Unlocked app. Take note of both the danger signals *and* the growth you're experiencing.

Make changes as contexts shift. When seasons change, proactively consider and complete adjustments. What was healthy may no longer be so due to your changing responsibilities or passions. Small shifts can be massively impactful, especially if you are regularly adjusting. Just like with dental care, intentional maintenance and minor adjustments are preferable to ignoring warning signs and ending up with a root canal.

Build practices for foundational health in advance. Value your body; it is the vessel through which you get to create over your whole lifetime. Experiment with approaches to healthy diet, exercise, and sleep until you find what works for you. These practices fuel a foundation of wellness and can spur experiences of community and creativity. Don't forget to have fun!

Stay fresh with your mindsets. Return to supportive affirmations and engage with core beliefs through spirituality or values that strengthen your sense of security. Challenges with pacing or priorities often stem from where we have begun to believe things, consciously or subconsciously, that provoke fear. There might be something to believe that helps you let go again and move at the speed of hope, not fear.

Invite people you trust to speak into pace and priorities. Honest feedback about our approaches is a gift. Find someone you trust and actively invite their honest, constructive input. Schedule periodic times with them, or give them the authority to share at any point. An enemy of long-term creative flourishing is when you arrive at a point when no one will be honest with you because they fear hurting their connection. Be someone who is open to receiving *and* giving honest feedback to others.

Embrace the Voyage

Your creative journey is a marathon, not a sprint. It is possible to be a great spouse, a great friend, a great parent, and a fulfilled, joyful creative being; it will just require intention and proactive choices. Though some decisions may feel difficult at first, they can become habits that feel natural and provide experiences supportive of your expression.

Stories from others' processes or from your own journey can inspire intention around pace that supports your goals. It's not a waste of time to slow down to do some maintenance to your foundation. At times you might recognize where you have more capacity, freedom, and grace to move forward than you thought. As your creativity develops and impacts your life in new ways, strengthening foundations and revisiting pace and priorities will be necessary.

You are designed to create beauty and goodness. You are not meant for dependency, broken relationships, compromise, addictions, fears, and the other unhealthy fruit that can occur when creative beings lose a healthy pace, carry too much weight, become isolated, or struggle with fixation. The world needs the light that your life is designed to reflect and the love your being is meant to express. I believe that this is because you are made by a Creator and designed to know and experience an unconditional love that brightens your process and propels you forward. You were not meant to run off and hide or to bear the weight of the world until you self-destruct. You carry a creative nature intended

CHAPTER 14 | LONGEVITY UNLOCKED

to release life-giving relationships, experiences, solutions, and art into the world. And your legacy will outlive you, especially if your creativity flows from intention and connection. This is the subject of our next and final chapter.

> ### 🖌 ONE-STEP ACTIVATION
> Time for a tune-up. Reflect on where you are seeing signs of irritation, stress, or exhaustion around your expressions. Identify one practical change in pace or priorities you can make. Or use the free Warning Light tool in the Creativity Unlocked app to reflect on your approach more deeply.

CREATIVITY STORIES

PAOLO | PHOTOGRAPHER

"I come alive when I'm behind the camera. When it's in my hands, I actually start to see the world differently," Paolo shares. As a product, event, and architectural photographer based in New York, he finds much to be explored, discovered, and appreciated. "I'm more aware of sights and angles. The camera gives me a lens and a voice to create with, and my brain operates on a different level."

Paolo's journey to discovering this passion includes multiple resonant themes. "Photography is an expression that incorporates the passion for visual art and design I've had for years and supercharges it with movement. I studied health and nutritional science, partly because I had to embark on a personal wellness journey around food and exercise, so I love the active nature of my craft." Leaning into this creative passion has aligned with discoveries about himself. "I'm a people person, but I didn't ever think that was true in my youth. Photography has helped me embrace this new identity. Now I find such joy and exhilaration being in front of people at events, on set, and planning shoots with others. In a sense, they're different aspects of my audience because they are each affected by my expressions."

Photography also connects Paolo to his heritage. "Being the son of first-generation immigrants from Italy, the table is such an important aspect of life. My background contributes to the appreciation and long-term dreams I have for the hospitality industry. Part of my passion for food and connecting to people from different backgrounds comes from the opportunities I had in my youth to return to the homeland." Paolo notes how his professional focus on photography focused on architecture links to other joyful childhood memories. "As a kid, I would spend a lot of time with my dad while he worked as a contractor. He would sketch out designs on napkins and make blueprints. It has influenced how I see and capture spaces, and it brings me to a deep sense of warmth and satisfaction in the midst of my creativity."

Translating a personal passion into a profession required that Paolo find an audience for his craft. "I just started showing up to events with a camera and looking for ways to serve those around me. It turns out that people like photos of themselves. Work started appearing as I engaged with people in an authentic and genuine way, and I appreciate the relationships that have developed in the process." Paolo notes how his craft provides connection on a deeper level. "My passion is to serve people. I love the interactions I have with people on the street via taking pictures, and there's meaningful connection in the process of hearing someone's story. It often starts with just seeing the innate value, the God image, in the person in front of me."

Paolo shared these words of advice around the creative process: "Follow the joy. How you express your creative nature may change and evolve over the years as your context changes and discoveries are made. Who you reach may shift. But true, heartfelt joy will help see you through the exploration and stick with expressions through the ups and downs. The more you practice, the more you will grow. Not every part of the creative process is fun; there's a lot of discipline in my journey. But there can be a delight in what you discover. Whatever you find the most joy in, that's probably a good indication you're supposed to pursue it, in some form or fashion."

LEGACY UNLOCKED

Recognize creativity's long-reaching impact and meaning. The outflows of your expressions will affect people who never know your name. Understanding your creativity's role in the broader tapestry of humanity can spark purpose and reinvigorate dreams. In this chapter, learn how to unlock creative legacy, starting with small everyday actions.

The Power of a Single Yes

Art instructor Etta Budd is not the answer to many trivia questions. Born in 1864, she taught at Simpson College, a small institution in Indianola, Iowa. But her creative expressions would contribute, indirectly, to advances that have saved at least a billion lives. In the late 1880s, she took note of a talented artist and gardener. Ms. Budd encouraged him to study botany at Iowa State University under her father, who headed the horticulture department.[70] This artist would become the university's first African-American student despite facing discrimination due to his race. Ms. Budd made a point to sit with him in the cafeteria during her visits until others did so as well. The student's name? George Washington Carver.

Over the course of his life, this legendary inventor and scientist developed over one hundred products stemming from peanuts and served as a leader of the groundbreaking Tuskegee Institute. George Washington Carver's discoveries helped small farmers introduce new crops and adopt agricultural practices that greatly strengthened their financial stability. Born a slave, he overcame momentous prejudice and obstacles, including refusal of admittance to multiple higher education institutions. As incredible as his personal achievements are, his creative legacy expands far beyond what he directly accomplished. As a nineteen-year-old graduate student, Carver imparted his fascination with plants on the six-year-old son of a professor during their walks through fields near campus.[71]

This young boy was Henry Wallace. His passion for agriculture eventually led him to become the U.S. Secretary of Agriculture before serving as Vice President of the United States. Wallace's creative accomplishments helped indirectly solve global problems, leaving a legacy that stretches beyond America's borders. In the 1950s and 1960s, large areas of Mexico's agricultural lands were being devastated by a fungus called rust. Wallace convinced a large U.S. philanthropic foundation to partner with the Mexican government in the development of rust-resistant crops for the country.[72] The resulting experimental program near Mexico City would soon become home for a young American plant pathologist named Norman Borlaug, whose discoveries would save over a billion lives and launch the Green Revolution.

After arriving in Mexico, Borlaug set to work crossing strains of wheat to find one that could solve the problem of rust and suit the local agricultural conditions.[73] Years of diligent work paid off with discoveries that transformed Mexico's agricultural output, leading the country to unexpected surpluses that made it an exporter of wheat. Borlaug's crops and practices would soon have tremendous impact on other continents. Experts had feared that rapidly growing populations and low agricultural yields in Pakistan, India, and other Asian countries would eventually lead to vast famines and kill tens or hundreds of millions of people.[74] Despite some initial resistance, Borlaug's keen insights and wheat strains played a significant role in increasing agricultural capacity in these places. This larger output raised the standard of living in many countries, reducing political tension and the risk of war. In the decades that have since passed, experts estimate that more than a billion lives have been saved due to these developments.[75] In 1970 Borlaug received the Nobel Peace Prize for his work.

Mapped out by Andy Andrews in his book *Your Life Matters,* this powerful example of creative legacy involves many individuals not named here.[76] You could track these stories back further, to the families, supporters, and communities of teacher Etta Budd, inventor George Washington Carver, businessman and politician Henry Wallace, scientist Norman Borlaug, and the various people who shaped their lives. The small (and big) yeses of many contributed to a legacy that surpasses what they likely imagined or could control. This is a wonder of our creative nature.

An Ever-Expanding Tapestry

Remember when we mentioned the world-changing impact of creativity, all the way back in the first chapter? It's time to return to this important reality. Like the other parts of the creative journey, this topic is best engaged with from the foundation of intrinsic motivation that you have been building. An internal sense of satisfaction and joy will fuel your process in ways that external impact cannot. But recognizing a generational perspective and the powerful possibilities of small creative choices can add momentum and strengthen approaches that serve humanity and make you fully alive.

People you never meet, in places and times far from your location and interests, can be impacted through your creative actions, whether big or small. Psychologist Lev Vygotsky believed that every expression, whether acknowledged or not, adds to the larger picture. He wrote, "When we consider the phenomenon of collective creativity, which combines all these drops of individual creativity that frequently are insignificant in themselves, we readily understand that an enormous percentage of what has been created by humanity is a product of the anonymous collective creative work of unknown inventors."[77] There is much that we experience today that has come from the risks, sacrifices, and dedication of people whose names we'll never know. And the journeys of those who crafted your coffeemaker, penned your favorite songs, or paved your commute to school were shaped by the contributions of many others. Recognizing the different aspects of your creative legacy can increase personal fulfillment and provide fuel and hope for your expressions.

Join me in an imaginative visualization. Read the instructions first, and then close your eyes. Picture in front of you a massive, beautiful wall tapestry that extends wider and higher than you can see. What colors does it hold? What are the images you notice woven into its threads? Then approach the tapestry in your mind. What do you see as you get closer? Stay in this place and explore the tapestry for as long as you'd like. When you're done, open your eyes and continue reading.

Your individual story is part of a much larger, multi-generational narrative that connects us all. Unlocking your creativity brings the richer colors of vibrancy and passion to the threads your life weaves into this tapestry. What you create can extend beyond your lifetime. You are weaving threads that intersect with the expressions of others and offer pathways for future generations. Somewhere in this masterpiece the threads of Etta Budd, George Washington Carver, Henry Wallace, and Norman Borlaug connected, formed relationships, activated vision, developed programs, discovered life-saving crops, and eventually fed families across the globe.

Being aware of the tapestry alters understanding of your role. You do not have to feel responsible for the whole tapestry. You simply get to discover and play your part in the artful weaving of humanity. Doing so will add to those around you. Parts of the tapestry near you have been dulled or even torn by fear, loss, and pain. Your creative potential can be part of reweaving these broken, dimmer places into something beautiful, even if you don't get to see the ultimate finished work in your lifetime. Finding what makes your heart come alive changes the tone of your outflows and offers new possibilities not only for your expressions but also for the broader tapestry. What could a world gleaming with joy-filled, meaningful creativity look like? The contributions of celebrated pioneers remain important, but what will transform the planet in ways yet unseen is the fresh activation of expressions and connection in multitudes of people.

Take heart in the truth that your creative legacy is not limited to dreams that are fully realized or as successful as you envision. A significant aspect of your legacy comes from where you impact others. The people you support, champion, or engage with, even in small capacities, will release their own creative expressions that affect others, and so on. The depth of impact depends not just on *what* you create but also on *how* you create. The businesses you serve, the art you produce, the experiences you share may fade from human memory, but the excellence, love, and goodness they release can continue to bear fruit through the hearts and values of the people they touch. This realization can influence how we approach pursuits, whether they take years or are daily creative acts.

Don't underestimate the power of your words and your kindness. They can help people recognize, brighten, strengthen, or mend their threads and those around them—or simply convince them not to throw it all away. The reach of individuals' creative natures extends in ways often unseen. We tend to focus on the entrepreneur, scientist, musician, or leader who achieves notoriety, without recognizing the importance of everyone who had a part in the process. Parents, teachers, friends, coaches, supporters, previous pioneers—all have an impact on what an individual adds to the tapestry. Competitors and rivals also play an important role. Whether in sport, art, business, or science, many of the luminaries who now have household names were inspired by others to go further, faster, higher, or deeper in their creative expression. Their predecessors and even their adversaries' dreams might appear as failure to some because they did not "win" or achieve fame, but they are also part of the tapestry. Public credit or recognition is not required for or indicative of one's impact.

You Are Walking in the Dreams of Those Who Came Before

The opportunities around you today, no matter how small or big, are the outflows of the dreams of those who came before. Many are far beyond what your ancestors could have imagined. Just picture the face of one of your great-great-great-great-great-grandmothers in the 1800s if you told her that you can cross the globe in a few hours inside a flaming aluminum tube. Or if you showed her your smartphone and a live video call with someone deep in the Himalayas or exploring pyramids in Egypt or Peru. She might think you were crazy, or into some heavy-duty herbal remedies.

Many of our ancestors were confined to a more limited context, with limited opportunity, and many other challenges. But we wouldn't be here without them. You are part of the fruit and fulfillment of seeds that have been planted for centuries. Your simple yes to life, to hope, to activating the creative capacity you have, can seed experiences for future generations, whether or not you see them sprout. Did you know that, if you go back nine generations from your parents, more than a thousand people were involved in your making—in a single generation? You have 1,024 eighth great-grandparents. You might gravitate to individuals who stand out as exemplary for positive or negative reasons—the greatest hero or villain who has contributed fame or shame to your lineage—but the truth is that the small creative choices of many played a role in you existing and in the strengths and positive qualities you carry.

A friend of mine wrote a condolence card to the wife of a recently passed former Sunday school teacher. My friend had not seen this man for fifty years but remembered him fondly as one who lived out what he taught and who left a mark that inspired her own spiritual journey that would jump-start decades later. This teacher never fully knew the impact of his faithful kindness. My friend has had an indirect role in supporting individuals in their own creative journeys in art, business, and beyond that have impacted millions of people, and it's a part of that Sunday school teacher's unseen impact.

Releasing the Weight of Legacy

Creative legacy is a fitting benediction for this book. It points to the importance of creative identity, grace-filled mindsets, and an approach rooted in longevity. Without these concepts, a focus on legacy can backfire. It can become a heavy burden to bear, something that adds pressure to your process or dredges up regret. The keys in this book are

CHAPTER 15 | LEGACY UNLOCKED

designed to help the reality of legacy increase inspiration and purpose for your creativity, via a life-giving process rooted in the tools you have acquired thus far.

We have all been impacted by the creative actions of those who came before us, some wonderful and others costly and wrong. There are likely creative choices in your life that you would make differently. Same here. None of us are perfect, and we all need help. But letting those low moments define our creative potential and legacy going forward doesn't serve anyone, including ourselves. I probably sound like a broken record, but this is the beauty, the power, the incredible wisdom of grace. It empowers creativity in connection, in love, beyond what we can offer or access on our own.

If thinking about legacy ever starts getting heavy, return to the keys in this book that enable experiences of connection and empower a childlike approach. Here are some examples of applying the concepts of previous chapters to this topic:

1. Remember that your creativity is multifaceted. Become aware again of *all* the ways that you are expressing yourself every day and the reality that you often can't fully control the end result.
2. Add affirmations about legacy to your list. Enunciate your choice to create with a longer-term perspective and from a place of value instead of needing to prove it. Intentionally strengthen this mindset through repetition.
3. Quiet external pressures and return to the prioritization of intrinsic joy. Allow that focus to fuel and nourish creative processes that take more time.
4. Lean into the meaningful connection activated by your expressions, and allow it to empower deep satisfaction whether or not you see your name in lights. The most impactful and beneficial works are sometimes the most unseen or those that are ahead of the time in which they will be celebrated.
5. Continue healing from past pain. Recognize that this process strengthens and brightens the gift—the thread—you pass along.
6. Get intentional about serving others in their creative journeys. You don't have to wait until you're an expert or a "known

quantity." Everyone needs encouragement. Take notice of the gifts you see and communicate this value to others.
7. Let go, again, of unhelpful pressures to reach a certain audience. Continue prioritizing what authentically connects to your passions and values, and incorporate refinement that increases depth of your enjoyment and excellence. Authentic, joyful, freedom-filled expression is the goal, and its reach and impact might surprise you.
8. Revisit the childlikeness activations. Dream again, with legacy in mind. What would the world look like if people created from connection and love around the topics and needs that they're passionate about? How can you support the childlike creativity of those who will come after you?
9. Connect more deeply with grace. Narratives and experiences of compassion and love help us keep creating in healthier ways, especially when we have recognized choices we would do differently now.
10. Celebrate the redemptive possibilities of creativity. Think about how your life can be a part of creating spaces and solutions for healing and transformation.

As you engage with and pursue creative endeavors, there will be many opportunities to learn, re-learn, and learn again how to (not) carry the weight. Here's an irony helpful to remember: letting go of the burden of sustaining or creating legacy actually empowers us to better build with legacy in mind. For me, letting go of the pressure to maximize the impact of the educational and financial experiences in my journey alleviated limiting stress I had carried for years. Experiencing connection and love that allowed childlikeness sparked a joy that fuels service and generosity daily. Creativity thrives in freedom, not in fear or control. The pressure to have or maintain a certain outflow or long-lasting impact can choke out the delight of the process and ultimately lead to decisions rooted in fear that sour or dim the influence we have.

Have you ever seen someone so driven in their creative pursuits that they don't know how to care for themselves or those around them? Or a parent who becomes disconnected from their children because they are so intensely passionate about their future academic or athletic achievements? We must value the people around us more than the outcome they can achieve, as we must do with ourselves, creating from value instead of for it. Our tendency to see people as only widgets in a gigantic plan reveals a need to revisit where we started: the innate value and beauty within ourselves, which helps us honor the innate value in the human beings around us.

Engaging with Beauty and Brokenness

The creative tapestry of humanity contains both magnificence and mess. Recognition of its imperfections is essential for authentic, congruent experiences of its goodness. It is important to both celebrate the beauty of the tapestry and understand where it has been imperfect, wrong, or unjust. Considering the generational aspects of creativity may bring up pain from past or present situations. Some of the traumatic experiences that your ancestors walked through may have had severe negative ramifications for their descendants that continue today, including cycles of poverty, predisposition to health challenges, and relational dysfunction. Pain begets pain, until healing—a creative act—intervenes.

No one determines where they are initially placed in the tapestry. Your origin story might contain more disadvantages or challenges than another's. No human being asks for the pain they are birthed into or the trauma they experience. There is much to grieve about the ways in which people have used their creative power in the world. Take the time you need to engage with these realities—just don't let the pain rob you of finding beauty or intimidate you away from the pursuit of weaving life-giving threads into the tapestry of your story.

If considering the topic of legacy is difficult for you, know that you're not alone. You can apply this topic through the lens of your family by birth or through people who have been part of your creative journey. The mentors, teachers, friends, coaches, or neighbors who demonstrated love are part of your story, and you are part of their legacy. Where you can see goodness and love passed down through your lineage, celebrate those gifts and choices. Let them inspire you to create and build similar values in your life. Where you see the opposite, let those points inspire you to be a part of creating something different. Discovering and becoming what was lacking in your journey or the journeys of others can be part of the redemptive aspect of creativity. Individuals can be part of the reweaving of the tapestry for people beyond themselves. Many who came before have contributed to this process, even if they did not fully get to see the fruit or overcome the challenges they experienced.

Tangible experiences of connection empower the change that influences generations. You, in the midst of your process, pain, and exploration, are part of this important work as you receive the kindness and grace that you need. Connection, in all of its imperfect, messy process and forms, is what holds the tapestry together. There's another name for this quality: love. The affection people have for one another, the willingness to sacrifice for another's benefit, the choice to keep fighting for the good while not ignoring messy and broken realities, the care and acceptance we experience in relationships—all these are what have helped sustain the tapestry. Within the painful history of human beings over the centuries, you can find acts of sacrificial love that contributed to the good we see in the world today and that helped keep it from greater tragedy. Honoring those choices can inspire us to make hard decisions that benefit those who come after us—even if we do not know who they will be.

A World of Possibility

Every day, your life holds opportunities to add beauty to the spaces around you. Your experiences of intrinsic creative delight and connection at home, in the workplace, or via other activities will bless your journey and overflow into others'. It's the conversation you have with a stranger who looks like they are going through a tough time. It's the new thought pattern you build to see yourself with kindness that empowers healthier parenting. It's the organizational or business solution you develop that adds value to someone's life. It's your daily words and actions rooted in gratitude that add light and beauty into the world. When we operate in this way, we are brightening, expanding, and restoring the tapestry.

CHAPTER 15 | LEGACY UNLOCKED

Who knows the future of the person you greet warmly, the friend you encourage, the teacher you celebrate, or the employee you mentor? Whether you are young or more advanced in age, your words and actions hold creative power. You might be the pioneer helping set someone up for their future via your words or generosity, the builder making space for others to flourish, the refiner who takes what has been developed and refreshes it for the next generation.

Your external expressions can all flow from the intrinsic joy and meaningful connection that you have been unlocking through this book. Allow the natural, emotional, and spiritual inputs that inspire you to nourish your work, your conversations, your art, your adventures. You are designed to be a refreshing, life-supporting stream, not a stagnant pond. The more we experience the creative goodness of our expressions, the more we have to give away. Your creative yes, whether on a single day or repeated for years, has the power to make your family, your community, and beyond better off than when you arrived. But even before your choice to give, you have a choice to receive. Connection. Grace. Acceptance. Love. Stories that inspire you.

Resist the temptation to be distracted by what others are doing or stymied by what you are lacking. There is a unique opportunity in your hands. Pick up the brush, the hammer, the phone, the map again. And again. And again. As you create, take time to rest and refresh the colors you release. Continue your healing journey, stepping into wholeness in places that have felt limited. Then keep hammering away with the chisel you carry at the problems that waylay or confound. There is a role that is uniquely yours and uniquely beautiful in a story that stretches beyond what you can see. It's not too late to start afresh, even if you have tried before.

Dream about what could be with whatever capacity you have. It may be hard to imagine that you could empower others to explore joyful creativity or become fully alive. But you're moving out of survival mode into a thriving creative life, and what you experience will overflow to others. Let the dreams for yourself, your family, and the world that are bigger than seem possible be an encouragement. Allow them to remind you of your need for community and a love greater than yourself. Celebrate the wonderful piece you represent in the generational tapestry.

Embracing the passions of your heart gives permission for those around you to do the same. Whether you sense them now or not, the eyes of others will observe your healing, your growth, and your progress. Your dreams and hoped-for plans can be suddenly interrupted or delayed, but that can't erase the love released through the process. There is so much that we cannot control in this constantly changing world. But we can make the choice to keep showing up and to pursue deeper connection on every level that fuels both what we create and how we do so. Your creativity is powerful. The world is your canvas; your daily activities are your brushes. Love, kindness, and beauty are your colors. What will you paint today? Choose what will help you live fully alive.

🔑 ONE-STEP ACTIVATION

Reflect on your own family or community history, whether or not it's based in blood. Identify a gifting, attribute, interest, or passion that you appreciate and want to carry forward. Allow it to inspire an experience or outflow you create this week. Write about this and other aspirations for your new creative story using the following pages.

REWRITE YOUR CREATIVE STORY

REWRITE YOUR CREATIVE STORY

REWRITE YOUR CREATIVE STORY

REWRITE YOUR CREATIVE STORY

REWRITE YOUR CREATIVE STORY

REWRITE YOUR CREATIVE STORY

ACKNOWLEDGEMENTS

It truly takes a village. First and foremost, I am writing this only as a result of the grace of God. You've heard in these pages how I was flying the metaphorical airplane of my life into the ground when Love saw me, found me, and believed in me when I was a blacked out mess under a bus stop (and in many other settings). The transformation I experienced and the subsequent adventures have been some of the greatest gifts of my life. *Soli deo gloria.*

To my parents and siblings, your love, support, and encouragement have made this and many other projects not only possible, but a delight. Thank you for teaching me how to love, how to see the best in people, how to be generous, and how to be sensitive to God's voice.

To Laura, Sandy, Jason, Mark, Jon, Dan, Richard, Libby, Judah, Dave, Rebecca, Peter, Julian, Mark, Bill, Kris, and many others, thank you for speaking, loving, encouraging, and challenging me into Love and Truth. I wouldn't be who I am today without you.

To Tedd, Tinasha, Eric, Topher, Kevin, Julien, Marco, Robby, Jake, Joel, Carol, Phil, Sam, Amanda, Janet, Nova, and many others, thank you for being part of unlocking creativity in my life via a range of expressions.

To Worth, Loren, Peter, Ben, Matt, Emil, Seb, Sandy, Amir, Bret, Gerard, Stan, Richie, the Rehfeld family, and the many other friends who have been there through the ups and downs of the journey.

To editors Eline and Aristomelia, researcher Kendra, readers Nicola, Rebekah, Jesse, and Lindsay, advisors Karla and Brandon, encouragers

CREATIVITY UNLOCKED

Vanessa and Rob, and many others, thank you for sharing your incredible skills and your heart in this project.

To the storytellers in these pages, thank you for the honor of getting to share pieces of your journeys. May they inspire and bless many.

To Josh, Amy, David, Kara, Tom, Hayley, Hannah, Flo, Dave and all of the other incredible folks and donors who have made the nonprofit OneStepHope possible, including our brave recovery storytellers, thank you!

To those reading this, thank you for allowing me to be part of your journey. May your creativity bring you great joy and connection that continues to grow.

ENDNOTES

CHAPTER 1

1. Yongtaek Oh, Christine Chesebrough, Brian Erickson, Fengqing Zhang, and John Kounios (2020), "An Insight-Related Neural Reward Signal," NeuroImage 214 (116757): 116757. https://doi.org/10.1016/j.neuroimage.2020.116757.
2. Adobe, State of Create, accessed September 2021, https://www.adobe.com/content/dam/acom/en/max/pdfs/AdobeStateofCreate_2016_Report_Final.pdf.
3. Arthur B. Markman and Kristin L. Wood, *Tools for Innovation: The Science behind the Practical Methods That Drive New Ideas*, (New York: Oxford Press, 2009).
4. Robert E. Franken, *Human Motivation* (Pacific Grove, CA: Brooks/Cole Pub. Co, 1994).
5. Robert and Michele Root-Bernstein, *Sparks of Genius* (Boston: Houghton Mifflin, 1999).

CHAPTER 2

6. Martin E. P. Seligman, *Learned Optimism: How to Change Your Mind and Your Life* (New York: Vintage Books, 2006).
7. David Eagleman, *Livewired: The Inside Story of the Ever-Changing Brain* (New York: Pantheon Books, 2020).

8   Caroline Leaf, *Switch on Your Brain* (Grand Rapids, MI: Baker Books, 2013).

9   Brené Brown (2013), "Shame vs. Guilt - Brené Brown," Brené Brown, January 15, 2013, accessed January 2021. https://brene-brown.com/articles/2013/01/15/shame-v-guilt/.

10 Brené Brown, *DARING GREATLY: How the Courage to Be Vulnerable Transforms the Way We Live, Love, Parent and Lead*, (London: Portfolio Penguin, 2013).

11 Mark Noble, "TEAM CBT and the Art of Micro-Neurosurgery: A Brain User's Guide to Feeling Great," in *Feeling Great: The Revolutionary New Treatment for Depression and Anxiety*, David Burns (PESI Publishing & Media, 2020), p 439.

12 James Clear, *Atomic Habits* (London: Random House, 2021), p 63.

13 Brene Brown, "Finding Shelter in a Shame Storm (and Avoiding the Flying Debris)," Oprah.com. March 21, 2013, accessed May 2022, https://www.oprah.com/spirit/brene-brown-how-to-conquer-shame-friends-who-matter/all.

14 Tamlin S. Conner, Colin G. DeYoung, and Paul J. Silvia (2018), "Everyday Creative Activity as a Path to Flourishing," *The Journal of Positive Psychology* 13 (2): 181–89. https://doi.org/10.1080/17439760.2016.1257049.

15 Jack Canfield and Janet Switzer, *The Success Principles: How to Get from Where You Are to Where You Want to Be* (New York, NY: HarperCollins e-books, 2004).

16 Andrew Weil, *Spontaneous Healing: How to Discover and Enhance Your Body's Natural Ability to Maintain and Heal Itself* (New York: Fawcett Columbine, 1996).

CHAPTER 4

17 Karl Weick, "Small Wins: Redefining the Scale of Social Problems," *The American Psychologist*, Vol. 39, No. 1, 40-49, accessed April 2022, https://zeno-organisatieontwikkeling.nl/zeno/wp-content/uploads/2021/05/Weick-K.-1984-Small-Wins_Redefining-the-Scale-of-Social-Problems-American-Psychologist-33-1-40-49.pdf.

ENDNOTES

18 Nordic Business, n.d, "More Is More, Less Is More, or Is There More to It?" Nordic Business Report, Nordic Business Forum, accessed April 18, 2022. https://www.nbforum.com/nbreport/more-is-more-less-is-more-or-is-there-more-to-it/.

19 Charlotte L. Doyle (2017), "Creative Flow as a Unique Cognitive Process," Frontiers in Psychology 8: 1348. https://doi.org/10.3389/fpsyg.2017.01348.

CHAPTER 5

20 "The Rock Cycle," National Geographic Society, November 21, 2019. https://www.nationalgeographic.org/encyclopedia/rock-cycle/.

21 Matthew D. Lieberman, Naomi I. Eisenberger, Molly J. Crockett, Sabrina M. Tom, Jennifer H. Pfeifer, and Baldwin M. Way (2007), "Putting Feels Into Words: Affect Labeling Disrupts Amygdala Activity in Response to Affective Stimuli," *Psychological Science*, accessed May 20, 2022. http://pss.sagepub.com/content/18/5/421.

22 Bessel A. Van der Kolk, *The Body Keeps the Score: Mind, Brain and Body in the Transformation of Trauma*, (Harlow, England: Penguin Books, 2015), p 184.

23 Oshin Vartanian, Sidney Ann Saint, Nicole Herz, and Peter Suedfeld (2020), "The Creative Brain under Stress: Considerations for Performance in Extreme Environments." *Frontiers in Psychology* 11: 585969, accessed March 2022. https://doi.org/10.3389/fpsyg.2020.585969.

24 L. Toussaint, et al. (2016), "Effects of lifetime stress exposure on mental and physical health in young adulthood: How stress degrades and forgiveness protects health," *Journal of Health Psychology*, 21(6), 1004–1014, accessed Feburary 2022. https://doi.org/10.1177/1359105314544132 https://pubmed.ncbi.nlm.nih.gov/25139892/

25 Kirsten Weir, "Forgiveness can improve mental and physical health," *Monitor on Psychology*, January 2017, Vol. 48, No. 1, 30, accessed November 2021. https://www.apa.org/monitor/2017/01/ce-corner

26 Ibid.

CHAPTER 6

27 Liz Mineo (2017), "Over Nearly 80 Years, Harvard Study Has Been Showing How to Live a Healthy and Happy Life," *Harvard Gazette*. April 11, 2017, accessed March 2021. https://news.harvard.edu/gazette/story/2017/04/over-nearly-80-years-harvard-study-has-been-showing-how-to-live-a-healthy-and-happy-life/.

CHAPTER 7

28 Brené Brown, *Gifts of Imperfection* (Hazelden Information & Educational Services, 2010).

29 Ibid.

30 M. Janssen, et al. (2018), "Effects of Mindfulness-Based Stress Reduction on employees' mental health: A systematic review," PLOS ONE 13(1): e0191332. https://doi.org/10.1371/journal.pone.0191332.

31 Colin A. Capaldi, et al. "The relationship between nature connectedness and happiness: a meta-analysis," *Frontiers in Psychology*, Vol. 5, 976, September 8, 2014. doi:10.3389/fpsyg.2014.00976.

32 Bryan Walsh, "Does Spirituality Make You Happy?" *Time*, August 7, 2017, accessed December 2021. https://time.com/4856978/spirituality-religion-happiness/.

CHAPTER 8

33 Basil Mahon, *The Man Who Changed Everything: The Life of James Clerk Maxwell* (Wiley, 2003).

34 Tiger Webb, (2015), "James Clerk Maxwell: The Greatest Physicist You've Never Heard Of," ABC Radio National, December 1, 2015. https://www.abc.net.au/radionational/programs/scienceshow/james-clerk-maxwell:-the-greatest-physicist/6990508#:~:text=Albert%20Einstein%20once%20said%2C%20.

35 Basil Mahon, *The Man Who Changed Everything: The Life of James*

Clerk Maxwell (Wiley, 2003).

36 Theerman, Paul. 1986. "James Clerk Maxwell and Religion." *American Journal of Physics* 54 (4): 312–17. https://doi.org/10.1119/1.14636.

37 Reframe Media, n.d. "The Unassuming Faith of Maya Angelou," Think Christian, accessed May 16, 2022. https://thinkchristian.net/the-unassuming-faith-of-maya-angelou.

38 Alice Calaprice, ed., *Dear Professor Einstein: Albert Einstein's Letters to and from Children* (Amherst, New York: Prometheus Books, 2002), pp. 127-129. https://quoteinvestigator.com/2011/12/16/spirit-manifest/; Max Jammer, *Einstein and Religion: Physics and Theology* (Princeton University Press, 1999), pp. 92-93.

39 Maya Spencer, "What Is Spirituality? A Personal Exploration" (2012). https://www.rcpsych.ac.uk/docs/default-source/members/sigs/spirituality-spsig/what-is-spirituality-maya-spencer-x.pdf?sfvrsn=f28df052_2.

40 Casper Ter Kuile, *The Power of Ritual: Turning Everyday Activities into Soulful Practices* (Harper: San Francisco, 2021).

41 Albert Einstein (1940), "Science and Religion," *Nature* 146, 605–607, accessed May 2022. https://doi.org/10.1038/146605a0.

42 Mary C. Lamia, "What Are Beliefs?" *Psychology Today*, September 20, 2021, accessed May 20, 2022. https://www.psychologytoday.com/us/blog/intense-emotions-and-strong-feelings/202109/what-are-beliefs.

43 "Daniel Kahneman." n.d. The Decision Lab. Accessed May 16, 2022. https://thedecisionlab.com/thinkers/economics/daniel-kahneman.

44 Tom Holland, *Dominion*, (La Vergne, TN: Basic Books, 2021).

CHAPTER 9

45 Jane Ellen Stevens, "The Adverse Childhood Experiences Study—the Largest, Most Important Public Health Study You Never Heard of—Began in an Obesity Clinic," ACEs Too High, June 3, 2015. https://acestoohigh.com/2012/10/03/the-adverse-childhood-ex-

periences-study-the-largest-most-important-public-health-study-you-never-heard-of-began-in-an-obesity-clinic/.

46 Jane Ellen Stevens, "The Adverse Childhood Experiences Study—the Largest, Most Important Public Health Study You Never Heard of—Began in an Obesity Clinic," ACEs Too High, June 3, 2015. https://acestoohigh.com/2012/10/03/the-adverse-childhood-experiences-study-the-largest-most-important-public-health-study-you-never-heard-of-began-in-an-obesity-clinic/.

47 Vincent J. Felitti, et al. "Relationship of Childhood Abuse and Household Dysfunction to Many of the Leading Causes of Death in Adults" *American Journal of Preventive Medicine*, The Adverse Childhood Experiences (ACE) Study, Volume 14, Issue 4, 245 - 258, May 1, 1998, accessed December 2021. https://www.ajpmonline.org/article/S0749-3797(98)00017-8/fulltext.

48 Centers for Disease Control and Prevention, "Preventing Adverse Childhood Experiences," last updated April 6, 2022, accessed May 2022. https://www.cdc.gov/violenceprevention/aces/fastfact.html.

49 Ibid.

50 Larry Vint (2005), "Fresh Thinking Drives Creativity Innovation," QUICK - *Journal of the Queensland Society for Information Technology in Education*, No. 94, accessed February 2022. https://research-repository.griffith.edu.au/bitstream/handle/10072/7880/33187_1.pdf

51 Scott Barry Kaufman, "The Neuroscience of Creativity: A Q&A with Anna Abraham," Scientific American Blog, January 4, 2019, accessed January 2022. https://blogs.scientificamerican.com/beautiful-minds/the-neuroscience-of-creativity-a-q-a-with-anna-abraham/.

52 Shashi K. Agarwal, "Therapeutic Benefits of Laughter," *Medical Science*, 12(46), 19-23, September 10, 2014, accessed March 2022. http://www.discoveryjournals.org/medicalscience/current_issue/v12-13/n45-53/A4.pdf.

53 Nathaniel J. Blanco and Vladimir M. Sloutsky, "Adaptive flexibility in category learning? Young children exhibit smaller costs of selective attention than adults," *Developmental Psychology* 55, No.

10 (2019): 2060, accessed March 2022. https://www.ncbi.nlm.nih.gov/pmc/articles/PMC6768747/.

54 Nathaniel J. Blanco and Vladimir M. Sloutsky, "Adaptive flexibility in category learning? Young children exhibit smaller costs of selective attention than adults," *Developmental Psychology* 55, No. 10 (2019): 2060, accessed March 2022. https://www.ncbi.nlm.nih.gov/pmc/articles/PMC6768747/.

55 Allana Akhtar and Marguerite Ward (2022), "27 People Who Became Highly Successful after Age 40," Insider, February 17, 2022. https://www.businessinsider.com/24-people-who-became-highly-successful-after-age-40-2015-6.

56 Allana Akhtar and Marguerite Ward (2022), "27 People Who Became Highly Successful after Age 40," Insider, February 17, 2022. https://www.businessinsider.com/24-people-who-became-highly-successful-after-age-40-2015-6.

57 Smithsonian American Art Museum,"Grandma Moses," accessed May 15, 2022. https://americanart.si.edu/artist/grandma-moses-5826

58 Renee Lockwood and Sean O'Connor (2016), "Playfulness in Adults: an Examination of Playfulness and Play and Their Implications for Coaching," Coaching An International Journal of Theory Research and Practice 10(1):1-12, accessed February 2022. doi.org/10.1080/17521882.2016.1268636

59 Kenneth R. Ginsburg (2007), "The Importance of Play in Promoting Healthy Child Development and Maintaining Strong Parent-Child Bonds," *Pediatrics* 119 (1): 182–191, accessed March 2022. https://www.publications.aap.org/pediatrics/article-split/119/1/182/70699/The-Importance-of-Play-in-Promoting- Healthy-Child

60 "The Father of Social Networking," (2014) Business Podcast for Startups, December 3, 2014. https://mixergy.com/interviews/andrew-weinreich-sixdegrees/.

61 "The Father of Social Networking," (2014) Business Podcast for Startups, December 3, 2014. https://mixergy.com/interviews/andrew-weinreich-sixdegrees/.

CHAPTER 10

62 Daniel Goleman, *Social Intelligence: The New Science of Human Relationships* (London: Arrow, 2007).

63 David Burns, *Feeling Great: The Revolutionary New Treatment for Depression and Anxiety*, (Eau Claire, WI: PESI Publishing & Media, 2020).

64 Mark Noble, "TEAM CBT and the Art of Micro-Neurosurgery: A Brain User's Guide to *Feeling Great*," in *Feeling Great: The Revolutionary New Treatment for Depression and Anxiety*, ed. David Burns (Eau Claire, WI: PESI Publishing & Media, 2020), p 429-430.

65 Carolina Herrando and Efthymios Constantinides (2021), "Emotional Contagion: A Brief Overview and Future Directions," *Frontiers in Psychology* 12: 712606. https://doi.org/10.3389/fpsyg.2021.712606.

66 J. N. Rosenquist, J. H. Fowler, and N. A. Christakis (2011), "Social Network Determinants of Depression," *Molecular Psychiatry* 16 (3): 273–81. https://doi.org/10.1038/mp.2010.13.

67 "A Quote by Thomas A. Edison," n.d., Goodreads.Com, accessed May 11, 2022. https://www.goodreads.com/quotes/8287-i-have-not-failed-i-ve-just-found-10-000-ways-that.

68 Joseph M. Demakis, *The Ultimate Book of Quotations*. (North Charleston, SC: Createspace Independent Publishing Platform, 2012), p 196.

69 University College London, "Humans are hard-wired to follow the path of least resistance," ScienceDaily, accessed May 9, 2022. www.sciencedaily.com/releases/2017/02/170221101016.htm

70 Tom Morain, "Connection Between Norman Borlaug and George Washington Carver," last modified 2011, accessed March 9, 2022. http://www.agbioworld.org/biotech-info/topics/borlaug/connection.html

71 Andy Andrews, *The Butterfly Effect: How Your Life Matters*. (Naperville, Ill.: Thomas Nelson, 2011), p 82.

72 Academy of Achievement, "Norman E. Borlaug Biography — Academy of Achievement," last modified February 1, 2022, accessed March 24, 2022. https://achievement.org/achiever/norman-e-borlaug/

73 Ibid.

74 Ibid.

75 Ibid.

CHAPTER 15

76 Andy Andrews, *The Butterfly Effect: How Your Life Matters* (Naperville, Ill.: Simple Truths, 2011).

77 Lev Semenovich Vygotsky. *Journal of Russian and East European Psychology*, Vol. 42, No. 1, January–February 2004, p. 7–97. Accessed Feburary 22, 2022.

GET THE CREATIVITY UNLOCKED APP

Find supportive community, access daily encouragements, and dive deeper with e-courses and tools that help you activate your creativity. Join for weekly challenges that help increase joy and connection in everyday life.

Questions or issues? Email contact@onestepguides.com or visit www.onestepguides.com/creativity-unlocked-app.

TAKE PART IN A CREATIVITY UNLOCKED WORKSHOP

Join a online cohort that provides personalized support and feedback for your creative journeys. Or learn about how to bring a customized version to your organization or business.

Visit www.onestepguides.com/creativity-workshop

LEARN MORE ABOUT OUR STORYTELLERS

Get information about the books, art, organizations, and resources of the individuals featured in these pages. Visit www.onestepguides.com/creativity-unlocked-stories for more details and links to their social media profiles or websites.